Demand, Supply and Welfare Aspects of Pipe-borne Water in Sri Lanka

Demand, Supply and Welfare Aspects of Pipe-borne Water in Sri Lanka

By

Dinusha Dharmaratna

CAMBRIDGE SCHOLARS
PUBLISHING

Demand, Supply and Welfare Aspects of Pipe-borne Water in Sri Lanka,
by Dinusha Dharmaratna

This book first published 2011

Cambridge Scholars Publishing

12 Back Chapman Street, Newcastle upon Tyne, NE6 2XX, UK

British Library Cataloguing in Publication Data
A catalogue record for this book is available from the British Library

ISBN (10): 1-4438-3384-3, ISBN (13): 978-1-4438-3384-4

Dedicated to my Parents and Sanjaya

TABLE OF CONTENTS

LIST OF TABLES

List of Figures

PREFACE

This book identifies under-pricing as the major problem faced by the pipe-borne water sector in Sri Lanka, as well as many developing countries. Recently, the water board of Sri Lanka restructured its pricing strategy for pipe-borne water with the objectives of reducing water consumption and expanding the network. However, the success of the current pricing structure in achieving these objectives is uncertain. Therefore, to overcome the problems of identifying efficient water pricing, this book examines the use of cost-reflective alternative pricing strategies for pipe-borne water distribution services. The book evaluates current and alternative pricing strategies for pipe-borne water against the criteria of efficiency and equity while maintaining the financial viability of the national water utility in Sri Lanka. In order to analyse the welfare impacts of alternative pricing regimes, the demand for pipe-borne water by different user groups and the cost of pipe-borne water provision must be considered.

Such an evaluation requires the examination of operations and costs of the water board, and demands for pipe-borne water by residential, industrial and commercial user categories. Therefore, this book identifies the importance of price and other factors in determining residential, industrial and commercial water demand and respective production technologies of the Water board and marginal costs of supply. The pricing policies are examined and the approximate welfare losses or gains arising when prices diverge from marginal costs are computed. This work is based on a panel data sample of all (14) water board districts for sixty months (January 2001 to December 2005).

In summary, the main objective of the book is to analyse the welfare changes associated with the movement from the current tariff structure to the marginal-cost pricing structure. Within the context of this main research objective, the book also has the following subsidiary objectives:

(i) Estimate the price responsiveness of residential water consumers.

(ii) Investigate the relationship between rate structure, household characteristics, weather variables and level of water use.

(iii) Evaluate the minimum level of residential water use insensitive to price changes.

(iv) Estimate the price responsiveness of industrial and commercial water consumers.

(v) Estimate the short-run marginal cost and long-run marginal cost of water supply services.

(vi) Investigate the economies of scale or diseconomies of scale for the Water board.

(vii) Estimate the efficiency gains realised with the alternative pricing schemes.

The water tariff is an important management tool; however, pricing of water services is controversial in the existing political and social context. Water pricing decisions affect several different objectives of policy makers, often in conflicting ways. Therefore, empirical work is necessary to know with reasonable confidence how different categories of water consumers respond to water price changes. Initiation of water tariff reforms requires government or policy makers and the water board operators to understand the financial costs of providing the water services and the demand for water by different customer groups. This information is then used to assess how changes in the water tariffs affect the welfare of the pipe-borne water customers.

There is a substantial literature on water demand and cost estimations for developed countries, but very little research has been carried out in the context of developing countries. There are only a very few studies on residential water demand for Sri Lanka (Gunathilake, et al., 2001; Hussain, et al., 2002; Nauges & van-den Berg, 2006) and only one published study on industrial and commercial water demand (Hussain, et al., 2002). However, no demand study for Sri Lanka has used panel data covering all the NWSDB districts. Moreover, no study has been undertaken to research the structure of costs for pipe-borne water for the water board in Sri Lanka. These estimations are pertinent to the evaluation of price reforms. A number of authors have been critical of the pricing practices of pipe-borne water supply, only a few have quantified the magnitude of the deviations between actual and optimal consumption levels or the welfare losses or gains associated with the deviations (Garcia & Reynaud, 2004; Renzetti, 1992b, 1999). Moreover, very few studies in the developing country context have analysed the welfare effects of pipe-borne water pricing.

This study is the first attempt at a comprehensive analysis of the welfare effects of pipe-borne water sector in the Sri Lankan context. The findings have significant policy implications because they provide information on impact of price and other factors on residential, industrial and commercial water demand management, importance of threshold of consumption by residential users, the extent of economies of scale in pipe-borne water production and the welfare implications of different water pricing practices. Further, the findings will inform policy makers, the water authority and consumers in Sri Lanka and will have applications for other developing countries too.

Demand analyses (residential, industrial and commercial) are carried out to estimate the price elasticities for water and to observe the influences of socio-demographic and climatic variables on water use (Billings, 1982; Garcia-Valinas, 2005; Renzetti, 1992b). Both SRMC and LRMC are estimated using the cost functions for the NWSDB (Martinez-Espeneira, 2003a; Renzetti, 1999). Simulation models are then applied to estimate individual household welfare impacts and aggregate efficiency effects. Welfare gains and losses for proposed pricing alternatives are calculated (Garcia-Valinas, 2005; Renzetti, 1999).

The book is organized in the following manner: chapter 2 details the institutional background of the pipe-borne water sector of Sri Lanka and lays the contextual background for the analyses undertaken in the later chapters. This chapter provides a general overview of the water board: the organization, services and pricing strategies adopted over time (1994 to 2005). The institutional changes which have influenced the activities and the performances of the water board are discussed. Chapter 2 also provides water tariff structures for residential, industrial and commercial users of the water board. This chapter identifies the need for sector reforms to facilitate private sector participation and decentralization of services to improve the performances of the water board. Chapter 3 discusses the theoretical framework for efficient water pricing. This is followed by a discussion of the general theory of alternative pricing structures in the context of a water utility. This chapter provides the theoretical foundation for the rest of the book in terms of efficiency, equity and financial viability and identifies the inefficiencies associated with the present multi-block pricing structure.

Chapter 4 estimates the residential water demand based on aggregate data. This chapter provides a literature survey of past demand modelling. It specifies the data used and presents the methodology adopted in estimating the residential demand function. Analyses of this chapter are based on panel data composed of 14 water board districts over 60 months (from January 2000 to December 2005 for all water board districts). This chapter presents the results of Stone-Geary specification in addition to the traditional Cobb-Douglas demand model. Finally, the discussion of the results of the demand function along with some implications concludes the chapter. The results of this chapter suggest that the residential consumers of pipe-borne water are relatively price and income inelastic.

Chapter 5 estimates the industrial and commercial water demand separately using aggregate data. This chapter begins by surveying past empirical studies on industrial and commercial demand modelling. Similar to chapter 4, this chapter specifies the data set used and presents the methodology adopted in estimating demand functions. The analyses of this chapter build on a set of panel data similar to that of chapter 4. The chapter concludes by presenting the results and discussion along with some policy implications for industrial and commercial water demands. The results of this chapter suggest that the industrial consumers are more responsive to price changes than the commercial and residential users of water.

The estimation of the cost function for pipe-borne water is reported in chapter 6. First, SRMC and LRMC are estimated using a trans-log functional form and monthly panel data. This chapter highlights the importance of the estimation techniques and the application of theory. Cost functions are re-estimated imposing theoretical properties such as monotonicity and concavity. Apart from determining the marginal cost, the estimations also provide measures of economic parameters of production cost such as cost-output elasticities, cost shares and economies of scale. The estimated cost functions demonstrate economies of scale and the SRMC differ from LRMC by a substantial margin.

Chapter 7 examines a number of welfare measures: consumer surplus, deadweight loss and Hicksian welfare measures – compensating and equivalent variations. This chapter discusses the derivation of equivalent variation and compensating variation using a log-linear Marshallian demand curve. The results of the previous chapters (chapter 4, 5 and 6) are then combined with the information of pipe-borne water pricing to generate estimates of deviations and welfare losses or gains. The welfare gains or losses are analysed by the deviations of current consumption levels from those predicted under marginal-cost pricing and other proposed pricing. According to the results of this chapter two-part SRMC pricing has the highest welfare gain.

Chapter 8 concludes and highlights the importance of the findings for government policy. The contribution of the book is discussed in terms of estimation of marginal cost, residential, industrial and commercial demands and simulation models. In order to provide a comprehensive analysis of pipe-borne water provision in Sri Lanka, conclusions from the four empirical chapters are placed under broad headings. Finally, policy implications and directions of future research are identified.

ACKNOWLEDGEMENTS

I am thankful for the motivation, feedback and guidance of my supervisors Yew-Kwang Ng, Edwyna Harris and Jaai Parasnis. I am thankful to Robert Brooks, who was not my supervisor, but from whom I have learned immensely. In addition, helpful discussions with National Water Supply and Drainage Board staff, especially R.S.C. George, Deputy General Manager (Planning) have been constructive to my work. I am totally indebted to the National Water Supply and Drainage Board, Department of Meteorology and Department of Census and Statistics of Sri Lanka for allowing me to access required data. I extend my appreciation to current and past staff members and students at the Department of Economics. I acknowledge the financial and other support received for this book from the Department of Economics, Faculty of Business and Economics and Monash Research Graduate School, Monash University. And last but not least, I would like to thank my husband, parents, sister and brother for their continuous support and encouragement throughout my candidature.

ABBREVIATIONS

2SLS	Two-Stage Least Square
3SLS	Three-Stage Least Square
AC	Average Cost
ADB	Asian Development Bank
ADF	Augmented Dicky Fuller
AIC	Average Incremental Cost
AP	Average Price
AR	Auto Regression
CES	Constant Elasticity of Substitution
CS	Consumer Surplus
CV	Compensating Variation
DBTS	Decreasing Block Tariff Structure
EV	Equivalent Variation
FAO	Food and Agriculture Organization
FGLS	Feasible Generalised Least Square
GLS	Generalised Least Square
IBTS	Increasing Block Tariff Structure
IV	Instrumental Variables
IWMI	International Water Management Institute
LR	Likelihood Ratio
LRAC	Long-run Average Cost
LRMC	Long-run Marginal Cost
MC	Marginal Cost
ML	Maximum Likelihood
MP	Marginal Price
MRS	Marginal Rate of Substitution
MRT	Marginal Rate of Transformation
NWRA	National Water Resources Authority
NWSDB	National Water Supply and Drainage Board
OLS	Ordinary Least Square
PCSE	Panel Corrected Standard Error
PP	Phillip-Perron
PWISC	Present Worth Incremental System Cost
RSC	Regional Support Centre
RSP	Rate Structure Premium

SLRS	Sri Lankan Rupees
SRAC	Short-run Average Cost
SRMC	Short-run Marginal Cost
SUR	Seemingly Unrelated Regression
WB	World Bank
WRB	Water Resources Board
WRC	Water Resources Council
WRS	Water Resources Secretariat
WRT	Water Resources Tribunal

CHAPTER ONE

INTRODUCTION

In Sri Lanka, the provision of water for drinking and irrigation on a sustainable basis is a national priority (Central Bank of Sri Lanka, 2005). Achieving sustainability requires economising on the usage and appropriate pricing to prevent wastage and over-exploitation. The annual consumption of pipe-borne water through individual services covering residential, commercial, industrial and institutional use has increased from 275 to 383 million cubic metres during the last decade (NWSDB, 2005). However, the pipe-borne water supply situation is deteriorating in terms of quality and quantity due to continuous population increase, lack of maintenance, improper pricing, poor spatial coverage and non-revenue water (Central Bank of Sri Lanka, 2005).[1]

Two major factors which threaten the long-term sustainability of water resources in Sri Lanka are improper pricing and deficiencies in regulation. Pipe-borne drinking water is subject to a price with a subsidy segment, but other forms of water supply (agricultural or irrigation water and water directly drawn from reservoirs, streams, wells and lakes) are not subject to any form of pricing. This has led to over-exploitation and inefficient utilisation of water resources in Sri Lanka. The water resources can be managed efficiently by using cost-reflective pricing. This book focuses on the pipe-borne water sector in Sri Lanka and evaluates alternative pricing structures for pipe-borne water in terms of economic efficiency, equity and financial viability. This requires research to understand consumer behaviour and the impacts of cost structures of the water utilities. Therefore, this book undertakes empirical analyses of demand, cost and welfare to address issues related to pipe-borne water management in Sri Lanka.

---

[1] Non-revenue or unaccounted water is the quantity of water not billed from the total production. This includes leaks from transmission, distribution mains and other structures in the systems, illegal connections, metering errors and consumption on way side and garden taps (Hussain, et al., 2002).

A major problem faced by the water sectors in many countries is that prices are almost universally below the level of full-cost pricing (Renzetti, 1992b). Under-pricing of pipe-borne water results in over-consumption of water, reduces new investments, diminishes the quality and quantity of water delivered, slows spatial coverage of water (especially for poor settlements), and jeopardizes financial viability of water supplying entities. Household expenditure on water usually comprises a very small proportion of the household budget and, therefore, the significance of price to decrease water consumption is over-looked. Average household monthly consumption of 20 cubic metres of water corresponds to a water bill of Sri Lankan Rupees (SLRS) 117.50 (according to the 2005 water tariffs) and is less than 1 per cent of average household income (NWSDB, 2005).[2] Twenty cubic metres of water per month for a household is about three times the lifeline standard set by the World Health Organization (WHO). The main reasons for inefficient pricing are; first, raw water is typically assigned no value, therefore, recorded expenditures are unlikely to equal the full economic costs of water supply (Renzetti, 1992b).[3] Second, because consumer demand is considered exogenous, there is no recognition of the role played by prices to signal resource scarcity. Third, governments use water as a political tool to strengthen their power base. In order to overcome the inefficiencies in the pipe-borne water sector, water prices need to be raised to cover the full costs. The recent World Water Commission strongly endorsed the need for full-cost pricing of water services in both developed and developing countries (WWC, 2000).

To achieve the Millennium Development Goals set by the United Nations, policy makers and relevant authorities are attempting to expand the pipe-borne water coverage in Sri Lanka. These goals require all citizens in a country to have access to safe drinking water and adequate sanitation facilities by 2015 (Central Bank of Sri Lanka, 2005). Access to safe drinking water is estimated by the percentage of the population using improved drinking water sources, such as household connection to pipe-borne water, public stand pipe, borehole, protected well, protected spring and rain water collection (World Health Organization, 2002). In 2005, 92 per cent of the Sri Lankan population had access to safe drinking water, of

[2] The exchange rate announced by the Central Bank of Sri Lanka as at 2005 is US$ 1=SLRS 102.

[3] Raw water is water taken from the environment, (water withdrawn from initial sources) and is subsequently treated or purified to produce potable water.

which only 39 per cent had access to pipe-borne water (Central Bank of Sri Lanka, 2005).[4]

The premier national organization for the provision of safe and adequate drinking water supply and sewerage facilities in Sri Lanka is the National Water Supply and Drainage Board (NWSDB). It provides water supply and sewerage facilities primarily for residential, industrial and commercial establishments in urban areas and has recently been extended the services to rural areas. The Government of Sri Lanka together with the NWSDB has formulated sector goals to extend the pipe-borne water supply to 100 per cent of the urban population and 75 per cent of the rural population by 2010 (NWSDB, 2002).

Recently, authorities have suggested many solutions to water scarcity problems including increasing storage capacity through the construction of new dams; recycling waste water; reduction of per capita water consumption to the internationally determined lifeline level; charging increased water tariffs to reduce wasteful water use; and allowing water trading between agricultural water and domestic water (Edwards, 2006).[5] In the Sri Lankan context, most of these solutions are difficult to achieve in the near future. Building a new dam requires an enormous amount of capital and, hence, may need more government and foreign agency funding than is presently available. Water trading between agricultural and domestic use is not possible due to the lack of property rights and institutional arrangements to support such reforms. Therefore, in order to achieve these goals, the only feasible options are to reduce water consumption to lifeline level and create a water tariff which encourages efficient water use (Imbulana, et al., 2006).

1.1 Purpose

This book identifies under-pricing as the major problem faced by the Sri Lankan pipe-borne water sector. Recently, the NWSDB restructured its pricing strategy for pipe-borne water with the objectives of reducing water consumption and expanding the network. However, the success of the current pricing structure in achieving these objectives is uncertain. Therefore, to overcome the problems, this study examines the use of cost-

[4] 95 per cent of urban and 75 per cent of rural population had access to safe drinking water and 75 per cent of urban and 14 per cent of rural population had access to pipe-borne water in 2005 (Imbulana, et al., 2006).

[5] The internationally cited standard for lifeline level is 4 – 5 cubic metres of water per month that is sufficient for essential needs of a household with 5 members (WHO, 1997).

reflective alternative pricing strategies for pipe-borne water distribution services. The book evaluates current and alternative pricing strategies for water against the criteria of efficiency and equity while maintaining the financial viability of the national water utility. In order to analyse the welfare impacts, understanding the demand for pipe-borne water by different user groups and the cost of pipe-borne water provision must be considered.

Such an evaluation requires the examination of operations of the NWSDB, and demands for pipe-borne water by residential, industrial and commercial user categories. The importance of price and other factors in determining residential, industrial and commercial water demand management are identified. The respective production technologies of the NWSDB are characterised and marginal costs of supply are estimated. The pricing policies are examined and the approximate welfare losses or gains arising when prices diverge from marginal costs are computed. This work is based on a panel data sample of all (fourteen) NWSDB districts for sixty months (January 2001 to December 2005) (Renzetti, 1999).

In summary, the main objective of the book is to analyse the welfare changes associated with the movement from the current tariff structure to marginal-cost pricing structure. Within the context of this main research objective, the study also has the following subsidiary objectives:

i. Estimate the price responsiveness of residential water consumers.
ii. Investigate the relationship between rate structure, household characteristics, weather variables and level of water use.
iii. Evaluate the minimum level of residential water use insensitive to price changes.
iv. Estimate the price responsiveness of industrial and commercial water consumers.
v. Estimate the short-run marginal cost (SRMC) and long-run marginal cost (LRMC) of water supply services.
vi. Investigate the economies of scale or diseconomies of scale for the NWSDB.
vii. Estimate the efficiency gains realised with the alternative pricing schemes.

1.2 Contribution

The water tariff is an important management tool; however, pricing of water services is controversial in the existing political and social context. Water pricing decisions affect several different objectives of policy makers, often in conflicting ways. Therefore, empirical work is necessary to know with reasonable confidence how different categories of water consumers respond to water price changes. Initiation of water tariff reforms requires government or policy makers and the NWSDB operators to understand the financial costs of providing the water services and the demand for water by different customer groups. This information is then used to assess how changes in the water tariffs affect the welfare of the NWSDB customers.

There is a substantial literature on water demand and cost estimations for developed countries, but very little research has been carried out in the context of developing countries. There are only very few studies on residential water demand for Sri Lanka (Gunathilake, et al., 2001; Hussain, et al., 2002; Nauges & van-den Berg, 2006) and only one published study on industrial and commercial water demand (Hussain, et al., 2002). However, no demand study for Sri Lanka has used panel data covering all the NWSDB districts. Moreover, no study has been undertaken to research the structure of costs for pipe-borne water for the NWSDB. These estimations are pertinent to the evaluation of price reforms. A number of authors have been critical of the pricing practices of pipe-borne water supply, only a few have quantified the magnitude of the deviations between actual and optimal consumption levels or the welfare losses or gains associated with the deviations (Garcia & Reynaud, 2004; Renzetti, 1992b, 1999). Moreover, very few studies in the developing country context have analysed the welfare effects of pipe-borne water pricing.

This study is the first attempt at a comprehensive analysis of the welfare effects of the pipe-borne water sector in the Sri Lankan context. The findings have significant policy implications because they provide information on impact of price and other factors on residential, industrial and commercial water demand management, importance of threshold of consumption by residential users, the extent of economies of scale in pipe-borne water production and the welfare implications of different water pricing practices. Further, the findings will inform policy makers, the water authority and consumers in Sri Lanka and will have applications for other developing countries too.

Demand analyses (residential, industrial and commercial) are carried out to estimate the price elasticities for water and to observe the influences of socio-demographic and climatic variables on water use (Billings, 1982; Garcia-Valinas, 2005; Renzetti, 1992b). Both SRMC and LRMC are estimated using the cost functions for the NWSDB (Martinez-Espeneira, 2003a; Renzetti, 1999). Simulation models are then applied to estimate individual household welfare impacts and aggregate efficiency effects.

Welfare gains and losses for proposed pricing alternatives are calculated (Garcia-Valinas, 2005; Renzetti, 1999).

1.3 Structure of the Book

The book is organised in the following manner: chapter 2 details the institutional background of the pipe-borne water sector of Sri Lanka and lays the contextual background for the analyses undertaken in the later chapters. This chapter provides a general overview of the NWSDB: the organization, services and pricing strategies adopted over time (1994 to 2005). The institutional changes which have influenced the activities and the performances of the NWSDB are discussed. Chapter 2 also provides water tariff structures for residential, industrial and commercial users of the NWSDB. This chapter identifies the need for sector reforms to facilitate private sector participation and decentralization of services to improve the performances of the NWSDB. Chapter 3 discusses the theoretical framework for efficient water pricing. This is followed by a discussion of the general theory of alternative pricing structures in the context of a water utility. This chapter provides the theoretical foundation for the rest of the book in terms of efficiency, equity and financial viability and identifies the inefficiencies associated with the present multi-block pricing structure.

Chapter 4 estimates the residential water demand based on aggregate data. This chapter provides a literature survey of past demand modelling. It specifies the data used and presents the methodology adopted in estimating the residential demand function. Analyses of this chapter are based on panel data composed of 14 NWSDB districts over 60 months (from January 2000 to December 2005 for all NWSDB districts). This chapter presents the results of Stone-Geary specification in addition to the traditional Cobb-Douglas demand model. Finally, the discussion of the results of the demand function along with some implications concludes the chapter. The results of this chapter suggest that the residential consumers of pipe-borne water are relatively price and income inelastic.

Chapter 5 estimates the industrial and commercial water demand separately using aggregate data. This chapter begins by surveying past empirical studies on industrial and commercial demand modelling. Similar to chapter 4, this chapter specifies the data set used and presents the methodology adopted in estimating demand functions. The analyses of this chapter build on a set of panel data similar to that of chapter 4. The chapter concludes by presenting the results and discussion along with some policy implications for industrial and commercial water demands. The results of this chapter suggest that the industrial consumers are more responsive to price changes than the commercial and residential users of water.

The estimation of the cost function for pipe-borne water is reported in chapter 6. First, SRMC and LRMC are estimated using a trans-log functional form and monthly panel data. This chapter highlights the importance of the estimation techniques and the application of theory. Cost functions are re-estimated imposing theoretical properties such as monotonicity and concavity. Apart from determining the marginal cost, the estimations also provide measures of economic parameters of production cost such as cost-output elasticities, cost shares and economies of scale. The estimated cost functions demonstrate economies of scale and the SRMC differ from LRMC by a substantial margin.

Chapter 7 examines a number of welfare measures: consumer surplus, deadweight loss and Hicksian welfare measures – compensating and equivalent variations. This chapter discusses the derivation of equivalent variation and compensating variation using a log-linear Marshallian demand curve. The results of the previous chapters (chapter 4, 5 and 6) are then combined with the information of pipe-borne water pricing to generate estimates of deviations and welfare losses or gains. The welfare gains or losses are analysed by the deviations of current consumption levels from those predicted under marginal-cost pricing and other proposed pricing. According to the results of this chapter two-part SRMC pricing has the highest welfare gain.

Chapter 8 concludes and highlights the importance of the findings for government policy. The contribution of the book is discussed in terms of estimation of marginal cost, residential, industrial and commercial demands and simulation models. In order to provide a comprehensive analysis of pipe-borne water provision in Sri Lanka, conclusions from the four empirical chapters are placed under broad headings. Finally, policy implications and directions of future research are identified.

CHAPTER TWO

BACKGROUND AND PERFORMANCES OF THE NWSDB

2.1 Introduction

Sound management of water resources and access to water and sanitation services are now regarded as key components of sustainable development, particularly as a precondition for the steady improvement in living standards in developing countries (United Nations Development Programme, 2006). However, the use, abuse and competition for increasingly scarce water resources have intensified over the past decades. Population growth, urbanization together with changes in lifestyle and economic development in developing countries has heightened the pressure on water resources that are already limited (UNESCO Division of Water Sciences, 2003; World Bank, 1992). These countries are particularly vulnerable to the problems linked to climate change, such as floods, droughts and tsunamis. These will affect prospects for economic and social development, political stability, as well as ecosystem integrity (UNESCO Division of Water Sciences, 2003). Therefore, careful economic and environmental management of water is required.

Water in most cities and towns in developed and developing countries are under-priced with damaging long-run consequences (ADB, 1993; J.J. Boland, 1997; J. J. Boland & Whittington, 1998). The price of pipe-borne water is low in relation to the cost that is incurred on its provision and this under-pricing has resulted in poor services and reduced incentives to expand the spatial coverage of services (J. J. Boland & Whittington, 1998). The problems associated with pricing of raw water and public infrastructure has resulted in under-pricing of water. The pipe-borne water sector is often characterised by high levels of subsidies on grounds of lack of affordability by the poor (Mathur & Thakur, 2003). Subsidies on pipe-borne water are ineffectual in improving welfare of poorer households since these households typically do not have private connections and, therefore, are unable to benefit from the subsidy (J. J. Boland & Whittington, 1998).

Appropriate institutions are required to improve incentives for both water users and providers. This chapter presents the institutional background and performance in the context of the pipe-borne water sector in Sri Lanka with a greater emphasis on the NWSDB. However, comprehensive analysis of institutional evolution and context in the water sector in Sri Lanka is not the primary objective of this chapter. One of the main purposes of this book is to test the efficiency of various price reforms. Therefore, this chapter provides a contextual background for the analyses undertaken in later chapters about efficiency, equity and financial viability in the pipe-borne water pricing. For the purpose of this book, the pipe-borne water sector in Sri Lanka is considered to cover consumptive uses like residential, industrial and commercial from surface or sub-surface water sources. Other consumptive uses like irrigation and non-consumptive uses such as power generation, navigation and ecological water needs are not considered.

In most developing countries, women and young girls often spend hours collecting and carrying water, restricting their opportunities in productive activities due to poor pipe-borne water coverage (United Nations Development Programme, 2006). Water-borne diseases like gastrointestinal illnesses, vector-borne diseases and water-washed diseases are caused due to insufficient water for basic hygiene and unsafe water use (UNESCO Division of Water Sciences, 2003).[1] These water related diseases are among the most common causes of illness and death and these limit poverty reduction and economic growth in some of the developing countries such as India, Ethiopia and Indonesia (United Nations Development Programme, 2006). Further, these put pressure on a country's economy due to lost productive labour time, increased health costs by the government and individuals and long run impacts of nutritional deficiencies. An expansion of pipe-borne water coverage, well-regulated water supply and full sanitation would reduce the burden of water-borne diseases (UNESCO Division of Water Sciences, 2003). Access to safe drinking water and improved water management practices has a great potential to reduce the vector-borne disease and gastrointestinal illness burden (World Health Organization, 1997a). Further, it will reduce

[1] Gastrointestinal illness is defined as an episode of vomiting and/or diarrhoea (Nygard, et al., 2007) and water-washed disease is caused by water scarcity or unsafe, unreliable water which fail to provide adequate quantities of water for hygienic purposes (World Health Organization, 1997a).

the time to secure water and leave more time for people to engage in productive activities.

However, authorities often misallocate, misuse water and damage the environment as a result of institutional weaknesses, market failures, distorted policies and misguided investments. The problems in the water sector have resulted not purely from the natural limitations of water supply but rather from inefficiencies in water management. The problems in the water sector has revealed the limitation of institutions in dealing effectively with resource allocation and management (Saleth & Dinar, 2004). The major underlying constraints to increasing access to safe drinking water are lack of well-functioning water institutions, shortage of investment capital for extending the service and the negligible or partial recovery of operating costs of service provision. More recently, policy makers paid attention to impacts of institutional design on water institutions and the way these institutions can be designed to cope with changes and facilitate the achievement of economic and social objectives (Saleth & Dinar, 2005).

Water institutions set the rules and thus define the action sets for both individual and collective decision-making in the realm of water resource development, allocation and utilization (Saleth & Dinar, 1999). In this way, they establish the incentives, information and compulsions that guide behaviour and influence economic outcomes (Livingston, 1995). Institutions operate at different levels and contexts. There are formal and informal institutions, macro-level and micro-level institutions (Saleth & Dinar, 2004). Formal institutions have the foundation in the laws and structures of organised society while the informal institutions spontaneously develop to address specific issues (Gandhi, et al., 2007; Williamson, 2000). Macro level institutions are rules that structure interactions (both formal and informal rules) and micro level institutions are institutions of governance including markets, transactions or economic activities (Gandhi, et al., 2007; Williamson, 2000).

Most developing countries have informal water economies, marked by heavy dependence of water users on self-provision (through private wells, streams, rivers, lakes, and ponds) or community managed water sources. The common characteristic of informal systems is absent or limited use of prices to recover the costs of resource use. In contrast, self-provision gives way to more formalised service provision in developed countries. Volumetric supply and economic pricing are commonly used in these sectors for cost recovery and resource allocation; therefore, water emerges as an industry (Shah, 2005).

Institutional stability is a necessary condition for complex transactions over time and space (D.C. North, 1996). Past studies on institutional economics have found several characteristics that are expected from effective water resource institutions. These include, clear objectives and greater acceptance by stakeholders resulting in less conflict, good interactions to bring formal and informal rules together, greater adaptiveness in facing internal and external challenges, appropriateness of scale of size and scope and compliance ability (Gandhi, et al., 2007). The extent of institutional changes varies by country depending on economic, political, historical precedents, constitutional provisions and resource realities (Samad, 2005).

Institutional arrangements governing the water sector are undergoing remarkable changes worldwide such as market-based water allocation, decentralized management and private sector participation (Saleth & Dinar, 2000). Like all institutions, water institutions are subjective in operation, dependent on history, hierarchical and embedded within cultural, social, economic and political context (Saleth & Dinar, 2005). This chapter presents a brief discussion on institutional changes in the water sector in Sri Lanka, background of the NWSDB and its performances. The main focus of this chapter is to provide the background for the empirical analyses presented in chapters 4, 5, 6 and 7 related to the pipe-borne water sector in Sri Lanka.

For analytical convenience, factors that lead to changes in water institutions can be classified as endogenous or exogenous factors. Endogenous factors are those internal to the water sector and include water scarcity (not naturally determined), water conflicts, financial and physical deterioration of water infrastructure and operational inefficiency of water institutions. Exogenous factors are those outside the strict confines of water institutions and include economic development, demographic growth, technical progress, economic and political reforms, international commitments, changing social values and natural calamities like floods, drought and tsunami (Saleth & Dinar, 2000).

Institutions affect economic performance through the effect on cost of exchanges and production (D.C. North, 1996). Efficiently functioning institutions minimize uncertainty and facilitate exchange directly by providing information and indirectly by reducing transaction costs (Saleth & Dinar, 2004). Most of the time institutions and institutional changes are brought by political dominant interest groups favouring their own interest. Such changes will not necessarily minimize transaction costs and increase social welfare.

Sri Lanka is a developing country and relatively well endowed with water resources in terms of aggregate statistics. Surface water sources dominate the water sector while ground water is largely limited to domestic water supply and small-scale irrigation (Samad, 2005). Irrigation accounts for approximately 90 per cent of total water use. However, there is a growing water demand for domestic and industrial use. Presently, though a considerable proportion of the population have access to safe drinking water at the national level, there are districts where over 40 per cent of the population does not have access to safe drinking water (Appendix 1 Table 1) (Central Bank of Sri Lanka, 2006). A persistent challenge facing the water supply and sanitation sector has been the large urban-rural disparity in the level and quality of services provided to urban and rural populations.

The pipe-borne water supply situation in Sri Lanka is deteriorating in terms of quality and quantity. Pipe-borne water is subject to a price with a large subsidy segment. This creates wrong incentives and leads to inefficient utilisation of water resources. The justification for the high level of government subsidy for water services is claimed to be the limited ability of the poor to pay for services. Often people in most countries, particularly in developing countries expect connection to the pipe-borne water supply and to be subsidised (J. J. Boland & Whittington, 1998). Consequently, pipe-borne water sector in Sri Lanka is experiencing dramatic changes in funding capacities, which makes it difficult for long-term maintenance and modernization of ageing infrastructure. In practice, it is the rich, not the poor, who almost always benefit disproportionately from subsidised water services in developing countries (J. J. Boland & Whittington, 1998).

The proportion of population in Sri Lankan urban areas will reach nearly 60 per cent of the total population in 2025 and will be higher in the Western province where more than half of the urban population in the country lives today (Sri Lanka Water Vision Committee, 1999). The development of industries and services are also concentrated in this region. These factors will place a severe strain on the water resources and infrastructure for water supply and sanitation. Water scarcity and pollution can be major impediments to an orderly transition from a largely rural to an emerging urban society and require different institutional arrangements (Sri Lanka Water Vision Committee, 1999).

The real cost of water supply and sanitation services is expected to increase drastically as more marginal sources will have to be exploited to meet rising demand in the long run (Central Bank of Sri Lanka, 2002). The demand for residential and industrial water use has escalated while the engineering and environmental costs are much higher for new water supplies than for sources already tapped. All these facts suggest the need for the removal of subsidies and adoption of full-cost pricing. Full-cost pricing will lead to economic efficiency, cost recovery and extension and continuity of piped water services in urban, semi-urban and rural areas. Moreover, relative prices provide incentives for the creation of efficient institutions (D.C. North & Thomas, 1973).

The population without access to piped water supply in Sri Lanka rely on untreated water from shallow wells, rainwater collection tanks, streams or ponds, local drains and watercourses. These substitutes for pipe-borne water are likely to conceal large social and economic costs. For example, the cost of medicine and medical treatments linked to water-borne diseases caused by poorer quality water which often lead children to miss school (reducing human capital in the long run) or adults to lose work opportunities; the cost of fuel if household decided to clean their drinking water by boiling it; the opportunity costs associated with not being engaged in other productive activities (which mostly affects women and children); and other social costs through poor health and lost employment, linked to the degraded environments in which poor households live.

The above facts suggest an urgent need for efficient pipe-borne water service expansion to urban, semi-urban and rural areas. This requires more efficient policies, institutions and investments to govern the pipe-borne water sector. Over fifty different acts govern the water sector, however, Sri Lanka has neither an enacted water law nor a declared water policy needed to provide the legal framework for an integrated approach of water resources management (Samad, 2005). The need for national water policy was recognized since 1990s and in addition, the Asian Development Bank (ADB), World Bank (WB) and other international donor agencies insisted on a permanent institutional arrangement for water sector coordination (Gunathilake & Gopalakrishnan, 2002).[2]

Many different authorities and committees set the pipe-borne water sector goals; however, the responsible authorities have not clearly set targets with time frames of achieving those. None of the parties have detailed the strategies to achieve these goals or reformulation of tariff structures. However, one of the Millennium Development Goals set by the United Nations requires all citizens in a country to have access to safe drinking water and adequate sanitation facilities by 2015 (Central Bank of Sri Lanka, 2005). Millennium Development Goals have put pressure on

[2] ADB and WB are the main donors for the development of the pipe-borne water sector in Sri Lanka (Appendix 1 Table 2).

the parties responsible for pipe-borne water supply, primarily the NWSDB. Therefore, provision of safe drinking water, sanitation and pipe-borne water has become one of the Sri Lankan Government's most crucial economic and social objectives.

This chapter begins by examining the institutional changes that took place over time in the water sector of Sri Lanka. This is done in sections 2.1 and 2.2. In section 2.3, the background of the NWSDB is presented. In section 2.4, performances of the NWSDB are reviewed in terms of economic efficiency and equity, physical and financial performances. A summary of the chapter discussion is presented in section 2.5.

2.2 Institutional Changes

Providing safe drinking water and access to sanitation services are essential and fundamental elements of the Government's program for the economic and social development of Sri Lanka. In spite of having over 50 legislative enactments and 40 institutions dealing with the subject of water, there is no single piece of legislation to rationally manage and allocate water resources in Sri Lanka (Ariyabandu, 2005). A relative abundance of water reduces the perceived need for Sri Lanka to manage water use. However, changes in spatial and temporal distribution of rain, increased competition among users and enhanced operational and maintenance costs are acting to constrain supply. While piped water coverage levels and service quality have improved over the past decade, the need for water services has outstripped the government's ability to provide sufficient water and sanitation (including pipe-borne sewerage infrastructure) and to ensure equitable access to the citizens throughout the country (Central Bank of Sri Lanka, 2005).

There are many institutions that manage irrigation water use but only a few for domestic water. The Water Resources Board (WRB) was established in 1966 by the parliament Act No. 29 of 1964 to advise the minister on various facets of water resources management and to coordinate activities of other departments related to the water sector (Samad, 2005). Sri Lanka adopted the federal system through a constitutional amendment in 1987. Following the constitutional amendment, water sector responsibilities were divided between central government and provincial councils in 1990 (Seneviratne, 2000). Then with the technical and financial support from the ADB, Food and Agriculture Organization (FAO) and International Water Management Institute (IWMI), government undertook a major legal and administrative reform on the basis of the Action Plan for Comprehensive Water Resource Management in 1996. As a result, a Water Resources Council (WRC) and a technical secretariat, the Water Resources Secretariat (WRS) were established. Cabinet approved the establishment of these two institutions in July 1995 (Samad, 2005). The action plan included development of water policy, water law, autonomous water administration, and basin planning and a water information base known as the Water Resources System. The WRC is an advisory body that briefs the minister on water issues related to inter-provincial allocation. The WRS is the technical secretariat assigned to carry out duties directed by WRC (Ariyabandu, 2005).

In 2001, the National Water Resources Authority (NWRA) was established and made responsible for the preparation of a national water resource policy, long-term river basin management, conducting and coordinating water research and the allocation of water resources issuing entitlements. The Water Resources Tribunal (WRT) is an independent appeals tribunal established to resolve conflicts regarding water entitlements (Gunathilake & Gopalakrishnan, 2002). The NWSDB and the Urban Development Authority are responsible for domestic and industrial water supply, however, there is no single agency, legislation or administrative procedure responsible for groundwater development and use (Samad, 2005).

In terms of water policy, Sri Lanka does not have an exclusive and formally approved water policy. Policy is often formed in official documents such as the public investment programs, annual budget speech or the President's address to parliament. Sri Lanka is politically unstable; therefore, institutions related to water sector are also exposed to various forces (Seneviratne, 2000). Any change in the government usually results in changes to Sri Lankan water policy. Established institutions are often moved to different water related ministries as government changes. Even the managerial staff of respective institutions will face changes in their tasks (Samad, 2005). The political instability increases the costs of water policy formulation and implementation.

There were attempts to develop a coherent water policy and related institutional reforms as far back as 1950s (Seneviratne, 2000). The ministry of finance and planning, and the WRS developed a water policy document entitled 'Water Resources Policy and Institutional Arrangements'. The policy document was approved by the Cabinet of Ministers in March 2000 (Gunathilake & Gopalakrishnan, 2002). The main objective of the policy document was to achieve water resource allocation to meet the social, economic and environmental needs of the country with an emphasis on effectiveness, efficiency and equity. The concepts of efficiency and equity are discussed in greater detail in chapter 3.

The Water Resources Policy (2000) did not suggest any institutional change in the domestic water supply and no apparent disagreements arose with the operations of the NWSDB (Gunathilake & Gopalakrishnan, 2002; MONLAR, 2006). However, it proposed some steps to improve the economic sustainability of the institution, which included the following factors: first, water tariffs in urban areas should be set at a level such that it recovers operating costs and depreciation. The tariff should be gradually increased to recover the full supply cost of providing services, including debt service and a reasonable rate of return. Second, low-income people should have an appropriate lifeline tariff to ensure the affordability of water in sufficient quantity and quality to satisfy both basic consumption and hygienic requirements. Third, operational efficiencies of the water supply systems should be improved and the levels of non-revenue water (quantity of water not billed from the total production) should be significantly reduced from their current high levels for both existing and new projects. Finally, water demand management programmes should be implemented to reduce current consumption levels (NWSDB, 2002; Tortajada, 2006).

While the proposed policy makes some progress towards addressing existing imbalances, policy objectives fail to cover some of the key areas that need immediate attention such as the need for funds for capital investments for new water supply and sewerage projects and efficient operation and maintenance of the existing projects. Thus, with the current and continued expected shortages in government funding, it is essential that the customers of the NWSDB pay at least the full operation and maintenance costs for the services received and an increasing percentage of the investment costs. Due to revenue constraints, it is not possible for the Sri Lankan Government to heavily subsidize the operation and maintenance costs of services, high capital investment costs for all new projects, replacement capital for existing projects and to meet service provision targets. It is argued that the Water Resources Policy (2000) was an unsuccessful attempt at formulating water policy in Sri Lanka due to major weaknesses such as donor-driven nature, lack of transparency historical and cultural perspectives, inadequate safety nets and inadequate environmental concerns (Gunathilake & Gopalakrishnan, 2002).

The Water Services Reform Bill (2002) was another attempt at instituting a coherent policy for the regulation of water service provision, tariff setting, consumer protection, water quality standards and facilitation for private sector participation in water services (ADB, 2007). The Water Services Reform Bill was approved by the Cabinet of ministers in mid-2003, and was subsequently submitted to Parliament in October 2003.

However, the Bill was challenged by public activists on the ground that it did not adequately reflect the mandates and roles of local authorities. Although the Bill was redrafted in December 2003, its approval had been further delayed, and it was subsequently abandoned due to political reasons. Further deliberations led to a decision in December 2005 to explore options to amend the NWSDB Act instead of pursuing a more comprehensive water services reform (ADB, 2007).

2.3 The National Water Supply and Drainage Board

The organization responsible for pipe-borne water supply and drainage had its beginnings as a sub-department under the Public Works Department in early 1960s. From 1970 pipe-borne water supply and drainage functioned as a separate department under the Ministry of Irrigation, Power and Highways and remained so until the NWSDB was established in January 1975 by an Act of Parliament. The Act No. 2 of 1974 and its various amendments describe the statutory functions of the NWSDB: to provide water supply for public, domestic and industrial purposes and to operate a coordinated sewerage system (NWSDB, 2002).

The NWSDB is the principal authority providing safe drinking water and sanitation in Sri Lanka. The NWSDB stands as the apex institution responsible for the development, distribution and operation and maintenance of 90 per cent of the pipe-borne water supply schemes in the country (Interim National Water Resources Authority of Sri Lanka, 2002). Rural water supply and sanitation programmes including deep well programmes are also being implemented by the NWSDB. The NWSDB is created with a mandate to extract water from any source for the provision of safe water to the people. The NWSDB is an autonomous body in law but is controlled by the government in practice (Samad, 2005).

In accordance with the Board Act, several major urban water supply schemes operated by local authorities were taken over by the NWSDB to provide more coverage and improved services. The administration and management of the NWSDB has undergone progressive transformation aimed at achieving greater operational efficiency of Regional Support Centres (RSC).[3] While overall revenue collections are managed at the NWSDB head office, financial administration is gradually devolved to the RSC. The RSC independently administer operation and maintenance

[3] There are six RSC: Greater Colombo, Central and Sabaragamuwa, North and East, North Central and North Western, Southern and Uva and Western.

budgets, while billing and metering are decentralized to the district offices (ADB, 2007). A list of RSC and districts are given in Table 2.1.

Table 2.1: Regional Support Centres and Districts

RSC	NWSDB Districts	Administrative Districts
Southern and Uva	Galle	Galle
	Matara	Matara
	Hambantota	Hambantota
	Bandarawela	Moneragala and Badulla
Western	Kalutara	Kalutara
	Gampaha	Gampaha
North Central and North West	Kurunagala	Kurunegala and Puttalam
	Anuradhapura	Anuradhapura and Polonnaruwa
Central and Sabaragamuwa	Kandy	Kandy, Nuwara Eliya and Matale
	Ratnapura	Ratnapura and Kegalle
North and East	Trincomalee	Trincomalee
	Jaffna	Mannar, Vavuniya, Kilinochchi, Jaffna and Mullativu
	Ampara	Ampara, Batticaloa
Greater Colombo	Colombo	Colombo

Note: NWSDB districts contain more than one administrative district; however, the same names as administrative districts apply. Source: NWSDB (2006a)

In 2003, a draft amendment to the NWSDB Act was prepared and submitted to the Parliament. Several clauses were included in the amendments to legally enable the NWSDB to facilitate and promote joint venture partnerships subject to the approval of the Minister of Urban Development and Water Supply. It also facilitates the entering into approved water services agreements with operators for the supply of water and sewerage services or with any local authorities and community-based organization. The new NWSDB Act has provisions for the recovery of damages caused to the property of the NWSDB and costs of water wasted, misused or unduly consumed. Further, actions of pollution of any stream, reservoir or waterworks are considered as an offence under the new NWSDB Act. Other changes as specified in the proposed amendment would enable the NWSDB to establish and fix rates and other charges for the supply of water and sewerage services with the approval of the Public

Utilities Commission. However, the proposed amendment to the NWSDB Act was not signed by the Speaker of the House (Parliament) and consequently not registered in the Official Gazette (ADB, 2007).

The Board consists of four Members appointed by the relevant Ministers: a commissioner of local government, an officer from the treasury and an officer from the ministry of planning and economic affairs (NWSDB, 2006a). The NWSDB senior staff comprises of a General Manager, seven Additional General Managers and twenty Deputy General Managers. Although existing legislation for the NWSDB gives adequate autonomy in terms of staff appointments, remuneration, financial ceilings for procurement, operations and policies, it has not had sufficient autonomy to achieve efficiency. This is partly due to relatively weak management in the NWSDB and poor implementation of policies. The securing and retaining qualified and experienced staff and the lack of political will to impose tariffs to attain financial viability are additional problems. Even after 30 years of operation by the NWSDB, only one third of the population have access to pipe-borne water (Central Bank of Sri Lanka, 2005).

As of 2006, the NWSDB functions under the Ministry of Water Supply and Drainage. The NWSDB started its domestic water billing in 1982 with a gradual implementation of a tariff policy. Nevertheless, due to the initial lack of political will the process was slow. Although there are ten provisions in the NWSDB Act (1974) for levying charges for the supply of water and sewerage services, water tariffs were not introduced in the country until 1982. Since 1982, about fifteen tariff revisions had been effected.[4]

The most recent revision to the water tariff was made in March 2005 (NWSDB, 2006b). This tariff structure is applied nationwide and is largely based on recovery of recurrent costs (primarily operation and maintenance costs) plus debt service costs and depreciation. The 2005 tariff revision was aimed at reducing existing cross subsidies, cost-reflective pricing, recovery of increased cost of water production and motivating people to conserve water (Central Bank of Sri Lanka, 2005). However, even after adopting the new tariffs, these objectives have not been achieved due to high rates of cross-subsidies and non-revenue water.

---

[4] The first tariff revision took place in April 1990, followed by a major tariff revision in January 1994. Subsequently, two tariff revisions followed in 1997, and one revision each in 1998, 1999, 2001 and 2002 reflecting an increasing awareness of the need for cost recovery and the necessary tariff adjustments (NWSDB, 2002, 2006b).

Under existing arrangements, significant cross-subsidies exist, for example: non-domestic consumers heavily subsidize domestic water consumers and low-volume water users by high volume water users. The limited numbers of non-domestic users and high-volume users have reduced the financial viability of the NWSDB due to heavy cross-subsidization. In order to make water supply affordable to poor households, a lifeline tariff is defined for a minimum quantity of water for domestic consumers. This lifeline tariff is applied to all households for their first 15 cubic metres of monthly water consumption which includes about 75 per cent of domestic consumers (NWSDB, 2005). Further, the operation and maintenance costs of pipe-borne water are very high due to use of inefficient old machinery. The replacement of old machinery with new machinery was not undertaken due to the lack of funding by the NWSDB (Central Bank of Sri Lanka, 2005).

The institutional changes are expected to make the market perform better and provide incentives to the suppliers to increase their productivity. The public utilities are encouraged to recover their costs by charging rates that are cost reflective and eliminate cross subsidies (Barkatullah, 1999). The water utilities need to rationalize water tariffs ensuring correct incentives to water users by reflecting the economic costs of providing clean water and phasing out the heavy cross-subsidies among different classes of water users (Renzetti, 1992b). Within the acknowledged limits of affordability, the responsible institutions need to seek full cost recovery in its tariff policy. The heavy cross-subsidization of domestic consumers by industrial consumers should be substantially reduced (Central Bank of Sri Lanka, 2005). This would result in more revenue being available for extending piped connections to the under-served poor. The strategy of charging the full cost of water is important to attract the private sector to enhance investment and to meet the targeted coverage expansion.

The WB and ADB insisted the government to increase prices charged for water by the NWSDB. In 1997, the ADB made an attempt to formulate a tariff policy and shift the responsibility for tariffs from the state to an independent agency. This tariff proposal ensured that domestic consumers pay at least as much as commercial and industrial customers and eliminated all state level subsidies on water. The government also agreed to ensure the NWSDB meets the operation and maintenance cost and debt service or depreciation from revenues derived from water supply tariffs and to progressively reduce the cross-subsidy from non-domestic to domestic consumers (ADB, 1997). However, these changes have neither been enforced nor implemented.

The final decision to increase the water tariffs in Sri Lanka is primarily a political process, which means that the tariff increases requested by the water board may or may not be considered and approved by the politicians in a timely manner (Tortajada, 2006). The general experiences in developing countries have often been that politicians may prefer to progress slowly in terms of increasing tariffs, especially before elections. At present, the NWSDB is required to pay back to the Government only 50 per cent of the foreign loans, at an annual interest of 10 per cent, over a period of 24 years. Furthermore, the water board returns the funds to the Government in SLRS and the government assumes the entire foreign exchange risk (Seneviratne, 2000).

Non-revenue water has become one of the major problems in the pipe-borne water sector and leads to economic losses for the NWSDB. Non-revenue water accounts for approximately 31 per cent of the total water produced in 2005 and it was about 29 per cent in 2004 (Central Bank of Sri Lanka, 2005). Non-revenue water in Greater Colombo area in 2004 was 37 per cent of total water produced for the Greater Colombo and decreased to 36 per cent in 2005. While non-revenue water reduced from 36 per cent of total water produced in 2002 to 31 per cent in 2005, these improvements were rather slow and more progress is needed (NWSDB, 2005). In addition, a greater proportion of non-revenue water is due to old decaying distribution pipes and these pipes need to be replaced to reduce the wastage. However, the NWSDB lacks the required funding for proper maintenance of existing network systems.

A higher rate of non-revenue water is experienced in the Greater Colombo area and occurs primarily because the old pipe water supply system needs major and costly renovations. In addition, losses from the informal settlements (stand post water use) are consistently high. It would be a difficult task to engage in metering of this water usage in the existing political and institutional context. The economic implication of non-revenue water was estimated by the Ministry of Finance in 2002. They reported the existing quantity of non-revenue water could be sufficient to supply 420,000 new households assuming 25 cubic metres per month per household (Tortajada, 2006).

The ADB also insisted that water should not be given free of charge and the government of Sri Lanka should reduce the sources of free water such as stand pipes or street taps or else insist on construction of stand posts with meters (reduction of non-revenue water). A project was initiated to establish 50,000 new meters including at stand posts to reduce non-revenue water. But only about 30,000 meters were installed because of the NWSDB's unwillingness to continue installation given the opposition from consumers, particularly stand post consumers (ADB, 2000).

Many problems encountered in providing water services are due to the lack of incentives both for performance by providers and for efficient use by consumers. Poor quality and unreliable water services result in consumer's unwillingness to pay and in turn generates inadequate operating funds which lead to further deterioration in services. Initially, pipe-borne water was supplied entirely by the government of Sri Lanka. Access to safe water is considered as an inalienable right of people, making it a top priority of the government. Water supply has some key features (specifically for under-pricing); costs, availability and quality of water resources vary substantially according to locality, very long average asset life and important health and environmental externalities of water use that frequently are very difficult to internalize or to regulate efficiently. These key features have made it difficult for the government to attract private sector participation.[5] The provision of clean drinking water, sewerage and sanitation services has exceeded the Government's institutional and financial capacity and major changes are required in the investment policy to fund these activities. The private sector will have to play a major role in this effort since the estimated investment requirements to rehabilitate and expand water supply and sewage services in the main urban and rural settlements for the next decade far exceed the Government's ability (Central Bank of Sri Lanka, 2005).

The WB and ADB are the principal funding agencies undertaking extensive policy dialogue on the subject of privatization of water. The WB and the ADB have provided financing of American dollars (US$) 450 million for the rehabilitation and expansion of piped water schemes from 1977 to 2003 (MONLAR, 2006). They have designed these projects with a view to implement steps towards privatisation of water. The projects of the 1970s and 1980s mainly focused on the rehabilitation and expansion of the piped water systems in Colombo and coastal region between Kalutara and Galle. In 1990s the WB initiated piped water supply schemes for rural areas while the ADB continued to focus on urban areas (NWSDB, 2005).

The argument for privatization of piped water schemes has been put forward since the 1980s. Proposed water sector policy in 2000 argues for privatization as an option of institutional change. The private sector needs to be attracted to participate in water supply to achieve the objectives of growth and profit (Central Bank of Sri Lanka, 2005; NWSDB, 2002).

---

[5] Government needs to convince the private companies that economically reasonable depreciation rules will stay in place long enough to allow capital costs eventually to be recovered.

Profitability will be a key criterion in attracting private investments and may require the installation of efficient systems of water supply to minimize the losses, reasonable return for their shareholders, stable Government and economic conditions and charging water at economic rates. The provision of all these conditions may not be appropriate given the level of economic development in Sri Lanka. The main arguments against privatization from the social welfare point of view are that water provision should be a basic responsibility of the Government. Privatization may avoid under-represented or underserved communities and often fail to include public participation and contract monitoring. These agreements may lack dispute resolution procedures and privatization may be irreversible.

One possible area for future outsourcing could be meter-reading. The current practices of the water board, where meter-readers are given specific areas to cover consistently over long periods of time, have not produced good results in most developing countries (Tortajada, 2006). Such territorial control by meter-readers often has resulted in increases in their unauthorized incomes, since for some staff members, personal interest may over-ride the overall public interest. Such a problem can be addressed in two ways. First, the meter-reading could be outsourced to a national private sector company, perhaps with an incentive payment which could be directly linked to the generation of additional income for the NWSDB. Second, the levels of corruption could be reduced if the meter-readers are regularly rotated in terms of areas they cover so that they do not have opportunities to establish individual fiefdoms.

It would probably be a difficult political process for the NWSDB to outsource meter-reading to the private sector or change the territories of the meter-readers, who are highly organised and are politically well-connected. It is highly likely that the meter-readers will resist such moves very strongly because of their own personal vested interests. Outsourcing of the meter-reading to the private sector is likely to improve the present situation. It could significantly reduce the systemic corruption in meter-reading and the overall cost of meter-reading appreciably (Tortajada, 2006).

Decentralisation can be another option for institutional change. Due to the limited financial and administrative resources, governments need to be selective in the responsibilities for water resources. Often lower levels of the government cannot satisfactorily implement the decisions taken by the higher levels of the government. In such situations, decentralization of the responsibilities to the local governments and transfer of service delivery functions to the private sector is appropriate. Arrangements for ensuring performance accountability, placing an appropriate regulatory framework, enforcing environmental protection standards and prevention of monopoly pricing should remain Government's responsibility.

The Government initiated decentralization in early 1990s. In response, the NWSDB undertook a major initiative to devolve decision-making in investment and operations and maintenance to local governments to encourage their participation and to increase accountability and sustainability in the provision of water supply and sanitation services. The NWSDB can be separated from the operational functions and separate regional cost centres can be established within the NWSDB to promote accountability and to provide incentives for increased operational efficiency planning. To date, only a few local authorities have accepted this responsibility due to limited capacity of local authorities to manage and operate water supply schemes, limited financial capacity to invest and the likely politicisation of the administration of such schemes (ADB, 2007). The NWSDB encouraged the transfer of management of water supply schemes with less than 1,000 connections to community-based organisations to minimize operations and maintenance costs, while retaining the ownership of assets (ADB, 2007).

Recently, the NWSDB has identified the advantages of beneficiary participation in decision-making and implementation. Beneficiary participation purportedly ensures the sustainability of community centred development programmes. They have implemented participatory management for the ADB funded third water supply and sanitation project in rural areas (NWSDB, 2005). The NWSDB has introduced participatory development concepts in urban water supply systems as well. Local authorities, community based organisations and small entrepreneurs can be encouraged to take over the management of rural water schemes. The NWSDB promotes the transfer of responsibility for operation and maintenance of small urban and rural water supply schemes to local authorities and community-based organisations (ADB, 2007).

The priority for drinking water supply remains an unwritten policy at present, with potential conflicts between sub-sectors evident since water resources planning to date do not consider aspects of water such as pricing, quality and service expansion. Growing competition for water among sectors and a lack of clear policy has resulted in substantial water shortages in some parts of the country. The poorer communities bear the costs of this through decreased production. Existing water pricing structures and cost structures for the pipe-borne water in Sri Lanka are discussed in the next section.

2.3.1 Water Pricing and Structure of Costs

Pipe-borne water pricing in Sri Lanka is extremely complex. Price discrimination is common across different categories of water users (residential, commercial, industrial), and household income groups based on the assumption that high income groups use more water. Cross subsidization is central to price discrimination. Typically higher rates are charged to industrial and commercial customers relative to the residential customers, allowing water utilities to cross-subsidize poor residential customers with revenues from rich firms. This is based on the misguided impression that the industrial and commercial sector can afford to pay more for water. Charging different prices for different user groups for the same resource could contradict the objectives of economic efficiency and equity. Water prices should signal to consumers the financial and other costs that the decisions to use water impose on the rest of the society. Charging very high prices for industrial and commercial users may cause them to exit the system and look for possible alternatives for pipe-borne water. This may disadvantage the residential users in the long-run as water utilities lose economies of scale in water provision (Renzetti, 2002).

Residential consumers are faced with an initial connection charge, monthly fixed fee and a volumetric charge. The connection charges for residential consumers depend on the diameter of the pipe line and connection charges are given in Appendix 1 Table 3. Water tariffs for residential consumers in Sri Lanka vary between decreasing block tariff structure (DBTS), increasing block tariff structure (IBTS) and a combination of both. Appendix 1 Table 4 shows the percentage change in the marginal price within each block for each rate structure from January 1994 to March 2005. Domestic water use generally attracts most of the attention of the policy makers. Therefore, there are more blocks for residential category but uniform water pricing for commercial and industrial categories. The price charged for industrial and commercial users is much higher than that for the residential users. Commercial institutions, industries, tourist hotels and others face only a uniform volumetric charge (no fixed charges). The uniform volumetric charge for these user categories is different for each category (for more details refer Appendix 1 Table 5).

In view of the considerable growth in the cost of water production and distribution in recent years, the most recent tariff revision was implemented from March 2005.[6] The main objective of this revision was to recover the

[6] Cost breakdown figures presented in Appendix 1 Table 6.

increased cost of water production, reduce existing cross-subsidies and motivate people to conserve water. Nevertheless, the tariffs structure was not a significant change from the previous levels of cross-subsidies. The most recent price reform for residential water users' monthly bills consist of two distinct components (two-part tariff): a part based on volume of water use and another part based on factors other than water use such as fixed capital expenditure. The charge based on the volume of consumption equals the volume consumed times the unit price. The unit price increases as usage increases; this structure is known as IBTS. The fixed charge reflects the cost of capital stock renewal and debt service while the volumetric charge covers operating expenses.

The main characteristic of the existing tariff structure is the lower rate for water usage up to 10 cubic metres per month (SLRS 1.25 per cubic metre), which is funded by a higher rate for water usage above 50 cubic metres per month (SLRS 75.00 per cubic metre). Another characteristic of the existing tariff structure is when household consumption increases beyond 20 cubic metres per month, then the final block price where the consumer belongs will be charged from 16 cubic metres. The IBTS for the NWSDB residential customers and details of existing water tariff structure are given in Appendix 1 Table 7.

Some aspects of the 2005 IBTS are worth noting: first, both first and second blocks are quite large. Ideally from an economic efficiency perspective, the first block should be for 4 – 5 cubic metres (the volume of water, as estimated by the WHO sufficient for an average household with 5 members per month). Setting a large initial block will directly benefit not only poor but also the middle and upper income households with private connections. Second, residential users face large price differentials between blocks. The price of the most expensive block is sixty times the price of the least expensive block (comparison of SLRS 75 and SLRS 1.25). Third, price per cubic metre is much less in the first two blocks resulting in very low monthly water bills. The majority of households fall into either the first or second block; hence, most households pay less than the average cost of water service. According to the NWSDB's 2005 annual report, average household monthly consumption per connection was 15.28 cubic metres; 19.14 cubic metres in Greater Colombo and approximately 15 cubic metres in all other regions. In contrast, in 2004 the NWSDB average was 16.7 cubic metres and Greater Colombo and all other region averages were 18.71 cubic metres and 16.46 cubic metres respectively (NWSDB, 2005). From an economic efficiency perspective, ideally, all households would be charged at the same volumetric rate since the system marginal costs are equivalent across all households.

An increase in total water usage and inadequate land for onsite sanitation has led to an emphasis on sewerage over the last decade. The NWSDB operates several waste water schemes and pipe-borne sewerage systems to minimize environmental pollution. Presently, the NWSDB maintains the sewerage system without any fee from consumers. However, immediate action needs to be taken to impose a sewerage service charge in all sewerage schemes maintained by the NWSDB. Furthermore, foreign lending agencies are insisting on the introduction of a sewerage charge to extend the loan facilities for new sewerage projects (NWSDB, 2005).

Production and distribution of water entails costs. These comprise of operations and maintenance costs including salaries and wages, electricity charges, chemicals for treatment of water, general repairs and maintenance of plant and machinery and cost of raw water (untreated water). In Sri Lanka, the NWSDB does not pay for water withdrawn from surface and ground water sources, referred as raw water. Therefore, the price of water supplied to the final user fails to account for the scarcity value of raw water. The price charged reflects the cost of storing, treating and distributing the water but not the value of the resource (Renzetti, 1992b). However, the capital requirement to access raw water generally increases when water becomes scarce. Marginal cost of water supply in reality will depend on the value of raw water (user cost or scarcity rent). Raw water may have a scarcity value; when there is abundant water, the scarcity values of raw water will approach zero; but when water supply is limited, raw water value can be significant. However, in the absence of market prices for raw water, economic valuation of scarcity rent is very difficult (Cavanagh, et al., 2002).

Water is drawn from different sources and distances for the NWSDB districts, therefore, cost varies between the RSC and districts (refer Table 2.2). Rivers are the main source of water supply to the regions; Greater Colombo draws water from Kelani Ganga river. Western region also draws from the Kelani Ganga and Kalu Ganga rivers and Southern and Uva region draw water from Gin Ganga river combined with streams and bore-holes. North Central and North Western RSC mainly draws water from irrigation tanks such as Nuwarawewa, Thissawewa and Thruwila and combined sources. Central and Sabaragamuwa and North and East RSC draw water from combined sources of rivers, streams, dams, tube wells and bore-holes (NWSDB, 2006a).

Salaries and wages along with electricity are the major costs in all districts in production and distribution of water. According to the NWSDB, the unit cost of water production and distribution (excluding capital costs) increased from SLRS 9.08 in 2003 to SLRS 14.60 in 2006

(NWSDB, 2007). The unit cost of water production and distribution including capital costs increased from SLRS 23.97 in 2003 to SLRS 26.93 in 2006 (NWSDB, 2007). However, according to the 2005 water tariff reforms residential consumers are able to consume 20 cubic metres of water per month at a tariff rate below the average operation and maintenance cost. Section 2.3 discusses the performances of the NWSDB in terms of economic efficiency, equity, physical and financial aspects.

Table 2.2: The NWSDB Cost Components (Year 2005)

NWSDB District*	Salary and wages cost (%)	Electricity cost (%)	Chemical cost (%)	Repair and maintenance cost (%)	Other cost (%)
Gampaha	50	27	5	3	15
Kalutara	45	28	3	7	17
Galle	47	31	3	12	7
Matara	52	33	3	8	4
Hambantota	54	25	4	10	7
Bandarawela	58	26	3	8	5
Kandy	44	25	3	9	19
Ratnapura	54	27	2	6	11
Anuradhapura	44	25	3	9	19
Kurunegala	54	27	2	6	11

Note: * Excludes Jaffna, Trincomalee, Ampara and Colombo,
Source : NWSDB (2005)

2.3 Performance of the National Water Supply and Drainage Board

2.3.1 Economic Efficiency and Equity

Economic efficiency, equity and financial viability are important objectives in the pricing and investment policies of a water utility (J. J. Boland & Whittington, 1998; S. Brown & Sibley, 1986; Ng, 1987; Whittington, 2003). Economic efficiency can be achieved by pricing according to the marginal cost, which will be sufficient to cover full costs and maximize social welfare (S. Brown & Sibley, 1986; Ng, 1987). Failure to adopt marginal-cost pricing leads to allocative inefficiency. Water tariffs should ensure financial viability in order to fund ongoing operation and maintenance costs, repay loans undertaken for supply expansion and to replace the capital stock. The revenue stream must be adequate to attract both equity capital and debt financing (Whittington, 2003).

Equity refers to fair distribution of economic prosperity among the members of the society (Just, et al., 2004). Two concepts of equity can be discussed; equity between different groups of consumers (residential verses commercial and industrial, poor verses rich) in the same time period and equity between present and future generations. In many countries water tariffs are used as tools of achieving income redistribution. However, achieving equitable distribution of income is a responsibility of the government and cannot be a primary function of the water authority. The government can use income and property taxes to redistribute the income. The water utility trying to achieve distributional objectives involves lower efficiency (Ng, 1987). The implications of this are discussed further in chapter 3.

A recent water policy document has noted that cross-subsidy from commercial or industrial consumers to domestic consumers should be reduced to a reasonable level (Gunathilake & Gopalakrishnan, 2002). Moreover, cross-subsidies between low-volume users and high-volume users should be reduced or eliminated since the wealthy are not necessarily high volume water users. Current water policy and water law on pipe-borne water are neither efficient nor equitable. Equity in pipe-borne water supply can be obtained by providing the opportunity for as yet unserviced consumers to join the pipe-borne water network.

2.3.2 Physical Performance

Since 1948, the government has implemented many programs to develop water resources and provide population with water supply and sanitation. During the world water supply and sanitation decade (1980-1990), the government embarked on an ambitious plan, targeting 100 per cent water supply coverage to urban population and 50 per cent coverage to rural population by 1990 (ADB, 2007). However, due to financial, physical and other constraints, these targets were only partially achieved. Although about 40 per cent of the population have access to the piped water supply, the proportion with a 24-hour supply is not more than half of those with piped water supply.

During the past 30 years, the organization has considerably expanded its scope of activities. Employee numbers have increased from about 1,000 in 1975 to around 7,981 in 2005. It was evident that the NWSDB was heavily overstaffed a decade ago (Tortajada, 2006). For example, in 1991 the ratio of staff members per thousand connections was extremely high, at thirty-three. The ratio has declined steadily, and by 2004, it was nine (NWSDB, 2005). This is illustrated in Figure 1 in the Appendix 1. In 2004, about 6.93 operation and maintenance staff were allocated for thousand connections and this staff to connection ratio was decreased to 6.63 in 2005 (NWSDB, 2005).[7] In spite of this progress, this ratio is still high when compared to the situations in other countries: for example, Singapore has 2 employees per thousand connections; and developed countries have a mean 2.1 to 2.2 employees per thousand connections (Tortajada, 2006). In 2002 the personnel cost as a percentage of the total operating cost was approximately 43 per cent. This has increased to 48 per cent of the total operating cost in 2005 (NWSDB, 2005). In developed countries the corresponding figure is around 30 per cent.

The number of water supply projects managed by the NWSDB increased marginally to 291 during 2005, while the number of new water connections increased by 7.9 per cent. The NWSDB has provided 66,117 new water connections in 2005, increasing its consumer network to 907,662. Total water supply by the NWSDB increased by 4.4 per cent to 383 million cubic metres in 2005 (Central Bank of Sri Lanka, 2001, 2002, 2003, 2004, 2005, 2006). A detailed summary of the pipe-borne water sector performances is given in the Table 2.3.

---

[7] In 2004, total staff per thousand connections was 9.17 and this reduced to 8.71 total staff per thousand connection in 2005 (NWSDB, 2005).

Table 2.3: Water Supply by the NWSDB

	2001	2002	2003	2004	2005
Water Supply Schemes	270	275	280	287	291
Total Water Supply (million m^3)	343	350	357	368	383
Total No. of Connections ('000)	660	730	780	840	910
Total Revenue (SLRS Million)	4,188	4,814	4,864	4,910	6,218

Source: NWSDB (2005)

The Greater Negombo and Kalutara to Galle water distribution projects have been identified by the government for private sector participation in 2002. The NWSDB has outsourced meter reading and spot billing in certain areas in 2003. The NWSDB implemented 47 upgrading and rehabilitation projects at a cost of SLRS 611 million during the 2003. Further, the NWSDB implemented a project aimed at reducing non-revenue water distribution in Colombo. The NWSDB handled 73 locally funded projects and 14 foreign funded projects during 2004 (Central Bank of Sri Lanka, 2005). The NWSDB continued to rehabilitate and improve existing water supply schemes using its own finances, which amounted to SLRS 177 million in 2005. The NWSDB implemented several water supply projects during 2006 to improve and expand water supply facilities.

2.3.3 Financial Performance

Public investment for water supply is mainly sourced from donors and is only sufficient to meet, at most, half of the total investment requirement. In 2005, the NWSDB estimated investment requirements of the water supply sector as SLRS 140 billion by 2010. However, the average annual investment by the government in the water supply sector was around SLRS 8 billion (Central Bank of Sri Lanka, 2005). Therefore, attracting private investment to the water supply sector is necessary to fill the investment gap and to achieve the set objectives. A prerequisite to this is the introduction of a water pricing policy that is based on the cost of delivering water as well as other economic criteria. Existing tariff arrangements are less attractive to private investors. If pricing policy can be advanced based on the cost of delivering water, it may not be necessary for private investments (since revised pricing will generate the required level of revenues) unless private sector is able to operate at a greater efficiency.

The NWSDB has made considerable progress in revenue collection since 1990, especially during the post-1995 period. The total bill collection efficiency has varied from 89 per cent to 100 per cent from 1993 to 2004, as shown in Figure 2 in Appendix 1. Though there have been continuous improvements in the methods used for revenue collection, considerable improvements are needed in the tariff structure setting, levels of the tariffs and reduction of non-revenue water.

Total revenue of the NWSDB rose due to the expansion in the consumer network, improvement in revenue collection and the upward revision of water tariffs over the past years. While the NWSDB reported net operating profits for 2001, 2002, 2003 and 2005, these operating profits are negligible compared to the required financial resources for maintenance and new investments.[8] Taking the depreciation of assets into account, the net financial results of the NWSDB record a significant loss, eroding its capital base and requiring the taxpayers to fund its replenishment. According to the NWSDB, the operating ratio (ratio of operation and maintenance expenditure excluding capital and total billing) varied between 0.92 in 2003 and 0.85 in 2006 (NWSDB, 2007).

2.4 Summary

The primary supplier of the pipe-borne drinking water is the NWSDB. In line with the Millennium Development Goals set by the United Nations, all citizens in the country should have access to safe drinking water and adequate sanitation facilities by 2015. To achieve these targets, the government has estimated that the pipe-borne sector will require investments at approximately SLRS 140 billion, average of SLRS 20 billion per year. During the last five years, even with assistance from foreign sources, the government was able to invest only around SLRS 8 billion per year. Therefore, the government has to find additional funding sources to fill this gap.

The availability of water services for the households is also uneven and only people who are living in some areas get water throughout the day, while households in most rural areas get uninterrupted water supply for a maximum of ten hours a day. A major problem that the NWSDB faces is the high percentage of non-revenue water. This problem has occurred mainly because of illegal and unmetered connections as well as damages

[8] The NWSDB reported a net operating loss in 2004.

to pipelines. The present water tariff does not reflect the cost of production and hence does not allow adequate revenue for the NWSDB. Therefore, the NWSDB is not in a position to maintain their pipeline network timely and provide subsidies to the people that need them the most. This situation will ultimately lead to inefficient sector operation as well as non-competitive pricing in the water sector.

In order to address these issues and to improve the performance of the NWSDB, policy makers have pursued sector reforms to provide an enabling institutional, legal and regulatory framework. These frameworks would facilitate the decentralisation of service provision, introduction of private sector participation and establishment of an independent regulatory framework. One of the main purposes of this book is to test the efficiency of various price reforms and the analyses of marginal cost of water supply and demand for pipe-borne water by various user categories. Therefore, this chapter provided a contextual background for the analyses undertaken in later chapters about efficiency, equity and financial viability in pipe-borne water pricing.

CHAPTER THREE

THEORY OF WATER PRICING

3.1 Introduction

A major task of regulatory commissions and water authorities is determination of the appropriate price for the pipe-borne water supply. The fact that water is a basic necessity for living and has a social and environmental value, makes it extremely difficult to select an appropriate price (Biswas & Tortajada, 2005). Water can be a public good or a private good depending on the context and its marginal utility varies as well. Many consumers believe there is an obligation to assure a reasonable level of water supply along with food, shelter and medical care to ensure that basic human needs are met. However, in the absence of external effects and ignorance or irrationality, all needs can be taken account of by appropriate income redistribution and not by specific water pricing policies.

This chapter reviews theoretical and conventional water pricing practices. One of the objectives of the book is to evaluate the welfare of various price reforms and a comparison with the current tariffs. This chapter discusses the objectives of water pricing and describes the advantages and disadvantages of the main types of tariff structures in use around the world. Further, this chapter establishes both the motivation for the use of marginal-cost pricing and understanding the limitations of its use. This chapter lays the theoretical background for the empirical analyses undertaken in chapter 4, 5, 6 and 7 by highlighting the importance of marginal-cost pricing. The following four chapters will then focus on empirical analyses of residential, industrial and commercial water demands, marginal costs and welfare effects of alternative price reforms.

Water is considered a lifeline service offered at lower prices to poor people and often as a form of redistribution of wealth to these groups from other consumers. Broadly, regulators design the pricing policy to serve the function by redistributing the wealth in the society and by signalling reallocation of resources in the society. From an economic viewpoint, efficient pricing is the central mechanism that determines the availability and allocation of water (Sibly, 2006). An efficient water tariff creates incentives that ensure users obtain the largest possible aggregate benefit for a given water supply cost. Setting appropriate prices is indispensable for providing adequate water to growing urban and rural population. Water in most cities and towns are under-priced, with damaging long-run consequences for households who have limited and poor quality water services, as water supplying entities are unable to invest and expand water coverage (Mathur & Thakur, 2003).

Governments should consider two important principles regarding water utility pricing (Sibly, 2006). First, water prices should be designed to avoid monopoly rents. In other words, a water utility should not accrue more revenue than required for the operational, maintenance and administrative costs, externalities, taxes, provision for the cost of asset usage and cost of capital. Second, in order to be viable, the water utility should recover at least the operational, maintenance and administrative costs, externalities, taxes, interest cost, dividends and provision for future asset replacement.

The economic basis of water pricing is founded in the notion that the supplier must be able to recover full supply costs. Full supply costs can be divided into private costs and external costs. Private costs are of two types; fixed costs and variable costs. The typical operation and maintenance costs can be referred to as variable costs and these include electricity for pumping, labour, repair materials, chemicals and other input costs. Capital costs are fixed costs which include capital consumption (depreciation charges) and interest costs associated with reservoirs, treatment plants and conveyance and distribution systems. External costs arise because of changes in the environment quality or stress on the local ecosystem and these costs are considered as variable costs (Sibly, 2006).

The opportunity cost of water addresses the fact that by consuming water, the user is depriving another user of water under a given fixed capacity. The opportunity cost of water is zero only when there are no other alternative uses. The opportunity cost is associated with physical scarcity of water where the absolute quantity of water is finite and cannot meet the needs of the human kind in the long run. However, water can be transferred from one place to another and utilize many alternative sources such as storm rainfall and sea water to increase the quantity of water. Therefore, water supply is constrained by economic scarcity. In water abundant areas and in its natural state, the opportunity cost of water will be zero. If consumption is close to capacity, the alternative forgone is the units of water that meet the demand with very high marginal valuation. Therefore, the short-run opportunity marginal-cost rises sharply as capacity is approached (capacity is low relative to the demand). If the next capacity expansion costs are very high, it is optimal to wait until the opportunity costs of excluded consumption (short-run opportunity marginal-cost) are very high before installing the new capacity (Ng, 1987).

Three types of instruments are generally used when charging for water. First, a connection fee or a fixed access charge is levied to provide the user with a connection to municipal water supply system and probably charged only once. These fees usually depend on the size of the connection, that is, the diameter of the pipe (refer Table 3 Appendix 1). It is often unclear the way that the connection fee is designed by the water utilities. However, it is suggested the connection fees should contain an element of capital cost that is involved with laying out the distribution network (Mathur & Thakur, 2003). Second, there is a periodic water tax or a fixed charge which is unrelated to water consumption. These fixed charges may be used for the purposes of construction, maintenance, capital renovation, extension and improvement of services. Third, a volumetric charge is levied on water and conceptually designed as a charge on consumption. These charges can be uniform, increasing or decreasing with the volume of water consumption.

Water pricing arrangements ideally should be transparent; reflect true economic costs of water provision (including environmental costs); include a component to reflect an appropriate return on investments; and provide a mechanism for users to have input into their level of service by reflecting their willingness to meet the cost of future investments and water quality improvements. A review of the pipe-borne water supply system in both developed and developing countries suggests higher water prices are desirable since charges to consumers typically cover an average of 35 per cent of the total cost of supply (Easter, et al., 1993). Annual recorded expenditures are unlikely to equal the full economic costs of the water service. However, the gains in economic efficiency resulting from the water tariffs are not easy to quantify (S. Brown & Sibley, 1986).

This chapter begins by explaining the multiple objectives of water pricing in section 3.2. Section 3.3 discusses first-best pricing by analysing the marginal-cost pricing and its limitations. The second-best analysis including discussions about uniform tariff structures and non-uniform tariff structures is given in section 3.4. The chapter concludes in section 3.5 with a summary discussion.

3.2 Objectives of Water Pricing

Economic efficiency, equity and financial viability are important objectives of the pricing and investment policies of a water utility (J. J. Boland & Whittington, 1998; S. Brown & Sibley, 1986; Ng, 1987; Whittington, 2003). Water prices should signal to consumers the financial and other costs that their decisions to use water impose on the rest of the society (J. J. Boland & Whittington, 1998). Economic efficiency results in pricing according to the marginal cost, which will be sufficient to cover full costs and maximize social welfare (S. Brown & Sibley, 1986).[1] Water tariffs should ensure financial viability in order to fund on-going operation and maintenance costs, repay loans undertaken for supply expansion and replace the capital stock. The revenue stream must be adequate to attract both equity capital and debt financing (Whittington, 2003). SRMC pricing does not generally lead to long term deficits, but may involve surplus or deficit cycles where there is lumpy investment and growing demand, because the price increases with demand and decreases with capacity expansion (Ng, 1987).

An efficient price signal leads to the consumption and production of an appropriate amount of a good or service by providing the correct incentives. Prices that are too low lead to over-consumption and will have a number of implications for water systems such as jeopardizing financial capacity by reducing revenues, postponement of necessary expenditures and investments and difficulties in catering to the increasing demand. It is very difficult to change these low water prices since these are politically motivated as discussed in chapter 2. This mismatch of supply and demand and the welfare loss associated with it has ripple effects throughout the economy, because society foregoes opportunities to use those resources or expenditure elsewhere.

Equity refers to the property of distributing economic prosperity fairly among the members of the society (Just, et al., 2004). In many countries, water tariffs are used as tools of achieving income redistribution. However, the government can use income and property taxes to redistribute wealth. If the water utility also tries to achieve distributional objectives then it generally results in lower efficiency (Ng, 1987). Only if governments need to incur very high costs to do general income redistribution will the use of water for equity purposes be justifiable (Ng, 1987). Most economists assert efficient pricing solutions are equitable

[1] Economists often use the sum of consumer surplus and producer surplus as an index of economic efficiency (S. Brown & Sibley, 1986).

(Ng, 1987; Sibly, 2006). Price is not only efficient but also equitable if costs are allocated to the 'cost causers'. This usually means that users pay monthly water bills proportionate to the costs they impose on the water utility by their water use.

The water tariff structure should be equitable and the implications of the equity objective for tariff design overlaps with the economic efficiency (J.J. Boland, 1997). Equity is defined as consumers in similar situations being treated in a similar manner while customers in different situations being treated in a dissimilar manner (Whittington, 2003). Using price as a way of allocating water enables marginal benefits to be equal to marginal costs and ensures that the marginal value of water across users and uses is equal. Raising the price for water will reduce consumption and will have a greater relative impact on low-income households than on high-income households (Cooper & Crase, 2006). However, increased water prices are likely to improve equity in few different ways; increasing supply by making marginal projects affordable; reducing the per unit cost of water to poor people by extending the water coverage for poor populations, reducing the reliance by the poor on water vendors (Rogers, et al., 2002) and reducing the extraction of water from non-hygienic sources.

In many countries, water tariffs are used as tools of achieving income redistribution. However, the government can use income and property taxes to redistribute wealth. If the water utility also tries to achieve distributional objectives then it generally results in lower efficiency (Ng, 1987). Only if governments need to incur very high costs to do general income redistribution will the use of water for equity purposes be justifiable (Ng, 1987). Water authorities achieve equity mainly by cross subsidisation. Cross-subsidies impose costs on society when consumers change their behaviour. The desire for equality itself cannot justify the implementation of subsidies. The ADB (2001) has identified the following circumstances to support subsidies in pipe-borne water services; first, if treated water uses have beneficial external effects in preventing health problems, second, transaction costs of measuring usage are very high and finally, a limited quantity of treated water for the poor is regarded as a basic human need. Subsidies or taxes should be based on the existence of external benefits or costs not the private benefits and costs.

Two concepts of equity can be discussed; equity between different groups of consumers (residential verses commercial and industrial, poor verses rich) in the same time period and equity between present and future generations (Ng, 1987). Equity between different groups of consumers can be categorised into residential verses non-residential users and different income groups. Often authorities charge different prices for water for different categories of users. The general assumption is that non-residential users of water are able to pay more for water than residential consumers. But there may be poor non-residential consumers and rich residential consumers. Further, under competitive markets, charging higher prices from industrial and commercial users may not improve the welfare of poor residential consumers due to the rise in commodity prices that will follow from increasing input costs (water) in the production process. If there is a significant difference in the price elasticity of demand for water between residential and non-residential users, then it could be used for price discrimination in order to raise a given amount of revenue (Ng, 1987). A water authority needs the information on different elasticities of demand for different separable market groups and this kind of pricing is known as Ramsey pricing. However, in this form of pricing, higher prices are paid by more inelastic users (residential users) while, lower prices are paid by elastic users (non-residential users) (Munasinghe, 1992).

Intergenerational equity implies that one generation of customers should not be forced to cover costs imposed by another generation. Intergenerational equity is an important issue in water supply because of the lumpiness of investments and long life span of the reservoirs. Intergenerational equity can be obtained by charging the full costs of water supply including the expenditures on long-lasting capital from consumers of each period (Ng, 1987).

Water authorities often use income as a variable to practice price discrimination and cross-subsidization across different consumer groups. Typically, a fixed charge is levied proportional to the value of the property and some amount of free water entitlements are given (Ng, 1987). The fixed charges based on the property values can be used in the form of two-part tariffs only if, the volumetric charge is in line with the marginal costs. Allowing people with high property values to subsidize the people with low property values is perceived to contribute to the distributional objective. However, this is an inefficient way of achieving distributional objectives. Often distributional function is a responsibility of the central government and not of the water authority. Moreover, if a government wants to achieve distributional objectives, they need to assess the values of all properties, not only water using properties (Ng, 1987). For the countries with property taxes, levying a fixed charge for water will lead to double taxation. Further, if the volumetric charge for water is in line with the marginal cost then levying a fixed charge will modify people's choices.

Supply of water at a higher price would encourage conservation and improve water service coverage to poor. The equity objectives of water tariffs are not fulfilled by IBTS. IBTS are structured with the critical assumption that water usage will be perfectly correlated with income (J. J. Boland & Whittington, 1998; Crase, et al., 2007). There is evidence of violations of this assumption in many instances (J. J. Boland & Whittington, 1998; Hajispyrou, et al., 2002). If water should be provided at lower prices for poor, water utilities can implement two-block tariffs (initial block provides water sufficient for basic needs at a low rate), two-part tariffs or lump sum transfers to low income consumers (J. J. Boland & Whittington, 1998; Crase, et al., 2007; Rogers, et al., 2002). A tariff with a single volumetric price would be simple, transparent, equitable, easy to implement and understandable (J. J. Boland & Whittington, 1998). Moreover, using a single volumetric charge will not exclude the possibility of other arrangements for the poor (Crase, et al., 2007). A single volumetric charge with fixed charges coupled with welfare considerations could be implemented to protect the objectives of efficiency, equity and revenues stability (Crase, et al., 2007). The fixed access charge can be modified for low income earners while the volumetric charge is set at the marginal cost. Government intervention can be an alternative mechanism for dealing with equity. A uniform quantity restriction of water where all consumers are restricted to use the same amount of water may be perceived as fair (Cooper & Crase, 2006). Since the different consumer groups value water in different degrees, the equity problems are inevitable (Cooper & Crase, 2006).

In addition to efficiency, equity and financial viability, resource conservation is also considered when setting tariffs. High tariffs are set to discourage over-use and waste thereby encouraging sustainable use of water sources (J. J. Boland & Whittington, 1998). However, this idea is already captured in the objective of economic efficiency. Sustainability, affordability and viability are intrinsically related. If water costs are exorbitant and the water rate required to cover the cost of service is considered unaffordable to the consumers served, long-term viability is jeopardized. From the water supplier's point of view, cost recovery is the main purpose of the tariffs. Cost recovery requires that on aggregate, tariffs paid by consumers should produce revenues equal to the financial costs of supply. Moreover, the revenue stream should be relatively stable and avoid financial difficulties for the utility.

The costs which form the basis for efficient prices should reflect the least-cost means of investing in capital facilities, operating the water delivery infrastructure and complying with applicable standards. Least cost options can be found through technological and institutional means. For example, the machinery used by the NWSDB is not energy efficient and thereby increases the expenditure on electricity. A key strategy for making any system more sustainable is to optimise the size. In the water sector, very small systems suffer from lack of economies of scale. A sustainable pricing scheme for water will achieve a balance among multiple complex goals as shown in Figure 3.1.

Figure 3.1: Multiple Goals in Sustainable Water Pricing

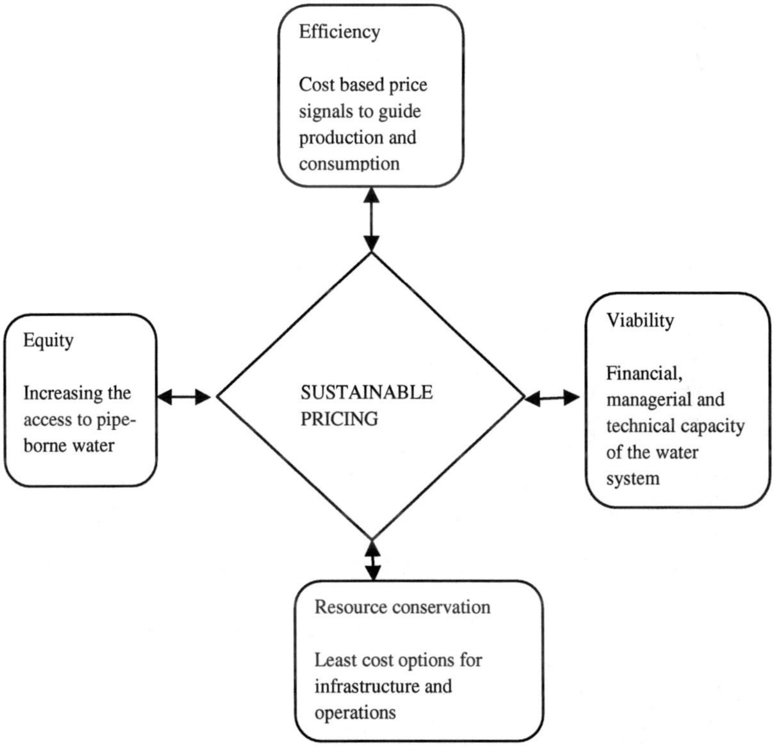

There are a variety of pricing methods in economic literature and in practice. Each has been developed to address a social concern of some type, including economic efficiency, cost recovery, water conservation and equity. Marginal-cost pricing is considered to be the preferred pricing method because it produces an efficient outcome. Industry practice often entails average-cost pricing to cover costs. Block-rate pricing is increasingly being adopted by water utilities to address water conservation needs, although there are serious reservations about the efficiency of this approach. A two-part tariff, consisting of a share of fixed costs and a price equal to marginal cost, has been proposed to cover costs optimally (Coase, 1946). Another theoretical approach focusing on efficient cost recovery is the Ramsey method (Baumol & Bradford, 1970; Ramsey, 1927). In the next sections, first-best and second-best analyses for water pricing are presented.

3.3 Analysis of First-best Approach

The first-best is an ideal situation and achievable only under ideal conditions where markets are assumed to be perfectly competitive (Ng, 1983). There are a number of assumptions such as homogenous product, perfect information, market price is exogenously determined and all buyers and sellers are price takers. These assumptions underlie two fundamental theorems of welfare economics. The first theorem states, "If everyone trades in the perfectly competitive market place, all mutually beneficial trades will be completed, and the resulting equilibrium allocation of resources will be economically efficient" (Pindyck & Rubinfeld, 1992).

The second welfare theorem states, "If individual preferences are convex, then every efficient allocation (every point on the contract curve) is a competitive equilibrium for some initial allocation of goods" (Pindyck & Rubinfeld, 1992). The redistribution is achieved through lump-sum taxes, where initial endowments are known and may be taxed or subsidised. Therefore, the government maximizes the social welfare with appropriate redistribution using lump-sum taxes and transfers (Barkatullah, 1999) but this may not be feasible in practice.

The first-best Pareto optimality requires the equality of the marginal rate of substitution (MRS) and the marginal rate of transformation (MRT) for each good produced and consumed (Ng, 1983). In the absence of factors such as external effects, this would be fulfilled if perfect competition prevails in all markets. The MRS can be defined as the amount of one good an individual will give up to gain one more unit of another good (and remain indifferent) and in free trade equilibrium, this is equal to the ratio of prices of two respective goods (Pindyck & Rubinfeld, 1992). The MRT is a measure of how much of one good must be given up to produce an additional unit of another good and is given by the ratio of the marginal costs of two respective goods (Pindyck & Rubinfeld, 1992).

First-best pricing is marginal-cost pricing since price is equal to marginal cost for all goods in all markets.

3.3.1 Marginal-cost Pricing

Economic efficiency results from pricing according to the marginal cost, which will maximize social welfare (S. Brown & Sibley, 1986; Ng, 1987). The economic efficiency argument for water pricing is based on the assumption that water users compare their marginal benefits with the marginal costs they face when deciding on water use patterns. If all water users face the same price, each will adjust their water use until their marginal benefits rise or fall to equality with the price (C. Howe, 2005). Producer surplus as well as consumers surplus increase as price moves towards marginal cost and total surplus is maximized when price is set equal to marginal cost. In the single commodity case, the price which maximizes total surplus is said to be efficient. But it is possible that a pricing scheme that maximizes total surplus may cause the firm to incur a loss, as marginal-cost pricing regime may not cover the fixed costs. However, pricing according to the marginal cost will not result in deficits in the long run (Ng, 1987). Pricing in accordance with economic efficiency is likely to result in surpluses for the water utility and is consistent with the objective of financial viability (Ng, 1987; Sibly, 2006). Pricing according to marginal cost and thus ensuring revenue sufficiency leads to the expansion of the network ensuring more households have an opportunity to be connected. Marginal-cost pricing is considered as the first-best pricing policy.

The long-standing problem troubling policy makers is whether to use the SRMC or LRMC pricing. Normally in water supply, storage capacity is fixed for a large number of years; hence, the short run for the water utility can be very long compared to the short run for other organizations. Therefore, it is plausible to price water according to the SRMC. According to Ng (1987), with an efficient schedule for capacity expansion, SRMC pricing will result in a lower unit price when capacity is large compared to demand and a higher unit price when the demand is large compared to the capacity. In other words, SRMC fluctuates with demand and capacity. In practice, small and infrequent fluctuations in SRMC may be used in pricing, given political feasibility, public ignorance, administrative costs and aversion to price variability (Ng, 1987).

The Figure 3.2 illustrates, if the demand is D_1 it is optimal to produce at Q_1 in the long run. SRMC pricing leads to losses at Q_1, breaks-even at

Q_2 and profits at Q_3.[2] Whether making losses, breaking-even or making profits will depend on whether the average cost curve is declining, flat or rising at the output level at which LRMC cuts the demand. LRMC is likely to increase above the LRAC and hence marginal-cost pricing will lead to surpluses for the water utility (Ng, 1987).

Figure 3.2: Capacity Expansion, $SRMC, SRAC, LRMC\ and\ LRAC$

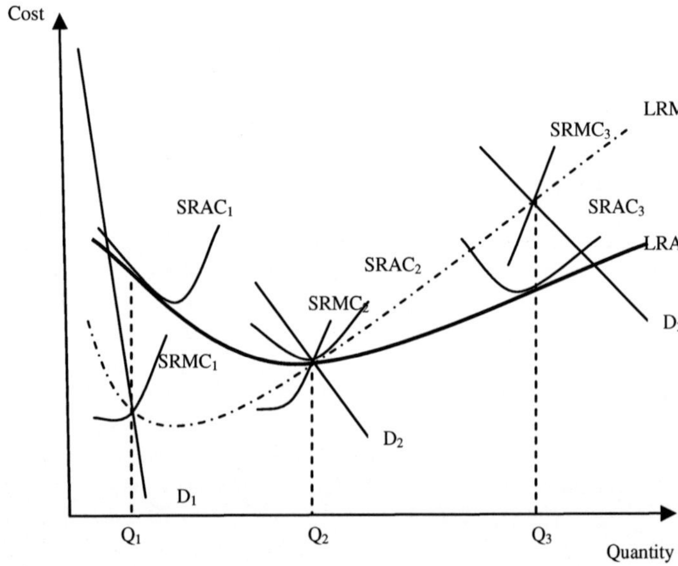

Source: (Ng, 1987)

SRMC gradually increases with increasing demand until a new capacity expansion has taken place. If the marginal cost of supplying water exceeds the average cost, setting price equal to marginal cost will result in profit for the water utility. Marginal-cost pricing will lead to surpluses represented by the rectangle $P_M BEC$ as shown in the Figure 3.3. If the marginal-cost pricing policy generates more than enough revenues to recover the costs of the service provider, then these revenues can be used

[2] $SRMC_1$ also intersects the D_1 at the same point as $LRMC$, because $SRAC_1$ is tangent to $LRAC$ means that the AC and the changes in AC as output changes are both the same in the short-run as in the long-run. $MC =$ change in total cost per output and total cost is AC times output, must also be the same for long-run and short-run (Ng, 1987).

to subsidize the poor households and used for expanding the services. As shown in the Figure 3.2, it can be concluded that SRMC pricing does not necessarily result in a deficit with the understanding of the principles of opportunity costs and the presence of capacity constraints (Ng, 1987).

Figure 3.3: Increasing Marginal Costs

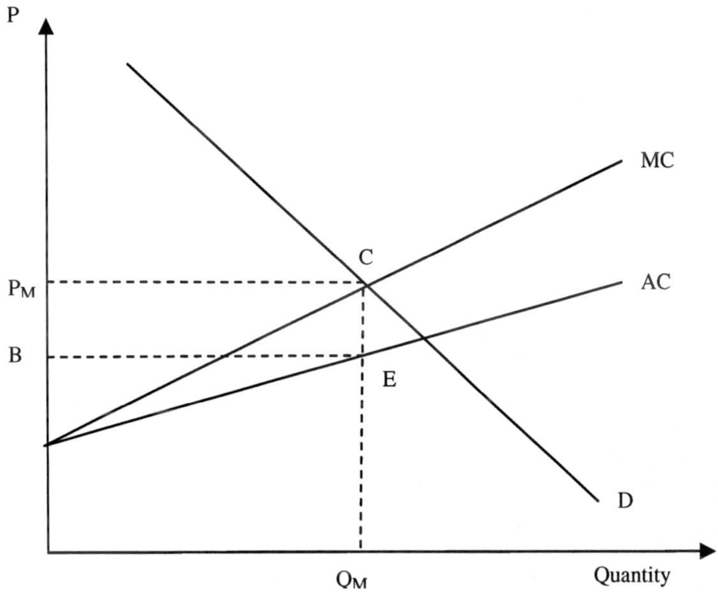

LRMC can be greater or lesser than the SRMC. However, if the SRMC is smaller than the LRMC, pricing according to the SRMC will result in excess consumption of water in the long-run. But if an optimal capacity expansion schedule and horizontal LRMC are assumed, SRMC fluctuates around LRMC and will not be lower than LRMC on average. It is likely that SRMC is greater than LRMC as SRMC may include the opportunity costs of excluded consumption opportunities. LRMC pricing is also reasonable to avoid frequent price variation, considering public ignorance, political infeasibility and administrative costs of fluctuating SRMC pricing.

Since SRMC fluctuates with demand and capacity, a compromise between SRMC and LRMC may be needed. In England, Wales and Portugal, privatized water services practice LRMC pricing to achieve efficiency and revenue sufficiency (Garcia & Reynaud, 2004). Garcia and

Reynaud (2004) argue that pricing according to the LRMC will raise government revenue and leave substantial surpluses for the water authority. These surpluses could be used to pay existing loans and to expand the capacity to supply pipe-borne water connections for unconnected users. Therefore, pricing according to the marginal cost enables society to achieve economic efficiency, equity and financial viability of the water utility.

It is important to discuss the limitations of marginal-cost pricing. Marginal-cost pricing leads to price fluctuations which may be unpopular with consumers and hold political risk for the Government. There are risks involved in managing supply at or near its demand level since unforeseen pressures on the supply could lead to critical water shortages. One well-known problem with marginal-cost pricing is that profit will not be zero unless cost is linearly homogeneous. Negative profit will result if marginal costs and average costs are declining; in this case the utility service will not be sustainable without subsidy from the Government (Loehman, 2003). In contrast, positive profits will result from increasing marginal and average costs. Funds for investment in capacity expansion may become available when marginal costs are greater than average costs. To overcome these problems water utilities adopt several different approaches which are discussed in section 3.4.

3.4 Analysis of Second-best Approaches

Limitations of marginal-cost pricing and market failures mean industries struggle to price at marginal cost without incurring a loss. The suggested solution to marginal-cost pricing under falling average cost is to impose an additional constraint for revenue of the utility. In other words, regulators implement a set of optimal prices (called second-best prices) subject to the revenue constraint. Utilities have implemented various pricing techniques within the second-best framework. These second-best pricing techniques are complex and can be categorised into uniform and non-uniform pricing. Under the uniform pricing average cost pricing, social marginal-cost pricing and Ramsey pricing are discussed while under the non-uniform pricing techniques two-part pricing, peak-load pricing and multi-part tariffs (IBTS, DBTS) are discussed.[3]

[3] Uniform pricing is considered as the first-best if it is set according to the marginal cost. There are also forms of uniform pricing that are considered as the second-best (average cost pricing, social marginal cost pricing and Ramsey pricing). However, in the presence of externalities social marginal cost pricing is the first-best.

3.4.1 Average-cost Pricing

A uniform price schedule is a tariff for goods in which the consumer's total outlay simply rises proportionately with the amounts of the purchased goods. The average-cost pricing technique is considered as uniform pricing. The shape of the average cost and the level of output decide whether marginal-cost pricing makes profits, breaks even or makes losses. If the water utility has decreasing average cost then pricing according to marginal cost will lead to losses to the water utility.[4] It is more likely the water utility faces a rising or horizontal average cost curve, hence marginal-cost pricing will not result in losses and over time SRMC pricing could ensure that the water authority breaks even (Garcia & Reynaud, 2004; Ng, 1987; OECD, 1999). Average cost is likely to rise due to increases in input prices and the increasing scarcity of suitable sites to construct reservoirs as easily accessible sources are progressively tapped.

Average-cost pricing aims to ensure that water charges will be sufficient to meet costs but not so high as to provide monopoly rents to the authority. The full-cost recovery pricing should include operation and maintenance costs, administration and overheads, externalities, taxes or tax equivalents, costs of asset consumption and returns on capital. Operation and maintenance costs, administration and overheads include the direct costs of labour, materials and services employed in water activities. In addition, they also include indirect costs of providing corporate support services such as human resources, administration and building occupancy. Capital costs involve two aspects; depreciation (costs of asset consumption) and the opportunity costs of capital or the rate of return on capital which could be achieved from an alternative use of the resources tied up in the assets. This method of cost recovery is relatively straightforward but has been criticized by economists because it does not result in economic efficiency.

Figure 3.4 shows the case of decreasing average cost where the marginal cost curve lies below the average cost curve. The associated output with marginal-cost pricing is Q_M and with average-cost pricing is Q_A. The efficiency gain associated with marginal-cost pricing in comparison to average-cost pricing can be measured by *CEG* (area under the demand curve less the area under the marginal cost curve between Q_A and Q_M). The subsidy required is the rectangle *ABEF* (loss to the water

[4] Whenever the average cost curve is falling marginal cost lies below average cost. Decreasing average cost (marginal cost < average cost), that is increasing returns.

utility). In this case it can be concluded that, when marginal-cost pricing leads to deficits, average-cost pricing can be an appropriate policy in view of the substantial extra costs of the government subsidies to water utilities (Ng, 1987).

Figure 3.4: Decreasing Marginal Costs

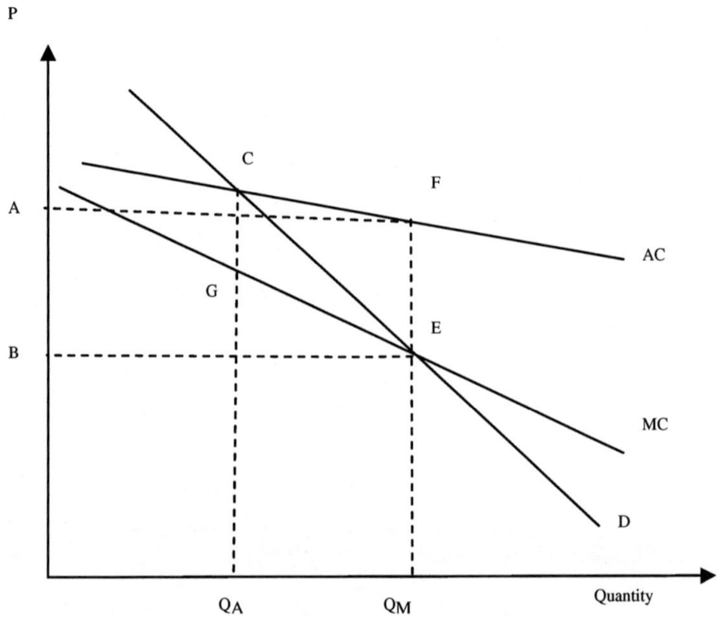

3.4.2 Social Marginal-cost Pricing

Another form of uniform pricing is social marginal-cost pricing. Maximizing aggregate net surplus leads to a price equal to social marginal-cost, thus pricing above marginal cost. If the price does not reflect the social marginal cost, consumers do not receive appropriate information about the societal cost of a marginal increase of demand (Garcia & Reynaud, 2004). Water resources exhibit externalities; on one hand, individuals take the clean water from the environment and dump waste water thus interfering with the use of clean water by themselves and others. In this situation, simple balancing of private marginal cost with the marginal benefits will lead to over-consumption of water since private marginal cost is less than the social marginal cost. These kind of negative externalities are often internalized using proper taxation. Therefore, it is important to evaluate the social marginal cost of water use.

$$p = mc + \lambda \tag{3.1}$$

In equation (3.1), p is price of water, mc is marginal cost of the water supply (short-run and long-run) and λ is marginal shadow price of water. This shadow price is positive when water is scarce or when water withdrawals have environmental impacts.

On the other hand, consumption of potable water by individuals in one household confers positive externalities on other households by reducing the risks of communicable diseases throughout the community. Since marginal social benefits are greater than the marginal private benefits, balancing private marginal cost with marginal benefits will lead to under consumption. This would support a minimal marginal price for an amount of water per month which would be required for adequate basic needs of a household and for a subsidised price of water.

3.4.3 Ramsey Pricing

Ramsey pricing is considered as another form of uniform pricing in the literature. If all prices are set at marginal cost in the presence of fixed costs and if the firm fails to break even, then it is necessary to modify prices including a mark-up over marginal cost. It would seem to be reasonable to impose high mark-ups in those markets where they will matter least (where quantity demanded is not too sensitive to price changes) (Baumol & Bradford, 1970). In other words, increasing prices in markets or market segments where price elasticity of demand is relatively low and low mark-ups in the markets with relatively high price elasticity of demand. This is also known as the inverse elasticity rule.

$$markup = \frac{P_i - C_i}{P_i} = \frac{\lambda}{\varepsilon_i} \tag{3.2}$$

In equation (3.2), P_i is price in market i, C_i is marginal cost, ε_i is price elasticity of demand and λ is proportionate constant or Ramsey number.

Household demand for water can be broken down into indoor and outdoor uses. It is generally argued that internal water uses (toilets, drinking, washing) are inelastic to changes in water tariffs relative to external water uses (gardening, lawn sprinkling, car wash). Many poor communities consume only the bare minimum volume of water which is sufficient to fulfil their basic needs. They would not be able to cut back on water consumption to any appreciable extent due to a change in water tariffs (Munasinghe, 1992). According to Ramsey pricing, higher prices will be charged to relatively less elastic users and these could be relatively poor households. Achievement of objectives like efficiency and equity is dubious with Ramsey pricing. Ramsey pricing of water presents a difficulty in terms of equity as lower income consumers with inelastic demand have to pay a higher unit price relative to more elastic users who typically belongs to high income groups (Altmann, 2007).

3.4.4 Two-part Pricing

A non-uniform price schedule is a tariff for goods in which the consumer's total outlay does not simply rise proportionately with the amounts of the goods one purchases. In the case where marginal-cost pricing cannot cover the total costs of the firm, non-uniform pricing can be used to increase the total surplus above the level using uniform pricing only (S. Brown & Sibley, 1986). Under the non-uniform pricing, two-part pricing, IBTS, DBTS and peak-load pricing are discussed.[5]

The simplest type of non-uniform pricing schedule is the two-part tariff which is composed of a fixed charge and a volumetric charge. Two-part tariffs can simultaneously satisfy the objectives of efficiency and revenue requirement (Sibly, 2006). In terms of water, two-part pricing has a fixed charge to cover the capital expenditure and the volumetric charge according to the marginal cost (Garcia-Valinas, 2005; Garcia & Reynaud, 2004; Ng, 1987). Two-part pricing can be used since some forms of water consumption are essential for all users. Two-part tariffs improve the efficiency of public pricing when average cost is decreasing and many consumers are inelastic with respect to the fixed charge within a reasonable range (Ng & Weisser, 1974). The costs for infrastructure are the most significant cost to water authorities; therefore, the revenue raised by efficient volumetric pricing alone is unlikely to cover the total cost. However, two-part tariffs can be used to achieve both economic efficiency and revenue requirements. The allocation of resources is Pareto efficient when the volumetric price is set equal to the marginal cost.

---

[5] Since the volumetric portion of the rate is still uniform and the fixed charge is independent of the volume, two-part tariffs can be considered as a form of uniform pricing too.

Fixed charges can be introduced with the SRMC pricing in order to cover the fixed costs or sunk costs (capital expenses) and debt service. A substantial fixed charge may be used when the capacity is abundant relative to the demand together with a low unit price (marginal cost is low when capacity is abundant) (Ng, 1987). The fixed charge can be reduced when the unit price increases in order to restrain demand in times when the demand is high relative to the capacity. If the water utility experiences increasing returns to scale, fixed charge can be used to recover deficits created by the marginal-cost pricing.

A moderate fixed charge along with marginal-cost pricing can be introduced without driving away any consumers. This will achieve some amount of surplus to the water utility without incurring an efficiency loss. The use of a two-part tariff may be politically acceptable since a low unit price with a substantial fixed charge be used when the capacity is abundant and vice versa. Determination of the fixed charge is important in designing two-part tariffs. The fixed component can be set at the level necessary to achieve the authority's revenue requirement after allowing for the revenue to be derived from the volumetric component. This could be in the form of a uniform charge for all customers. It can be determined by the difference between the revenue target and the revenue estimated to be achieved from the direct usage component.

Equal allocation of fixed charges between customers of particular class can be adopted due to its simplicity. But it may be inequitable between different categories of customers. In some instances, a fixed charge may be allocated in proportion to the cross-sectional area of the supply pipe. Under this method consumers who require more capacity will be charged more and hence it will achieve improved equity. Some water authorities allocate the fixed cost on the basis of the property values.

3.4.5 Increasing Block Tariff Structure (IBTS)

Another form of non-uniform pricing is an IBTS, where marginal prices increase with the quantity consumed. IBTS is considered as multi-part tariffs (this is an extension of a two-part tariff but usage charges vary with the quantities) (Bos, 1997). IBTS were first introduced in industrialized countries to assist poor households through revenue neutral cross-subsidies. However, recently IBTS have grown in popularity in developing countries while their use is in decline in industrialized countries (Whittington, 2003) and increasingly popular in the U.S.A.

The system design of IBTS requires the utility to determine the number of blocks, volume of water associated with each block and the price charged for each block. IBTS allows the utility to support the poor by providing a certain amount of water below the cost rate and charging higher prices for use beyond a minimum volume (refer to Figure 3.5) (J. J. Boland & Whittington, 1998). The basis for determination of price for each block is often unknown and often subject to rent-seeking by interest groups (Hall & Hanemann, 1996). The size of the initial blocks with lower rates should be determined by the amount of water essential for sanitation that is likely to have external benefits. Furthermore, utilities have indicated major concerns about cost recovery when conservation rates are adopted (Bishop & Weber, 2001). Bishop and Weber (2001) found that with demand reduction, utilities faced revenue losses that were greater than cost savings, implying the need for a rate increase of 1 to 14 per cent in the studied utilities.

Figure 3.5: Increasing Block Tariff Structure

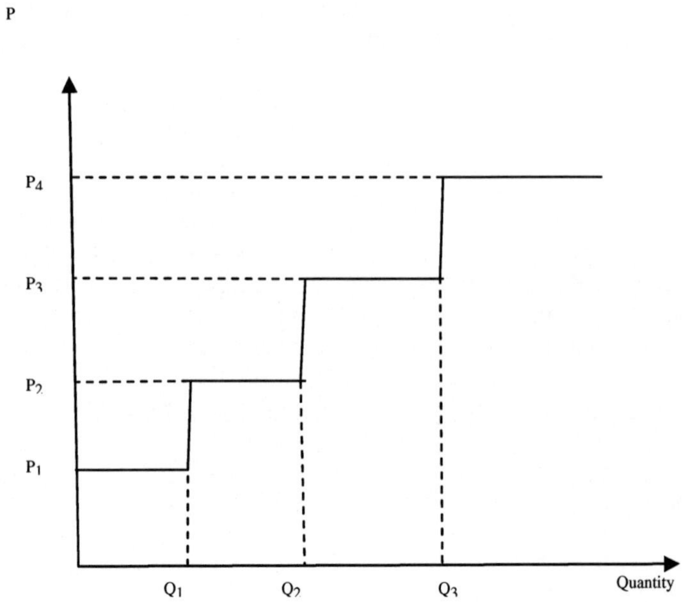

There are several economic arguments both for and against the use of IBTS. First, IBT promote equity as they force rich households to cross-subsidize poor households, assuming that wealthy households will use more water than the poor households (Whittington, 2003).[6] A low price in the initial block and designing the size of this block to be sufficient for essential needs will target the poor to obtain a sufficient quantity of water at a low monthly cost (J. J. Boland & Whittington, 1998). However, in most developing countries, pipe-borne water coverage level for the poor communities is already low and cross-subsidies will not correctly target the poor. In addition, researchers have found that the quantity of water consumed depends not only on household income but on many other household characteristics such as number of household members, water using equipment, size of the garden, personal preference for water use and weather conditions (David & Inocencio, 1998; Fernando Arbues, et al., 2003). Rietveld et al., (2000) concluded for Indonesia, a block rate system is beneficial for small households who are not necessarily low-income households.

Designing the size of the initial block is crucial in IBTS. The internationally cited standard for the initial block is 4 to 5 cubic metres of water per month which is sufficient for essential needs of a household consisting of 4 to 5 members (World Health Organization, 1997b). Most countries set the initial block as high as 10 to 20 cubic metres due to political and other pressures. A lower tariff in initial blocks may not necessarily target only the poor as middle and high income categories may also benefit. This leads to more water consumption than required and violates the efficiency, equity and revenue sufficiency arguments.

Second, it is argued that an IBTS is desirable because the price associated with the highest block can be set very high to prevent wasteful use. Nevertheless, if the volume of the initial block is large and the starting block prices are below marginal cost, this will encourage more water use. Therefore, setting the size and price of the initial block and proceeding blocks are crucial. If price is set equal to the marginal cost, then each user is required to pay the full cost of replacing each unit of water used. IBTS do not provide appropriate incentives to users without marginal-cost pricing. Consumers may not face the marginal cost of water until the third, fourth or final block under a multi-block design.

Third, under IBTS, it is difficult to raise revenues to meet financial constraints without large departures from marginal-cost pricing due to a lack of knowledge of household demand. Forecasting revenue from an IBTS requires the knowledge of the probability distribution of users under the tariff structure. This is difficult to estimate for a developing country due to data limitations. Fourth, IBT lacks transparency and is difficult to

[6] Water is a normal good, consumption increases with increasing income.

administer because it creates complications for users to understand the average or marginal price that is actually paid for water. The kind of price signal most customers rely on becomes confusing when their water use moves from one block to another. Further, IBTS cannot be easily understood and may create problems by making it difficult for the water utility representative to explain the bills to customers.

Finally, IBTS creates problems when a household with a metered connection supplies unconnected neighbours or when households have shared connections. In developing countries, not all households have metered connections and primarily middle and high income households are likely to have separate metered connections (J. J. Boland & Whittington, 1998). If the poor buy water from neighbours with private connections, water use is likely to exceed the initial blocks and will move into the higher priced blocks. Therefore, the poor household may pay a higher price for their water use. Moreover, households with shared connections are also likely to be poor and they will end up consuming at the higher block price. As a result, IBTS may have an opposite effect than intended as the poor will pay higher average prices than the rich (J. J. Boland & Whittington, 1998; Whittington, 2003).

Under block pricing, consumers face a piece-wise linear budget constraint. The consumers can either consume on the interior of each segment or at each kink point (the quantity at which the marginal price increases occurs). The use of increasing block pricing creates a wedge between the marginal price and the average price and prices are endogenous to the water use decision of the consumer. For the consumers above the first linear segment of the budget constraint, marginal price is not the price paid for every unit of consumption. There is an implicit subsidy given to consumers in the case of an IBTS (an implicit tax in case of a DBTS) which is the difference between what a household would pay if all units were charged at the marginal price and what they actually pay. These consumers face a 'virtual income' which is the summation of income and the difference variable (Cavanagh, et al., 2002).

Figure 3.6 shows a piecewise linear budget constraint for an IBTS with two blocks. The first block price is P_1 and the second is P_2 and income is given as Y and the virtual income is Y_v only for consumers who prefer to consume the full first block. Consumer's indifference curves can be placed in the first segment, on the kink or in the second segment. For simplicity, in Figure 3.6 it is assumed that the consumer's utility will be based on the amount of water and the total amount of other goods consumed and there is only one kink. The ideas discussed below can be generalized for more goods and more kinks.

Figure 3.6: Piece-wise Linear Budget Constraint with an Increasing Block Tariff Structure

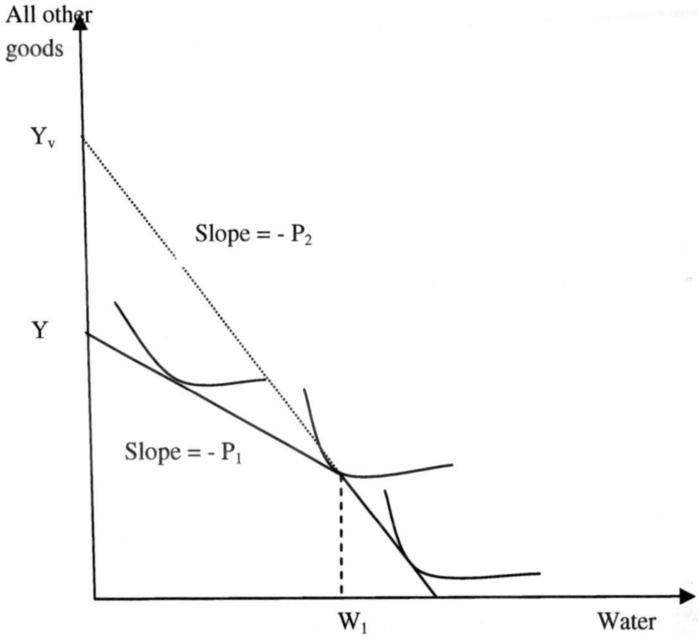

A consumer's utility function U is a function of water q_1 and other goods q_2. Assuming q_1 is a normal good, the prices of q_1 are given below in equation (3.3),

$$P(q_1) = P_1 \qquad (q_1 \leq k)$$
$$P(q_1) = P_2 \qquad (q_1 > k) \tag{3.3}$$

k is the value of q_1 at the kink point, P_1 and P_2 are prices of q_1 where $P_2 > P_1$. The price of q_2 is normalized at 1. The consumer expects to maximize utility subject to the budget constraint which is non-linear in q_1 (equation (3.4)).

$$\min(k, q_1)P_1 + \max(q_1 - k, 0)P_2 + q_2 \leq Y \tag{3.4}$$

Where Y is the consumer's income. The above expression can be rewritten as follows:

$$q_1 P_1 + q_2 \leq Y \qquad (q_1 \leq k)$$
$$q_1 P_2 + q_2 \leq y + k(P_2^1 - P_1) = Y_v \qquad (q_1 > k) \qquad (3.5)$$

Y_v is called the virtual income, the difference between Y and Y_v is $(P_2 - P_1)q_1$ (the difference between what a household in block two would pay in total if all units were priced at P_2 and what it actually pays under an increasing block pricing structure) (Cavanagh, et al., 2002).

3.4.6 Decreasing Block Tariff Structure (DBTS)

DBTS is a form of non-uniform pricing and is categorised as a form of multi-part tariffs. In terms of DBTS, consumers face a high volume charge up to the specified quantity in the first block and then for water consumed in addition to this amount, consumers pay a lower price in every additional block. The DBTS was designed to reflect the fact that when raw water supplies are abundant, large industrial customers often impose lower average costs as they enable the utility to capture economies of scale in water transmission and treatment. In addition, large industrial users typically take their supplies from the larger trunk mains and thus do not require the expansion of neighbourhood distribution networks.

Although it is still used in some communities in the United States and Canada, the DBTS has gradually fallen out of favour, in part because properly defined marginal costs are increasing in many parts of the world and an increased interest in promoting water conservation by the largest customers. The DBTS is often politically unattractive as it results in high volume users paying lower average water prices.

3.4.7 Two-block Tariff Structure

To retain the beneficial properties of block rate structures and to address the three important objectives of pricing (efficiency, equity and revenue sufficiency), utilities can consider two block tariff structures. This can be considered as a form of multi-part tariffs. The first block price can be set below or above marginal cost and the size of the block can be reduced to the lifeline level sufficient for a household and the second block price can be set equal to the marginal cost (J. J. Boland & Whittington, 1998; Whittington, 2003). Economically, the size of the initial block with the subsidy should be determined by the amount of water that is likely to have external benefits.

IBTS or DBTS with two blocks may reduce the inefficiencies of multi block system. Under the IBTS two block arrangements, the first block price is set below marginal cost and the second block price is set at the marginal cost. If water use by one household provides incidental benefits to other households, balancing marginal cost with marginal benefits will lead to under-consumption. This would support a minimal marginal price for an amount of water per month which would be required for adequate basic needs (Agthe & Billings, 1987; Billings, 1982). The size of the first block can be set such that relatively fewer users terminate their consumption in this block (J. J. Boland & Whittington, 1998). Then the subsidy would not be an issue, as nearly all users would face marginal cost price while cross-subsidies are limited to those who are generally considered to be the target of the redistribution.

On the other hand, almost all the consumers are relatively inelastic with respect to water use in the first block within reasonable limits (if the size of the first block is designed to provide sufficient water for basic needs). Economic efficiency implies maximization of community net benefits. Considering the extra cost of government funding, the regulator can set the first block price above marginal cost and the second block price at the marginal cost (DBTS with two block structure). This structure is rarely practiced due to political pressures and public perceptions.

3.4.8 Peak-load Pricing

The marginal cost of water supplies may be high during the dry season or peak season because water demand will be high and water supplies will be constrained. The cost of one consumer using water supply services should include the opportunity cost of someone else not getting that water. In these situations it makes sense to implement seasonal pricing to allocate available water supplies to high-value users (Ng, 1987).

$$p^{peak} = MC^{peak}$$
$$p^{off-peak} = MC^{off-peak} \tag{3.6}$$

p^{peak} and $p^{off-peak}$ are prices of water at the peak period and off-peak periods respectively, MC^{peak} and $MC^{off-peak}$ are marginal costs of water supply at peak and off-peak periods and usually $MC^{peak} > MC^{off-peak}$.

Peak-load pricing is used when the demand for water exhibits substantial variation from season to season. Peak-load pricing is expected to shift some of the demand from the peak time period to the off-peak time period, thus improving the efficiency of the system. This shift depends on customer response to time differentiated prices. Peak-load pricing encourages conservation when water is at its most valuable. The timing and accuracy of the price signals are crucial in peak-load pricing.

The utility requires maintaining an excess capacity above the average level of demand it can expect, due to variation in demand. If the variation in demand is systematic then the price for services during the peak periods should include the cost of capacity that makes consumption at the peak level possible. A variant marginal-cost pricing is based on the observation that demand varies seasonally and capacity constraints are evident. Renzetti (1992b) investigated peak-load pricing and found positive welfare effects and entailed pricing according to the SRMC in off-peak demand and LRMC in peak demand periods (Renzetti, 1992b).

Seasonal water pricing has been carried out in some parts of Europe and it has been found that it would have a significant negative impact on larger households. Moreover, seasonal pricing would require all meters to be read regularly (monthly or bi-monthly intervals) which results in additional costs. Grafton and Kompas (2006) propose a system in which peak pricing increases according to the dam storage levels. This was done by implicitly weighting the marginal supply cost by a scarcity factor.

3.5 Summary

The design of the water tariff structure is challenging because there are a number of objectives that need to be understood and met efficiently. A tariff design that contributes to the achievement of one objective may be detrimental to the achievement of another. The theoretically proven way of achieving all the objectives (efficiency, equity and financial viability) is the use of marginal-cost pricing (Ng, 1987). A wide range of water tariff structures have been developed and are currently practiced around the world.

In a survey of Asian countries, the ADB found that 20 out of a sample of 38 countries use an IBTS (ADB, 2001). Although increasingly popular, an IBTS have often failed to deliver on the promise of simultaneously meeting all of the different objectives of tariff design. This is partly due to poor design of block structures, political influence and also reflects the fact that low income households are not necessarily small consumers of water and there are many situations in which several poor households share a single connection. More importantly, an IBTS convey incorrect pricing signals to water users. Uniform volumetric rates and two-part tariffs structure perform comparatively well in meeting different objectives of pricing.

Pipe-borne water tariffs must not be used to deliver subsidies to poor households as too often they have failed to reach the majority of poor households and merely succeeded in creating a large financial drain on the sector. It is important to evaluate whether pipe-borne water distribution networks are the best option for the delivery of subsidies to the poor. The fact that water is a basic need by itself will not succeed to be the efficient and effective way to deliver subsidies to the poor. Moreover, food, health services and housing are also basic needs and no minimum quantity of these is usually offered free of charge. Therefore, the relevant issue is to identify the subsidy mechanism that will reach the poor most efficiently and effectively; while allowing water pricing structure to reflect the need and costs of the pipe-borne water sector.

One of the objectives of the book is to evaluate the welfare of various price reforms and a comparison with the current tariffs. This chapter lays the theoretical background for the empirical analyses undertaken in chapter 4, 5, 6 and 7 by highlighting the importance of marginal-cost pricing. The following four chapters will then focus on empirical analyses of residential, industrial and commercial water demands, marginal costs and welfare of alternative price reforms.

CHAPTER FOUR

PRICE RESPONSIVENESS OF RESIDENTIAL WATER DEMAND

4.1 Introduction

Appropriate water pricing policies can improve water use efficiency and augment revenues, thereby improving and expanding pipe-borne water supply services. Designing an appropriate pricing policy and efficient planning and management of pipe-borne water supply systems require an understanding of the determinants of water demand. The quantification of pipe-borne water demand assists water utility operators and policy makers in predicting consumption responses to changes in water pricing, by indicating the effectiveness of demand management. The total water consumption of pipe-borne water supplies has increased from 275 million cubic metres in 1995 to 396 million cubic metres in 2006 (Figure 4.1). The annual consumption of water through individual services covering domestic, commercial, industrial and institutional use has increased by 116 million cubic metres during the last decade (1995 to 2005). Residential water use was estimated at 243 million cubic metres accounting for 63.5 per cent of total water produced by the NWSDB and 46 per cent of the total revenue collected in 2005.

This chapter presents the analysis of residential demand for pipe-borne water in Sri Lanka in order to quantify residential consumer's responses to pipe-borne water price changes. One of the main objectives of the book is to evaluate the welfare effects of alternative water pricing rules. Therefore, the parameter estimates of this chapter, along with the findings of chapter 5 and 6 will be used to test the efficiency of various price reforms in chapter 7. The price responsiveness of residential water demand is dependent on a number of factors including prices, size of the household, income, temperature and rainfall.

At present, residential water use accounts for the largest share of total pipe-borne water consumption and is subjected to extensive subsidies. Continuous supply of water at the current rates may eventually lead the collapse of the water supply system (Gunathilake, et al., 2001). This chapter provides insights into the potential role of prices as a residential demand management tool. Price elasticity of residential demand, defined as the percentage change in quantity demanded of water in response to one per cent change in the price of water, is the key policy variable of interest that can be derived from the water demand function.

Figure 4.1: Total Water Production – Year 1995 to 2006

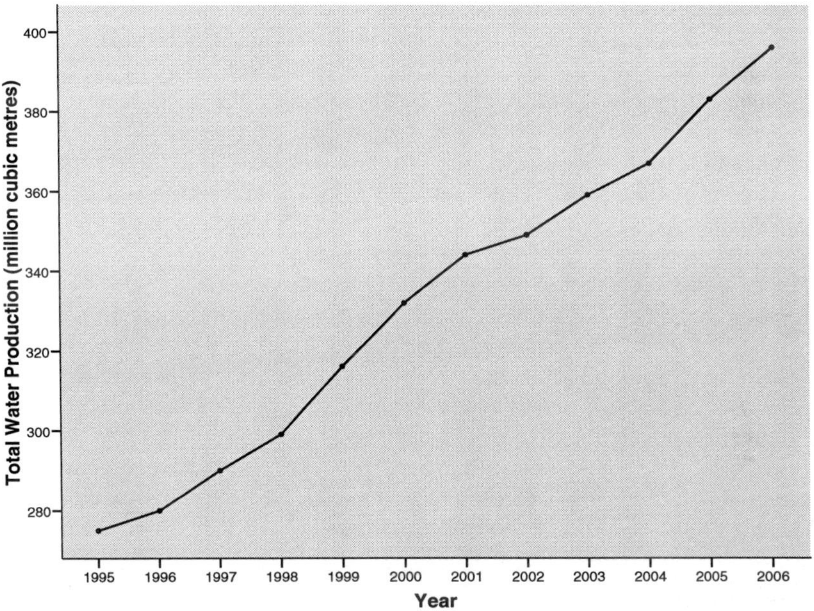

There are very few studies that investigate residential demand for pipe-borne water in Sri Lanka (Gunathilake, et al., 2001; Hussain, et al., 2002; Nauges & van-den Berg, 2006). Previous studies that have used Sri Lankan data have employed cross-sectional approaches (Gunathilake, et al., 2001; Nauges & van-den Berg, 2006); time series data (Hussain, et al., 2002); and econometric techniques such as Ordinary Least Squares (OLS) and Instrumental Variable techniques (IV) (Gunathilake, et al., 2001; Hussain, et al., 2002). Of these studies, those that have estimated residential price elasticity suggest magnitudes from -0.18 to -0.74 (Gunathilake, et al., 2001; Hussain, et al., 2002; Nauges & van-den Berg, 2006). These studies were undertaken using data from the mid-1990s to early 2000 with limited geographical coverage.

This chapter utilizes a new set of panel data covering all districts of Sri Lanka for sixty months (January 2001 to December 2005) to estimate elasticities. Further, this chapter uses more extensive and recent data compared with the previous studies thereby allowing for more policy relevant estimates. Moreover, the analysis includes identification of the proportion of household water use that may not be responsive to price changes. This will produce a better understanding of price responsiveness of residential consumers in the water sector of developing countries.

The findings of this chapter conform to previous studies that suggest demand for water is price and income inelastic. Moreover, by using the Stone-Geary specification this chapter provides water managers with important information about the consumption threshold below which demand is non-responsive to price changes. However, Stone-Geary form is relatively inflexible as it is predominantly linear and forces upon the data a particular type of outcome. Average household consumption is much greater than this estimated threshold value, therefore, this must be considered in the design of water pricing policies. In addition, the inelastic nature of water consumption creates opportunities for water utilities to raise revenues by increasing water charges. While one concern of increasing water prices is the impacts on the poor, the revenue raised can be used to increase pipe-borne water supply services to these groups and thus substantially improving their standard of living.

Section 4.2 reviews the literature providing the background to the empirical estimations of residential demand for water. It outlines the factors that need to be considered in estimating residential water demand and also elaborates on the commonly used estimation techniques. Section 4.3 provides an overview of data used in this chapter. Section 4.4 discusses the methodology, models and econometric techniques applied in this chapter while section 4.5 discusses the results. Section 4.6 gives some concluding remarks for residential water management.

4.2 Literature Review

Evidence suggests that water demand is inelastic but not perfectly inelastic. Weak sensitivity of consumption to price changes is a result of several factors: the intrinsic nature of water as a necessity to life; the fact that water bills constitute a small portion of household's budget and because of imperfect price information (Gaudin, 2005). Higher elasticity estimates are associated with long-run analyses (Agthe, et al., 1986;

Nauges & Martinez-Espineira, 2004). Arbues et al., (2003) suggest that long-run price responsiveness is likely to be greater due to the changes to capital investment by consumers through purchase of water efficient appliances. In addition, price elasticity of water can vary in the presence of income heterogeneity. For instance, Agthe and Billings (1987) and Renwick and Archibald (1998) have concluded that the price elasticity of residential water demand is lower for low income households compared to middle and high income households.

A meta-analysis of 124 estimates of water demand elasticity for both developed and developing countries between 1963 and 1993 found the mean price elasticity as -0.51, a short-run median estimate of -0.38 and a long-run median estimate of -0.64 with 90 per cent of estimates between zero and -0.75 (Espey, et al., 1997). This signifies that the percentage reduction in the quantity of residential water demanded is less than proportionate to the percentage increase in price (Worthington & Hoffmann, 2006). While some estimates are very low, for example, Renwick et al., (1998), Martinez-Espineira and Nauges (2004), Barkatullah (1996) and Pushpangandan and Murugan (1998) have estimated price elasticity to be less than -0.25, many estimates lie in the range of -0.25 and -0.75 (Billings & Agthe, 1980; Chicoine & Ramamurthy, 1986; Gaudin, et al., 2001; Martinez-Espeneira, 2003a; Nieswiadomy, 1992; Nieswiadomy & Molina, 1989).

A large number of studies estimate residential water demand for developed countries with most concentrating on the United States and Europe. For example, Howe and Linaweaver (1967), Gibbs (1978), Danielson(1979), Foster and Beattie (1979), Billings (1982), Schefter and David (1985), Chicoine and Ramamurthy (1986), Nieswiadomy and Molina (1989), Renwick and Archibald (1998), and Renwick and Green (2000) have used U.S. data. Some studies that used European data are Hansen (1996), Hoglund (1999), Nauges and Thomas (2000), Martinez-Espineira (2003b), Garcia and Reynaud (2004) and Martinez-Espineira and Nuages (2004). There are relatively few studies estimating the residential water demand in developing or low income countries (Worthington & Hoffmann, 2006). Of the few available, there are estimates for Philippines (David and Inocencio, 1998), Indonesia (Rietveld et al., (2000), India (Pushpangadan and Murugan (1998) and Cambodia (Basani et al., 1999). However, price elasticity estimates for developing countries are comparable with those for developed countries.

In contrast to developed countries, where almost all households obtain water from the water utility through a piped network, the residential water sector has more variation in developing countries. In developing countries, households may have a private metered connection with water collected from wells, public taps, rivers, lakes or water vendors or they may have no private metered connection and rely entirely on other sources. Very little is known about the household behaviour in developing countries regarding the factors influencing water consumption choices and the substitutability or complementarity of piped water and water from other sources (Nauges & van-den Berg, 2006). Many studies on residential water demand are in the form of contingent valuation to derive willingness-to-pay for getting a house connection to a piped water network (J. H. North & Griffin, 1997; Pattanayake, et al., 2006; Whittington, et al., 2002).

Most empirical studies on developing countries report price elasticities varying between -0.2 to -0.6 (David & Inocencio, 1998). David and Inocencio (1998) studied Manila's water supply and sewage treatment network which was being considered for privatisation. The estimated price elasticity of demand for water was -0.5 and the price elasticity of vended water was -2.1. A study based on Indonesia found that the price elasticity of demand is as large as -1.2 and the income elasticity is quite small (Rietveld, et al., 2000). A study conducted for Kerala, India produced very low short-run price elasticity values varying from -0.04 to -0.07 (Pushpangadan & Murugan, 1998). Cambodian towns exhibited price elasticity of demand values for water as -0.5 in a model using household level cross-sectional data (Basani, et al., 1999).

Only a handful of studies investigated residential demand for pipe-borne water in Sri Lanka. The study by Gunatilake et al., (2001) estimated the demand function for residential water use within the Kandy municipal limits in Sri Lanka. They used primary and cross-sectional data which was collected through a survey of 58 households. However, this is not considered a sufficient number of observations for robust estimation. The marginal price elasticity of demand obtained by simple OLS regression was -0.34 (Gunathilake, et al., 2001). The study by Hussain et al., (2002) estimated separate water demand functions for residential, commercial and industrial sectors using monthly time series data for 60 months from January 1994 to December 1998. The country level residential price elasticity of demand was estimated at -0.18, after excluding the price variable to capture intra-marginal price effects (difference variable) (Hussain, et al., 2002).

Nauges and Van-den Berg (2006) illustrated the impact of water price increases on consumption of piped water through a study of the demand for water of piped and non-piped households using cross-sectional data for 1,800 households in the Southwest of Sri Lanka. The marginal price elasticity was estimated at -0.74 for households exclusively relying on piped water and as -0.69 for households using piped water but supplementing with other water sources (Nauges & van-den Berg, 2006). In addition, Pattanayak et al., (2006) conducted a study to show how willingness to pay surveys can be used to gauge household demand for an improved network of water and sanitation services. Approximately 1800 households in Southwest of Sri Lanka were surveyed in 2003 and poverty and costs were found to be the key determinants of water demand (Pattanayake, et al., 2006).

One of the controversial issues considered in the literature is the estimation of water demand in the presence of block tariffs (due to non-linear pricing and kinked budget curves). Over the past 40 years, improvements in water demand estimation involved correction for the endogeneity of price and quantity under block pricing, proper price specification, accounting for implicit income effects and the use of time series or panel data rather than cross-sectional data (Cavanagh, et al., 2002).

Residential water demand has been extensively studied with the presence of increasing and decreasing block tariff structures. For example, Billings and Agthe (1980), Renwick and Archibald (1998), Gaudin et al., (2001), Martinez-Espineira (2003a, 2003b), Rietveld et al., (2000) and Hajispyrou et al., (2002) have conducted analyses of an IBTS. Studies by Chicoine and Ramamurthy (1986) and Williams and Suh (1986) have examined DBTS, while Foster and Beattie (1981), Schefter and David (1985) and Nieswiadomy and Molina (1989) have included both increasing and decreasing block tariff regimes (Worthington & Hoffmann, 2006).

Early studies used only a single price variable (either average or marginal price) as an independent variable when estimating the demand for water under block pricing. Marginal price refers to the price prevailing in the last consumption block and intra-marginal price refers to the prices prevailing in the intermediate blocks. The average price is calculated by dividing the total revenue or water bill by the total quantity consumed.

Average price has been used by Foster and Beattie (1979), Chicoine and Ramamurthy (1986) and Nauges and Thomas (2000). They found using average price as the only price variable tends to produce large estimates for price elasticity of demand. It is possible for average price to remain constant or to decrease when marginal price increases with constant intra-marginal prices. This is assuming that the price elasticity is not zero and only fewer units will be purchased at a higher marginal price (Billings, 1982). In addition, since average price is derived ex post, it fails to account for changes in intra-marginal prices. Authors considering average price argue that households are rarely well informed on the price structure and are thus more likely to react to average price rather than marginal price (Beattie & Foster, 1979; Chicoine & Ramamurthy, 1986; Nauges & Thomas, 2000). Howe and Linaweaver (1967), Gibbs (1978) and Hansen (1996) used marginal price as the only price variable. This would have lead to erroneous estimates as marginal price alone fails to account for the income effect of a change in intra-marginal rates with constant marginal price. Both average and marginal price variables were used by Nieswiadomy (1992) and Billings (1982), however, they failed to account for changes in intra-marginal rates.

If average and marginal prices are positively correlated then the use of a single price variable can lead to upward bias in the estimates of price elasticity (Taylor, 1975). Taylor (1975) and Nordin (1976) suggested the use of two price variables to overcome the above problems. Marginal price and a difference variable, D, are now increasingly added in demand estimations under block pricing. The difference variable is also called a Rate Structure Premium and is defined as $(AP - MP) * Q$. AP is the average price paid for water, MP is the marginal price paid for water and Q refers to the quantity of water consumed. The difference variable is the difference between the actual total bill and what the user would have to pay if all units were charged at the marginal price.

In the case of increasing (decreasing) block pricing, the difference variable represents a saving (an additional cost) to the consumer and thereby providing an implicit subsidy (tax) for water consumed in the intra-marginal blocks (Billings & Agthe, 1980). The difference-variable elasticity measures the income effect of changes in intra-marginal rates and the marginal-price elasticity measures the income and substitution effects of a change in marginal price. Most researchers have adopted the strategy of using two price variables instead of a single price variable (Billings & Agthe, 1980; Chicoine & Ramamurthy, 1986; Martinez-Espeneira, 2003a; Nauges & Martinez-Espineira, 2004; Nieswiadomy & Molina, 1989; Renwick & Archibald, 1998; Renwick & Green, 2000; Schefter & David, 1985).

Taylor (1975) hypothesized that in linear models, the coefficients of the difference and income variable should be equal in magnitude but opposite in sign. Since water is a normal good, the income coefficient is positive and the difference-variable effect is negative. Therefore, for a given marginal price, the higher the difference variable, the lower the intra-marginal prices and the higher the subsidy leads to higher real income of consumers. Increasing intra-marginal rates decreases the difference variable and decreases the implicit subsidy and reduces water use.

The theoretical expectation of the difference variable should be equal in magnitude and opposite in sign to the income variable has been tested in empirical literature but with little success (Agthe, et al., 1986; Arbues, et al., 2003; Billings & Agthe, 1980; Hewitt & Hanemann, 1995; Nieswiadomy & Molina, 1989). Shin (1985) argued that it might be due to price illusion or incomplete information concerning the full budget constraint. Shin (1985) introduces a perceived price variable to capture the pure income effect. Perceived price is a function of marginal price, average price and the price perception parameter (k) $P^* = MP(AP / MP)^k$ (Shin, 1985; Worthington & Hoffmann, 2006).

If the expected marginal benefits of learning the true nature of the rate schedule are less than the expected marginal costs, it is likely that consumers will react to a proxy of marginal price, such as the ex post calculated average price. If the expected marginal benefits are greater than the expected marginal costs, it is likely that consumers investigate the problem carefully and react to the true rate schedule. If consumers stop searching for information when the expected marginal benefit equals expected marginal cost, perceived price may lie between marginal and average price and the difference variable may be embedded in the perceived price. Nieswiadomy and Molina (1991) used a price perception model to compare increasing and decreasing tariffs and found that customers react to marginal price when facing an IBTS and average prices when faced with a DBTS (Worthington & Hoffmann, 2006). Sri Lankan residential consumers are faced with IBTS; therefore, this chapter uses marginal price and the difference variable in the residential demand estimation.

Researchers found the quantity of water consumed depends on many factors other than price, such as number of household members, income, temperature and rainfall (Arbues, et al., 2003; David & Inocencio, 1998; Rietveld, et al., 2000). An income variable is included in most residential demand estimations and occasionally the assessed value of the property is used in addition to money income (Hewitt & Hanemann, 1995; C. W. Howe & Linaweaver, 1967). Since the property value is correlated with income and other variables, Jones and Morris (1984) developed a proxy for family income based on the educational level of the head of the household, vehicle ownership, assessed property value and age of the residence. Several researchers found different income elasticities for different income levels (Agthe & Billings, 1987; Arbues, et al., 2003; Billings, 1987; Gunathilake, et al., 2001; Saleth & Dinar, 2000).

Water is considered to be a normal good and the demand for normal goods should increase with income. The estimates of income elasticities are almost income inelastic and small in magnitude (Barkatullah, 1999; Chicoine & Ramamurthy, 1986; Garcia & Reynaud, 2004; Gaudin, et al., 2001). This could be explained by the fact that water bills often represent a lower proportion of income for households (Arbues, et al., 2003). In addition, there is a complication that increasing and decreasing block rates potentially encompass income effects and this may serve to reduce the significance and the magnitude of the income effects (Worthington & Hoffmann, 2006). Moreover, since the estimated income elasticities are short-run and hence cannot capture activities like buying new appliances, moving houses or house extensions which may influence water demand over the longer term.

The average number of household members and average household income of each district are included in the present residential demand analysis. Number of household members is included as an independent variable in most residential demand estimations. Household size is expected to positively affect household water use, however, due to economies of scale, the increase in water use is less than proportional to the increase in household size (Arbues, et al., 2003; Hoglund, 1999). Studies like Nauges and Thomas (2000) confirmed that age distribution within the household members have varying impacts on residential water use. They argued water consumption in areas with a higher proportion of younger persons is likely to be higher due to more frequent laundering and use of water-intensive outdoor leisure activities (Worthington & Hoffmann, 2006).

Climatic effects in residential water demand models have been introduced in different ways. These range from temperature (Griffin & Chang, 1990), minutes of sunshine, precipitation, rainfall (Stevens, et al., 1992) and number of rainy days (Worthington, et al., 2006). Some used precipitation during the season (Beattie & Foster, 1979, 1981) while others used evapotranspiration from Bermuda grass minus rainfall (Billings, 1982; Billings & Agthe, 1980; Hewitt & Hanemann, 1995; Nieswiadomy & Molina, 1988). Stevens et al., (1992), Hussain et al., (2002) and many other researchers used temperature together with annual or monthly rainfall. Espey and Shaw (1997) and Dalhuisen et al., (2003), in their meta-analysis argued that incorporation of rainfall results in significantly less elastic estimates of the price elasticity of demand, since in some cases water prices and rainfall are positively related (Worthington & Hoffmann, 2006). Nevertheless, seasonal water pricing is not practiced in Sri Lanka and hence these concerns are not relevant here. Therefore, monthly average temperature and rainfall for each district are included in the demand estimation.

The availability of accurate data at an appropriate frequency has plagued attempts at modelling residential water demand (Worthington & Hoffmann, 2006). Estimating residential water demand functions with household data would be the most valuable, however, only a few, for example, Beattie and Foster (1981), Nieswiadomy (1992) and Hajispyrou et al., (2002) have used household level survey data. There is a high level of data re-use from previously published work due to lack of data availability. For example, Agthe and Billings (1980), Agthe et al., (1986) and Agthe and Billings (1987) used 1974 to 1980 data for Tucson Arizona, while a 1976 to 1985 Denton data set was repeatedly employed by Nieswiadomy and Molina (1989, 1991), Griffin and Chang (1990), Hewitt and Hanemann (1995) and Gaudin et al., (2001) (Worthington & Hoffmann, 2006).

The most common research focus is on aggregate data at community or utility level (Ruijs, 2007; Stevens, et al., 1992). This needs the matching of average water consumption with the averages of the household related characteristics from different sources. These other characteristics include household income, household size and household demographics (Worthington & Hoffmann, 2006). In keeping with this approach, aggregate data for all the NWSDB districts are matched with household demographics and climate data for each district in this chapter.

Panel data techniques have dominated the literature, for example, Agthe and Billings (1980), Martinez-Espineira (2003a), Hewitt and Hanemann (1995), Gaudin et al., (2001) and Chicoine and Ramamurthy (1986). Cross-sectional techniques are the next most popular and found in studies such as Beattie and Foster (1981), Stevens et al., (1992), Rietveld et al., (2000) and Hajispyrou et al., (2002) (Worthington & Hoffmann, 2006). The difficulties in gathering accurate and consistent data means that time series techniques are rarely used; Hussain et al., (2002) is a recent example of the few studies using time-series data.

Various econometric techniques are employed to analyse panel data in water demand models. These include OLS, Generalized Least Squares (GLS), two and three Stage Least Squares (2SLS and 3SLS), IV and Maximum-likelihood (ML). OLS technique dominated the water demand literature (Billings & Agthe, 1980; Hewitt & Hanemann, 1995; Martinez-Espeneira, 2003a; Worthington & Hoffmann, 2006), however, with the presence of block pricing this technique yielded bias and inconsistent estimates (Billings, 1987; Nieswiadomy & Molina, 1988).

Nieswiadomy and Molina (1991) used the 2SLS procedure where in the first stage the observed price is regressed against all explanatory variables and the predicted price is then specified in the second stage as a regressor. Another approach involved the regression of the observed water demand on the actual price schedule to linearize the tariff structure to obtain instrumental marginal price and the difference variable (Worthington & Hoffmann, 2006). In the second stage the instrumented marginal price and the difference variable are used to estimate the demand function (Agthe & Billings, 1987; Agthe, et al., 1986; Barkatullah, 1996; Hewitt & Hanemann, 1995; Worthington & Hoffmann, 2006). Both of these techniques are likely to improve the reliability of estimates (Worthington & Hoffmann, 2006). To address the short comings and to test the robustness of the results, a comparison of estimates from OLS, IV and 2SLS techniques is used later in this chapter.

This chapter presents the estimation of residential water demand for Sri Lanka using Cobb-Douglas and Stone-Geary functional forms. A variety of functional forms have been employed in estimating residential water demand. Cobb-Douglas water demand equations are widely used in the literature, including Beattie and Foster (1981), Garcia and Reynaud (2004) and Hewitt and Hanemann (1995) (Worthington & Hoffmann, 2006). It is important to look at the most commonly used functional forms where the water demand function can exhibit different elasticities at different levels of use in different price ranges. In fact, the same demand curve can be elastic over some ranges and inelastic in others. Intuitively, this could be expected because water is used for different purposes; some uses are more willingly substituted than others. Essential uses of water are drinking, cooking, and personal hygiene and these are expected to be highly inelastic.

The use of a demand equation derived from the Stone-Geary utility function is proposed explicitly to consider that water consumption includes two components: a fixed quantity that cannot be adjusted immediately after a price increase and a residual that can adapt instantaneously. This specification has been rarely used in residential water demand studies (Al-Quanibet & Johnston, 1985; Gaudin, et al., 2001; Nauges & Martinez-Espineira, 2004). This has an advantage of being theory-compatible as well as explicitly modelling a minimum level of consumption that does not depend on prices. The limitations implied by this specification are not restrictive because water has always been proved to be a normal good and price inelastic (Nauges & Martinez-Espineira, 2004).

According to Martineiz-Espineira and Nauges (2004), for Seville in Spain, the estimated minimum consumption level or threshold was 4.7 cubic metres per capita per month and the average price and income elasticities were -0.10 and 0.10 respectively (Nauges & Martinez-Espineira, 2004). After relaxing the restriction that the threshold remains constant over the period, the estimated threshold was 2.6 cubic metres per capita per month (lower than previous model). Gaudin et al., (2001) used a Stone-Geary utility function to derive residential water demand for Texas using a five year panel. Stone-Geary results gave elasticities ranging from -0.19 to -0.28. The results suggested approximately three quarters of total water usage is not responsive to price changes and the values ranged from 8 to 10 cubic metres per capita per month. A study by Al-Qunaibet and Johnston (1985), used monthly data from Kuwait and the estimated price and income elasticity were -0.77 and 0.211 respectively. They estimated the subsistence water use level in Kuwait to be about 1.26 cubic metres per capita per month.

As discussed in the literature review, two price variables, marginal price and a difference variable, must be used to reliably estimate demand in the presence of block pricing (Nordin, 1976; Taylor, 1975). It is apparent from the literature that the panel data has several advantages over cross-sectional data (Billings & Agthe, 1980; Gaudin, et al., 2001; Martinez-Espeneira, 2003a) and household survey data is ideal, but due to data unavailability aggregate data are commonly used (Ruijs, 2007; Stevens, et al., 1992). Keeping with these past approaches, aggregate panel data techniques covering fourteen water utility districts for sixty months are used to estimate residential water demand in Sri Lanka. Data on average household incomes, average numbers of household members, average monthly temperatures and average monthly rainfall intensities are matched with districts and months. The Cobb-Douglas is the most widely used functional form for estimations of residential water demand (Beattie & Foster, 1981; Garcia & Reynaud, 2004; Hewitt & Hanemann, 1995) and Stone-Geary functional form is rarely used in the water demand literature (Al-Quanibet & Johnston, 1985). The residential water demand in Sri Lank is analysed using both Cobb-Douglas and Stone-Geary functional forms to estimate more policy relevant parameters.

Data used in the current study do not take into account the differences in households within each district and fail to take into account household specific characteristics influencing residential water demand in Sri Lanka. However, use of aggregate data will provide useful information to policy makers by providing estimates of price elasticity of demand, the quantity of water that is not responsive to price changes and the prospects for residential water demand management through the pricing mechanism.

4.2.1 Residential Water Pricing in Sri Lanka

Sri-Lankan residential water consumers' face non-linear pricing and the same pricing schedule is administered across all the NWSDB districts. The pricing system consists of two types of charges: fixed and volumetric. The volumetric charge is variable and subjected to increasing block pricing consisting of eight blocks. Under the IBTS, consumers' monthly water bills with different blocks can be mathematically expressed as follows (equation (4.1)):

$$
\begin{aligned}
&B_1 = [MP_1 * Q] + F \;\; if \;\; 0 < Q \leq q_1 \\
&B_2 = [MP_2 * (Q - q_1) + MP_1 * q_1] + F \;\; if \;\; q_1 < Q \leq q_2 \\
&B_3 = [MP_3 * (Q - q_2) + MP_2 * (q_2 - q_1) + MP_1 * q_1] \\
&+ F \;\; if \;\; q_2 < Q \leq q_3 \qquad\qquad (4.1) \\
&\Lambda \\
&B_8 = [MP_8 * (Q - q_7) + MP_6 * (q_7 - q_6) \\
&+ MP_6 * (q_6 - q_5) + MP_5 * (q_5 - q_4) \\
&+ MP_4 * (q_4 - q_3) + MP_3 * (q_3 - q_2) + MP_2 * (q_2 - q_1) \\
&+ MP_1 * q_1] + F \;\; if \;\; q_7 \leq Q
\end{aligned}
$$

In equation (4.1), B_i is monthly water bill of a customer using Q units of water; MP_i is the marginal price $(MP_8 > ......MP_4 > ....MP_1)$; q_i is the break point of the price schedule *(i=1-8)*; and F is the monthly fixed charge.

Table 4 in Appendix 1 shows the price over the period of study (January 2001 to December 2005). In 2001, the initial 10 cubic metres of water were charged at a rate of SLRS 1 per cubic metre. The charges gradually increased to SLRS 40 per cubic metre when consumption exceeded 50 cubic metres. In mid-2002 prices were changed even for the first 10 cubic metres and raised by SLRS 0.25 per cubic metre. This price structure under went further revision in 2005, however, there was no change to the rates of the initial two blocks and this schedule remains in operation. The following section describes the data used for analysing residential water demand in this chapter.

4.3 Data

As noted, analysis in this chapter uses a panel data sample of 14 districts for 60 months from January 2001 to December 2005, yielding a total of 840 observations. Information on aggregate residential water consumption, number of residential metered customers and respective price structures was obtained from the NWSDB. Socio-economic variables were obtained from the two sources: 2001/02 and 2005/06 Household Income and Expenditure Survey of the Department of Census and Statistics and 2003/04 Consumer Finances and Socio-economic survey of the Central Bank of Sri Lanka. Interpolation was used to derive monthly income and the number of household members for the intervening periods. The average household income values for each of the NWSDB districts were obtained by weighting incomes from administrative districts. Weather data for the period for relevant districts were collected from the Department of Meteorology, Sri Lanka.

The dependent variable, monthly average household water quantity is calculated by dividing monthly total residential water quantity by the total number of residential connections for each district. The marginal price measures the changes in the price of the final units of water purchased by the consumer and is calculated for each district and month from the respective rate schedules. The marginal price variable absorbs both income and substitution effects of a price change. Assuming people purchase lower volumes of water as price increases, the expected sign is negative.

The difference variable absorbs the income effect of changes in intra-marginal rates. In the presence of increasing block pricing, it is assumed that this variable will be negative; representing an implicit subsidy. The reasoning is as follows: as intra-marginal rates increase, the difference becomes larger (less negative), causing a reduction in the implicit subsidy, thereby decreasing water use. The sign for the difference elasticity of demand would be positive (derivative is negative and difference is also negative). To facilitate more intuitive interpretation, the difference variable under increasing block pricing schedules is multiplied by (-1) in this analysis. The anticipated sign of the estimated coefficient is hence, positive, implying an increase in the difference variable leads to an increase in the implicit subsidy and hence higher household water consumption. Respective rate structures and average water consumption are used to calculate the relevant difference variable.

Income is one of the main determinants of consumption and may act as a proxy for the water using appliances. Assuming consumption of water increases with the level of income, the expected sign on the derivative of water use with respect to income is positive. Household water consumption decisions are affected by household size and age structure of the household and other relevant variables such as possession of washing machines, vehicles and gardens. However, due to the lack of data availability, the model presented here includes only the number of household members. It is expected that water consumption is positively related to the number of household members.

Weather patterns exert the following influences on water demand: high temperatures increase water demand while high rainfalls decrease water demand. Outdoor water use depends on climatic conditions which are represented by weather variables. To capture the influence of climate, monthly and district average temperature and rainfall data are used in models discussed in the next section. The coefficient of temperature with respect to water use is expected to be positive while the coefficient of rainfall is expected to be negative. The next section provides the summary statistics of the variables used in the residential water demand analyses. Use of intensity of rainfall as an independent variable in the residential demand analysis has limitations, since high intensity of rainfall may not always reduce the monthly water consumption. Therefore, inclusion of number of rainy days or rain-free days would provide a better indication of influence of climatic variables on residential water consumption (Worthington & Hoffmann, 2006). However, above variables were not used in the present analysis due to data unavailability.

4.3.1 Summary Statistics

Table 4.1 displays the minimum, maximum, mean and standard deviation of the input variables used for estimating residential water demand. The dependent variable, average monthly household water consumption, ranges from a minimum of 10 cubic metres to nearly 33 cubic metres with a mean at 17 and a standard deviation of 2.49 cubic metres. Therefore, the majority of households benefit from the subsidy given through lower tariffs for the initial 20 units of water. On average households receive SLRS 38 as a subsidy (fixed charge included) and SLRS 97 (fixed charge excluded).

Table 4.1: Summary of Variables in Residential Water Demand Analysis

Variable	Units	Mean	Std. Dev.	Min	Max
Monthly household water demand	m^3/month	17.06	2.49	9.65	33.21
Real marginal price	SLRS/ m^3	8.00	6.06	1.25	61.37
Real difference without fixed charge	SLRS	-97.03	124.91	-1338.17	0.00
Real difference with fixed charge	SLRS	-37.99	125.29	-1288.07	57.78
Real average price	SLRS/ month	6.38	1.06	5.00	21.18
Number of residents in household	persons	4.24	0.19	3.72	4.80
Real mean income	SLRS/ month	21301.72	6674.82	11143.80	44755.81
Monthly temperature	^{0}C	27.23	2.17	18.90	31.70
Monthly rainfall	mm	158.01	140.32	0.00	1337.00
Real instrumented marginal price	SLRS/m^3	28.32	10.67	17.63	52.88
Real instrumented difference variable with fixed charge	SLRS	338.53	162.60	183.05	711.60

Table 4.2 provides average monthly household water consumption for each district from 2001-05. Figure 4.2 provides an indication of a declining trend in household water use over time in most districts. This declining trend in average household water use may be due to reduction in system transportation losses or leaks.

Table 4.2: Annual Average of Household Water Consumption

Year	2001	2002	2003	2004	2005
Ampara	16.24	16.65	15.69	16.65	16.11
Anuradhapura	18.91	18.12	17.76	17.12	16.69
Bandarawela	16.08	15.35	14.52	14.81	14.43
Colombo	23.74	21.48	19.23	18.58	18.10
Galle	18.43	17.42	17.56	17.01	15.79
Gampaha	20.44	19.01	18.04	18.13	17.80
Hambantota	17.14	16.29	15.69	15.83	15.59
Jaffana	21.70	23.98	19.49	19.14	18.56
Kalutara	14.98	14.10	13.90	14.62	14.68
Kandy	16.48	15.81	16.06	15.88	15.55
Kurunegala	18.96	16.69	16.61	16.48	15.83
Matara	17.45	16.80	15.65	15.68	14.96
Ratnapura	16.92	15.72	15.40	16.34	15.93
Trincomalee	18.55	17.76	16.46	17.10	16.34

Figure 4.2: Monthly Household Water Consumption – Year 2001 to 2005

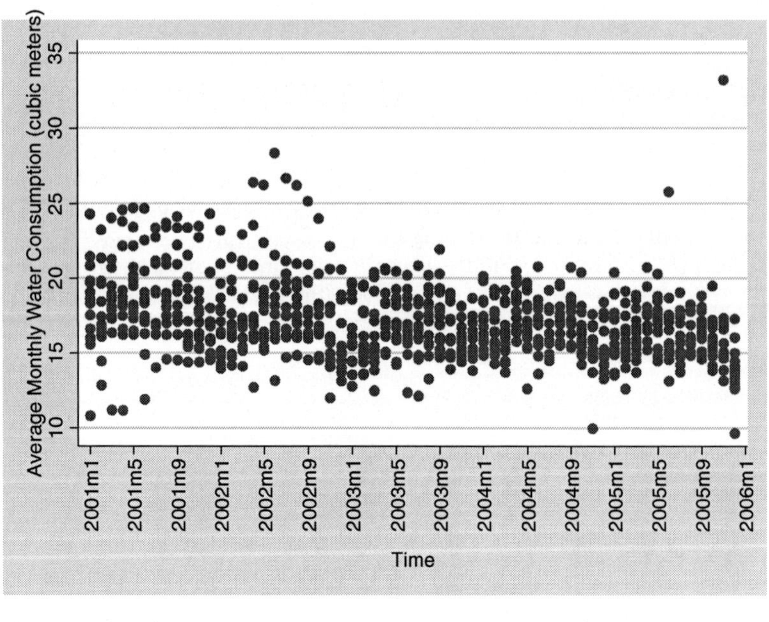

Figure 4.3 and 4.4 represents the average household water consumption for each district over the period being examined. On average, Jaffna, Colombo, Gampaha and Anuradhapura districts consume more water than the other districts. Kalutara and Bandarawela districts represent the lowest average water consumption.

Figure 4.3: Average Monthly Household Water Consumption for NWSDB Districts

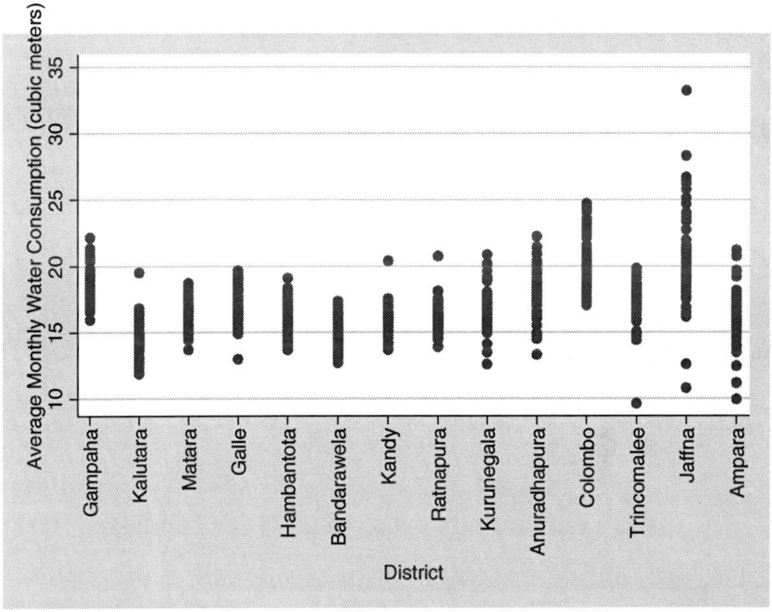

Figure 4.4: Average Monthly Household Water Consumption by District over Time

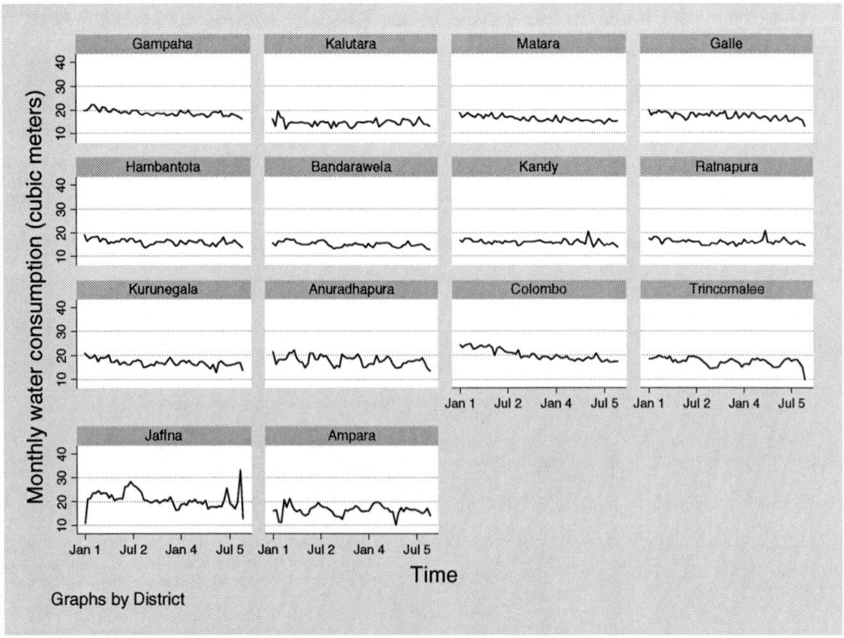

4.4 Methodology - Marginal Price Models

Marginal price and the difference variable are used in the analysis to allow for the possibility that households know the marginal price. The prices in each block vary significantly and monthly metering assumes households have some control over their consumption. Therefore, the residential water demand model is expressed as follows:

$$Q = f(MP, D, W, Y) \quad (4.2a)$$

$$MP = f(Q, rate\,structure) \quad (4.2b)$$

$$D = f(Q, rate\,structure) \quad (4.2c)$$

In above equations, Q is monthly water consumption for an average household, MP is marginal price for the last unit purchased, D is the difference between the actual water bill and what would be paid if all units were purchased at MP, W is a vector of weather variables (rainfall and temperature) and Y is a vector of socio-economic features (household income and number of household members).

The marginal price model includes three structural equations because quantity, marginal price and difference variable are simultaneously determined and are all dependent variables. The first model utilizes observed quantity values and solve for marginal price and difference variable. Then the solved values for marginal price and difference variable are used in the demand equation.

The marginal price and difference variable specification normally requires individual household level data. However, aggregate data can also be used, but the results may be biased unless the aggregate marginal price and difference variables are weighted by the proportion of households actually consuming in each block (Stevens, et al., 1992). Unfortunately, this requires information beyond that which is available at present.

A potential problem in estimating demand under discrete pricing is that the quantity consumed and the prices are determined simultaneously. Simultaneity arises because the quantity of water determines the price under the pricing schedule. With block-rate pricing causality goes in both directions, from price to quantity and from quantity to price. Consumers choose the amount of water to be purchased depending on some measure of price, and the price paid depends on the amount of water consumed. As a result, the OLS assumption of independence between the error term and the explanatory variables is violated as water price depends on the quantity. This will yield biased and inconsistent estimates (Hensen, 1984).

To overcome the simultaneity problem in the presence of block pricing, instrumental variable approaches have often been used in the literature (Billings, 1987; Nauges & Martinez-Espineira, 2004; Nieswiadomy & Molina, 1988). Consistent parameters may be obtained by an instrumental variable method. The objective of the instrument is to provide a proxy for the endogenous variables that are price variables in water studies. The instrument should fulfil the requirement of being uncorrelated with the error structure while being correlated with the stochastic regressor. The linearizations of the tariff structures and 2SLS procedure are employed in this chapter to overcome the problem of simultaneity.

4.4.1 Linearization of the Tariff Structure (Model A)

The approach described below is labelled as Model A. It uses an artificial linearization of the tariff structure from which instruments for marginal price and difference variable are derived. This assumes that consumers, instead of making the effort to learn how the tariff works and which block they are consuming in at each moment in time, will roughly estimate the whole tariff as a ray line given by an intercept and a constant marginal price (Martinez-Espeneira, 2003b). Since both *MP* and *D* are limited to one value for every household under a particular rate structure, the inference is that all households subject to the same pricing schedule are consuming in the same block.

$$TR = \alpha + \beta Q + \mu \tag{4.3}$$

The total revenue (TR) function is computed using the range of quantity values encountered in the entire data set. These values of the total revenue are then regressed against the corresponding quantity values (10 – 33m^3) from the data used in this chapter. The first derivative of the estimated function gives

$$\beta = \frac{\partial TR}{\partial Q} = MP^* \tag{4.4}$$

The estimated parameter β is the instrumental marginal price variable for the consumer and marginal revenue for the water utility.

Estimating the parameter α in equation (4.3) gives the difference between what consumers actually pay and what consumers would pay if all units were sold at the marginal price MP^*, that is the instrumental difference variable D^*. This procedure results in the representation of each rate schedule by MP^* and D^*, which are constant for all observations under each specific rate structure.

This approach has several advantages. First, substitution of the estimated values of *MP** and *D** into the demand equation frees the model from any asymptotic covariance between these two explanatory variables and the error structure (Deller, et al., 1986). Second, any simultaneity resulting from quantity dependent price is eliminated by using a marginal price that is constant for all households subject to the same price schedule. Finally, instrumental marginal price varies only over the rate structure and not over quantities consumed, thus no feedback of quantity on price can occur.

The measurement problems of the quantity that biases the *MP* and *D* can be overcome with the use of aggregate data, as suggested by Oshfeldt (1983). Aggregate data are generally less sensitive to outliers and measurement errors compared to specifications based on observations corresponding to individual users and billing periods (Moeltner &

Stoddard, 2004). However, there are no problems arising from errors in the measurement of quantity because the marginal price instrument does not vary with quantity, thus making it impossible to assign a wrong marginal price ex-post from the rate schedule.

4.4.2 Two-stage Least Square (Model B, C and D)

The second approach for estimating instruments is used (Model B, C and D) in order to test the robustness of results. This approach is much more common in the literature and has been employed in a number of studies such as Deller et al., (1986), Nieswiadomy (1992) and Nieswiadomy and Molina (1988, 1989, 1991). This procedure not only deals with missing price data, but also provides instrumental variables and effectively avoids measurement errors and simultaneity problems (Deller, et al., 1986). This technique is increasingly used in the literature because exact information on household location on the rate schedule is difficult to obtain for most studies.

A set of instrumental variables is estimated using a 2SLS estimation procedure for Model B, C and D. In the first stage of Model B, the observed marginal price and the difference variable were regressed against rate-structure characteristics such as the minimum charge, fixed charge, average marginal price, average change in the marginal price, income, number of household members and weather variables (Deller, et al., 1986; Nieswiadomy, 1992; Nieswiadomy & Molina, 1988, 1989). The predicted marginal price and difference variable are used in the second stage. The benefit of this approach is that it makes an attempt to capture the characteristics of rate structures faced by consumers. Nevertheless, the shortcoming of this approach is that it does not account for the quantity consumed and the consumer's location in the rate schedule directly.

In the 2SLS estimation procedure of Model C, the first stage consists of regressing the observed marginal price and difference variable against rate-structure characteristics such as block prices, fixed charges, incomes, numbers of household members and weather variables (Nieswiadomy, 1992). The predicted marginal price and the difference variable are used in the second stage. Model D is similar to Model C, in the first stage observed marginal price and difference variable are regressed against rate structure characteristics such as lagged block prices, fixed charges, incomes, numbers of household members and weather variables (Renwick, et al., 1998). The block prices were lagged by one period to avoid contemporaneous correlation with water use under block pricing (Renwick, et al., 1998).

As noted above, Model A uses artificial linearization of the tariff structure to obtain the instrumented marginal price and the instrumented difference variable. Model B, C and D are estimated using a 2SLS estimation procedure to account for endogeneity of the marginal price and difference variables. The predicted marginal price and difference variable are used in the second stage.

4.4.3 Econometric Models

The demand function is first estimated using the OLS technique and the results are presented to investigate the bias in these estimates. Since the study uses a panel data set, use of the OLS technique involved model specification problems. The complex stochastic error structure is likely to include cross-section disturbances, time-series disturbances and a combined disturbance term (a combination of cross-section and time-series). The use of OLS would also assume constant intercept and slope parameters which is unreasonable in the case of panel data.

The issue of model specification in the case of panel data sets has been addressed by the common variance and error component models. The covariance models are also known as fixed-effects or the least square dummy variable models, since they make an allowance for the intercept term to vary over time across cross-section units. The error-component model is also called random-effects, where the intercept is treated as a random variable.

4.4.3.1 Fixed-effects Regression Model

In the fixed-effects regression model, it is assumed that the local effects are fixed for each district and not random. The fixed effects model is used to control for omitted variables that differ between cases but are constant over time. The fixed effects model allows the intercept term to vary across districts and dummy variables are considered as a part of the intercept (Park, 2005). The fixed-effects estimator is computed by transforming observations into deviations from the district means eliminating all static variables (equation (4.5)) (Martinez-Espeneira, 2003b).

$$Q_{it} = (\alpha + \mu_i) + \beta MP_t^* + \gamma D_t^* + \rho W_{it} + \delta Y_{it} + v_{it} \quad (4.5)$$

In equations (4.5) and (4.6), Q_{it} is consumption in period t for average household in district i, MP_t^* is instrument marginal price of water in period t, D_t^* is instrument difference variable for period t, W_{it} is a vector of weather variables which change across district levels as well as over time (rainfall, temperature), Y_{it} is a vector of socio-economic features, which change across district levels and temporally (household income, number of household members), μ_i is individual effects and v_{it} is the econometric error term, independently and identically distributed random variables with $E[v_{it}] = 0 \; and \; E[v_{it}^2] = \sigma_v^2$.

$\beta, \gamma, \rho \; and \; \delta$ are the slope coefficients to be estimated. This specification is usually employed when specifying a different intercept coefficient for each cross-sectional unit that can adequately capture differences in cross-sectional units; the changes across districts in the present case. Fixed-effect models estimate household water use as a deviation from the household's average use, based on the deviations of the explanatory variables from their averages.

Several problems have been identified with fixed-effects models. For example, the inclusion of many dummy variables leads to substantial losses of degrees of freedom and the dummies included might not directly identify the shift in the regression line (Pindyck & Rubinfeld, 1981).

4.4.3.2 Random-effects Regression Model

If some omitted variables are constant over time but vary between cases while others are fixed between cases but vary over time, then both types can be included using a random-effects regression model. The random-effect estimator used in this analysis is the weighted average of fixed effects and between effects as implemented in STATA.[1] The random-effects model estimates variance components for districts and error assuming the same intercept and slopes (Park, 2005). This model is estimated using GLS if the variance structure among cross-sections is known and if the variance structure is unknown, the feasible generalized least squares (FGLS) is used (Greene, 2003).

---

[1] Regression with 'between effects' is used to control for omitted variables that change over time but are constant between cases. This allows use of variation between cases to estimate the effect of the omitted independent variables on the dependent variable.

4.4.3.3 Panel-corrected Standard Errors Model

Different error variances are usually expected from the different cross-sections. This technique calculates panel-corrected standard error (PCSE) estimates for linear cross-sectional time-series models where the parameters are estimated by OLS or Prais-Winsten regression. This method assumes the disturbances are, by default, heteroscedastic and contemporaneously correlated across panels when computing the standard errors and variance-covariance estimates (Og & Schulz, 2006). The PCSE model allows for correction for heteroscedasticity and serial correlation adjusted using Prais-Winsten regression (Stata Press, 2003).

4.4.4 Stone-Geary Model

The Stone-Geary model assumes consumers have a given level of income and prices. The consumer first purchases a subsistence level of each good and then allocate residual income in fixed proportions to each good according to their respective preference parameters (Deaton & Muellbauer, 1980).

Let Q_w and Q_z be demands for water and all other goods respectively and P_w and P_z are unit prices. γ_w and γ_z are minimum amounts and β_w and β_z are preference parameters and I is virtual income (difference between the household income and the difference variable).[2]

The Stone-Geary utility function can be written as:

$$U = \beta_w \ln(Q_w - \gamma_w) + \beta_z \ln(Q_z - \gamma_z) \tag{4.7}$$

Where $\beta_w > 0, \beta_z > 0\ \beta_w + \beta_z = 1, (Q_z - \gamma_z) > 0\, and\ (Q_w - \gamma_w) > 0$

Normalizing the price of the aggregate goods to one results in the following budget constraint:

$$I = Q_w P_w + Q_z \tag{4.8}$$

Maximizing utility subject to the budget constraint yields the following demand function (with the assumption $1 = \beta_w + \beta_z$):

[2] Subscript w denotes water and z denotes all other goods.

$$L = \beta_w \ln(Q_w - \gamma_w) + \beta_z \ln(Q_z - \gamma_z) + \lambda(I - Q_w P_w - Q_z)$$

$$\frac{\partial L}{\partial Q_w} \rightarrow \frac{\beta_w}{(Q_w - \gamma_w)} = \lambda P_w$$

$$\frac{\partial L}{\partial Q_z} \rightarrow \frac{\beta_z}{(Q_z - \gamma_z)} = \lambda$$

$$\frac{\partial L}{\partial \lambda} \rightarrow I = Q_w P_w + Q_z$$

Assuming $\beta_w + \beta_z = 1$

$$Q_z = \frac{\beta_z P_w (Q_w - \gamma_w) + \gamma_z \beta_w}{\beta_w}$$

substituting in $I = Q_w P_w + Q_z$

$$Q_w = \frac{I\beta_w - \gamma_z \beta_w + P_w \gamma_w \beta_w - P_w \gamma_w}{P_w} \tag{4.9}$$

$$Q_w = \beta_w \frac{I - P_w \gamma_w - \gamma_z}{P_w} + \gamma_w \tag{4.10}$$

Preference parameter for water can be given as;

$$\beta_w = \frac{P_w Q_w - P_w \gamma_w}{I - P_w \gamma_w - \gamma_z} \tag{4.11}$$

It is assumed that $\gamma_z = 0$, so the demand function for water is given as;

$$Q_w = (1 - \beta_w)\gamma_w + \beta_w \frac{I}{P_w} \tag{4.12}$$

This simple specification of $\gamma_z = 0$ is preferred since γ_z does not provide any relevant information for the study. After assuming $\gamma_z = 0$, γ_w can be renamed as conditional water use threshold below which consumption is not affected by prices (Gaudin, et al., 2001). The term conditional emphasizes that this threshold is dependent on the available technology, pricing structure and price of durable goods during the period of estimation. β_w represents the marginal budget share allocated to water.

The main advantage of the Stone-Geary utility function is it uses only two parameters for each good while allowing for non-constant elasticities that may increase with price. The assumptions of the Stone-Geary utility function of strong separability, positive marginal propensity to consume and a positive threshold implying inelastic demand are appropriate for water demand estimations. In all studies estimating a single water demand equation, the assumption of strong separability between water and other goods is very common. Moreover, empirical evidence suggests that water is normal good and is found to be price inelastic implying that the rest of the assumptions are suitable for this analysis (Espey, et al., 1997; Worthington & Hoffmann, 2006)

$$Q_{it} = (1-\beta_w)\gamma_w + \beta_w \frac{I_{it}}{MP_{it}} + \alpha_1 hh_{it} + \alpha_2 tp_{it} + \alpha_3 rf_{it} + \varepsilon_t \tag{4.13}$$

In equation (4.13), β_w and γ_w are structural parameters representing respectively the share of water expenditure in the supernumerary income and the fixed component of monthly consumption. The study explicitly accounts for the number of household members (hh_{it}), rainfall (rf_{it}) and temperature (tp_{it}) with ε_t as the usual econometric error term. The implicit assumption is that threshold (γ_w) does not vary over time. Marginal price and the difference variable are obtained by the method proposed in Model A.

Price and income elasticities can be derived from these estimates. In this particular case, the two elasticities have the same magnitude and opposite sign as shown in the equation (4.14).

$$\xi_P = \beta \frac{I}{PQ} = -\xi_I \tag{4.14}$$

A GLS procedure is used to formulate estimates of the demand function structural relationships using Stone-Geary utility function since disturbance terms from the OLS model solution exhibited properties of autocorrelation, heteroscedasticity and mutual correlation. This procedure was used to estimate the model. The error term is assumed to be panel correlated and independent for GLS estimation.

4.5 Results and Discussion

Panel unit root tests are conducted to provide an overall aggregate statistic to examine whether a unit root exists in the panel data and to judge the time series properties of the data accordingly (Wang, 2003). Panel data unit root tests have been proposed as more powerful alternative tests than those based on individual time series unit roots tests. One of the advantages of panel unit root tests is that their asymptotic distribution is standard normal. The test proposed by Levin, Lin and Chu (2002), is applicable for homogeneous panels where the autoregressive (AR) coefficients for unit roots are in particular assumed to be the same across cross-sections. Im, Pesaran and Shin (2003) allow for heterogeneous panels and propose panel unit root tests which are based on the average of the individual Augmented Dicky Fuller unit root tests computed from each time series. One major criticism of the Levin, Lin and Chu (2002) and Im, Pesaran and Shin (2003) tests is that they require cross-sectional independence (Im & Pesaran, 2003; Levin, et al., 2002).

In addition, there are two Fisher-type tests: ADF and Phillip-Perron (PP) (Baltagi & Kao, 2000). The tests of Levin Lin and Chu and Breitung assume a common unit root process across cross sections while other tests assume an individual unit root process across different cross sections (Breitung, 2000; Levin, et al., 2002). All above specified tests were carried out using Eviews statistical software and found no variables were non-stationary. Panel unit root test results are given in the Appendix 1 Table 8.

Regression results provide insight into the variables that influence the variation in residential water demand. Panel regression results for OLS, IV and 2SLS techniques using STATA statistical software are reported in Table 4.3 and Table 4.4. The Cobb-Douglas model results are presented in Table 4.3 and 4.4 and the coefficient itself is the elasticity (Greene, 2003) while Stone-Geary results are presented in Table 4.5 and Table 4.6. In all the analyses robust standard errors are used. Robust standard errors are developed to compensate for the existence of the unknown pattern of heteroscedasticity which cannot be totally eliminated. The use of robust standard errors in fixed effects model will unequal variance along the predicted line (Wooldridge, 2001). Moreover, robust standard errors can also improve the statistical inference from pooled-time series data with autocorrelated errors and from panel data. However, occasionally, autocorrelation is inherent within the panels from one time period to another and these problems can be handled using the PCSE model.

Both fixed and random effect regressions are conducted. The Hausman test investigates the null hypothesis that the coefficients estimated by the efficient random effects estimator are the same as the ones estimated by the consistent fixed effects estimator. It compares the fixed versus random effect under the null hypothesis that the individual effects are uncorrelated with the other regressors in the model (Hausman, 1978). If they are insignificant (probability>chi2 larger than 0.05) then it is safe to use random effects while with a significant probability value, fixed effects should be used. If the null hypothesis is rejected, the random effect model produces biased estimators, violating one of the Gauss-Markov assumptions (Greene, 2003).

Table 4.3: Residential Water Demand Model Estimates – Cobb-Douglas Model

Variable		OLS - fe	Model A IV- fe	PCSE $AR(1)$ (Model A)
Constant		0.8008 (0.8274)	-1.4893 (1.2845)	-0.2771 (0.3488)
Marginal price		0.0412 (0.0312)	-0.0563 (0.0153)***	-0.1131 (0.0275)***
Difference variable		0.0575 (0.0175)***	-0.0043 (0.0092)	-0.0145 (0.0177)
Mean income		-0.0581 (0.0332)*	-0.0317 (0.0581)	0.1251 (0.0224)***
Household size		0.5134 (0.3271)	0.9832 (0.5156)**	0.3441 (0.1596)**
Temperature		0.4697 (0.0702)***	1.0428 (0.0892)***	0.5616 (0.0672)***
Rainfall		-0.0014 (0.0021)	-0.0052 (0.0031)*	-0.0078 (0.0044)***
Rho		0.5254	0.6416	0.4753
R-sq	Within	0.6241	0.3187	
	Between	0.5787	0.1373	
	Overall	0.6021	0.1839	0.7006

Notes: Column one: log-linear water demand model is estimated using OLS technique; Column 2: log-linear water demand model is estimated using IV technique given in Model A; Column 3: log-linear water demand model is estimated using IV technique given in Model A with PCSE technique; fe – fixed effects estimator *** Significant at $\alpha = 0.01$, ** Significant at $\alpha = 0.05$ and * Significant at $\alpha = 0.10$ standard error values (robust) in parentheses below estimates; Dependant variable is natural log of monthly residential quantity of water

The demand function is first estimated using the OLS technique and the estimates are presented to investigate the biasness in these estimates. The bias of the price coefficient is expected to be positive in the presence of an IBTS. OLS estimates of price elasticity of water demand yield biased estimates since the price variable is correlated with the random error term. As described by Henson (1984), the coefficient on marginal price is expected to be biased toward zero and the coefficient on the difference variable to be biased away from zero, under an increasing block structure (Hensen, 1984).

The Hausman test compares the results of OLS and IV techniques. The test uses the result that the OLS will be consistent and asymptotically efficient under the null hypothesis that the price variables are exogenous but will be inconsistent under the alternative hypothesis (Nieswiadomy & Molina, 1989). The test statistic has degrees of freedom equal to the number of explanatory variables. The calculated Hausman test statistic is 181.9 which greatly exceed the critical value of chi-square at 1 per cent level of significance with 6 degrees of freedom. Therefore, OLS estimates presented here are biased. The results improve with instrumental estimation of the marginal price and the difference variable and are statistically different to OLS estimates. The instrumental estimation provides a proxy for the endogenous price variables and solves the problem of simultaneity.

Before estimating the IV and 2SLS models, an augmented regression test was conducted to determine whether it is necessary to use instrumental variables. The 2SLS estimator is less efficient than OLS when the explanatory variables are exogenous because 2SLS estimates can have very large standard errors (Wooldridge, 2001). Hausman (1978) suggests direct comparison of OLS and 2SLS estimates to determine whether the differences are statistically significant. Following Davidson and MacKinnon (1993), residuals of each endogenous variable is included as a function of all exogenous variables in a regression of the original model. The endogeneity of marginal price and the difference variable were tested and it was found that the OLS is inconsistent as marginal price and the difference variable are endogenous.

Model A represents the artificial linearization of the rate schedule and the estimation results are reported in Table 4.3. Both fixed and random effects estimations were carried out. The Breusch and Pagan Lagrangean multiplier test for random effects was conducted and the random effects estimator violated the primary assumption that the unit specific residual is zero. Therefore, results of the fixed effects estimator are presented. The instrumental variable technique provided expected signs except for mean income which is not significantly different from zero. The marginal price coefficient has the expected sign and is statistically significant. The marginal price elasticity is -0.06, that is a 10 per cent increase in marginal price of water will lead to a 0.6 per cent decrease in water consumption. The difference variable was found to be statistically insignificant but with the expected sign. Temperature and number of household members are positively correlated with water use while rainfall has a negative effect, as expected. On warm days, it is expected that users consume more water for bathing, drinking and garden watering compared to wet days where people are expected to take less baths and reduce garden water use.

The PCSE model was estimated to account for the unique variance of disturbance in each case. It takes into account the panel structure and uses the information from all the data for the estimation (Og & Schulz, 2006). Model A is estimated using the PCSE technique. This model uses instrumented marginal price and instrumented difference variable from artificial linearization of the tariff structure. The overall goodness of the fit for the PCSE model (R^2) is 0.70. This analysis includes a correction for serial correlation and for heteroskedasticity, both within panels and across panels (Jansen A. & Schultz, 2006). The analysis uses a Prais Winston Regression that also adjusts for serial correlation using first-order $AR(1)$ adjustment with an estimated rho of 0.48.[3]

The PCSE technique shows a negative price elasticity implying a 10 per cent price increase in water will reduce the water consumption for an average household by 1.13 per cent. This estimate is comparable with Hussain et al., (2002) results but less than that estimated by Nauges and van-den Berg (2006) where they included availability of alternative water sources. Household size and mean household incomes contribute positively to water consumption and the respective coefficients are significant. The income elasticity was found to be positive and a 10 per cent rise in income leads to a 1.25 per cent increase in water consumption. The coefficient of the number of household members implies that a one per cent increase in the household size will increase the household water consumption by 0.34 per cent. This implies a change in water use is less than proportional to the increase in household size or population because of economies of scale in water usage, including cooking, cleaning, car washing and gardening (Worthington & Hoffmann, 2006).

---

[3] Both common $AR(1)$ autocorrelation structure and panel specific $AR(1)$ autocorrelation structure are estimated, results of the common $AR(1)$ autocorrelation structure estimator are presented here (due to a large number of significant coefficients).

Table 4.4: Residential Water Demand Model Estimates – 2SLS Techniques

Variable		Model B 2SLS – re	Model C 2SLS – re	Model D 2SLS – re
Constant		1.5310 (0.4277)***	1.4002 (0.4895)***	1.6159 (0.4356)***
Marginal price		-0.3702 (0.1550)**	-0.5858 (0.2433)**	-0.4090 (01679)**
Difference variable		0.3930 (0.0936)***	0.5343 (0.1493)***	0.4196 (0.1021)***
Mean income		0.0426 (0.0207)**	0.0438 (0.0205)**	0.0324 (0.0179)*
Household size		0.2130 (0.1425)^	0.2827 (0.1698)*	0.2308 (0.1604)^
Temperature		0.1143 (0.0799)^	0.1621 (0.0952)*	0.1270 (0.0904)^
Rainfall		-0.0053 (0.0039)^	-0.0077 (0.0049)^	-0.0058 (0.0042)^
Rho		0.0157	0.0084	0.0208
R-sq	Within	0.4496	0.3805	0.4344
	Between	0.9296	0.9073	0.9223
	Overall	0.5835	0.5068	0.5651

Notes: Column one: log-linear water demand model is estimated using 2SLS technique on Model B; Column 2: log-linear water demand model is estimated using 2SLS technique on Model C; Column 3: log-linear water demand model is estimated using 2SLS technique on Model D; re – random effects estimator *** Significant at $\alpha = 0.01$, ** Significant at $\alpha = 0.05$, * Significant at $\alpha = 0.10$ ^ Significant at $\alpha = 0.20$ standard error values (robust) in parentheses below estimates; Dependant variable is the natural log of monthly residential quantity of water

In terms of weather variables, as expected, water consumption increases with temperature and decreases with the rainfall and both effects are significant. The coefficient of monthly temperature is relatively larger than the coefficient of monthly rainfall. The small size of the estimated coefficient for monthly rainfall suggests that it does not play a great role in water consumption decisions. The coefficients suggest that if the monthly rainfall increases by 10 per cent, monthly household water consumption will decrease approximately by 0.07 per cent while a 10 per cent increase in the monthly temperature will increase the monthly residential water use by 5.6 to 9.9 per cent according to PCSE technique and Model A.

Model B, C and D are estimated using the 2SLS procedure and the results are reported in Table 4.4. The instrumented marginal price and instrumented difference variable are obtained using different combinations of exact rate structure characteristics such as minimum block prices, fixed charges, average marginal prices, average change in marginal prices and lagged block prices (Deller, et al., 1986).[4] The instrumental variable must satisfy two requirements: it must be uncorrelated with the error and correlated with the endogenous explanatory variable (Wooldridge, 2001). If there is more than one instrumental variable then it can be tested to check whether they are uncorrelated with the structural error. The regressing of 2SLS residuals on exogenous variables produces $R^2 = 0.0003$ with the Model B, therefore, the null hypothesis could not be rejected ($840 * R^2$ is value in a Chi-square distribution with one degree of freedom).[5] Therefore, instrumental variables used in model B pass the over-identification test and the instrumental variables are exogenous (Wooldridge, 2001).

Further, a rank test was conducted to determine whether the matrix of reduced form coefficients for the endogenous regressors is full rank. Rank test implements the Kleibergen-Paap (2006) *rk test* and test for the rank of a matrix. Heteroskedastic robust test for full rank rejects the null

[4] Average marginal price for relevant rate structure is computed by $\Sigma_{a=1}^{n} MP_a / n$. Average change in the marginal price is computed by $\Sigma_{a=1}^{n-1} \Delta MP_a / n-1$ (Deller, et al., 1986).

[5] Over-identification tests were conducted for all the 2SLS procedures with the null hypothesis of excluded instruments are valid instruments, uncorrelated with the error term and correctly excluded from the estimated equation. Across all 2SLS estimates (Model B, C and D) the null hypothesis could not be rejected. Over-identification statistics that is robust to arbitrary heteroskedasticity and within-group correlation was used in all models.

hypothesis of $rank = 1$ and therefore, the model is identified.[6] All of these models (Model A, B, C and D) are likely to improve the reliability of the estimates. The method in Model A may overcompensate for OLS bias as a result of artificial linearization of the tariff schedule (Terza, 1986). Model C and Model D produced similar results to Model B and the estimated results are presented in Table 4.4.

The overall goodness of fit varies from 0.51 to 0.58 and the coefficient on marginal price is negative and significantly different from zero at the 95 per cent confidence level. The magnitude of the coefficient ranges from -0.37 to -0.58 implying a 10 per cent increase in marginal price would reduce the water consumption by 3.7 to 5.8 per cent. The instrumented difference variable and mean household income are significant with expected signs and an income elasticity of 0.03 to 0.04. The coefficient of the difference variable varies from 0.39 to 0.53 and it is different from the magnitude of the income coefficient. This suggests consumers mistake the average price to be the marginal price and that the difference variables are only a very small fraction of household income. This implies that a 10 per cent increase in the intra marginal prices will decrease the implicit subsidy and reduce monthly household water consumption by 3.9 to 5.3 per cent. Further, the coefficient of the number of household members has the expected sign and is significantly different from zero at the 80 per cent confidence level.

The Stone-Geary functional form results are given in Table 4.5. In the Stone-Geary functional form, for all techniques, coefficients are estimated with the expected sign and significance, except the coefficient of rainfall with common $AR(1)$ and Panel-specific $AR(1)$ techniques. The share of water expenses in the income (β_w) is small but significantly different from zero. The low value of the β_w coefficient is not surprising because the share of water expenses in overall household budget is low. Temperature is significant and has expected positive sign while rainfall is not significant in common $AR(1)$ and panel specific $AR(1)$. The insignificant results on the rainfall variable may be due to the use of intensity of rainfall rather than the frequency of rainfall (number of rainy or rain-free days). Consumers are likely to be more price responsive to the number of rainy days than for intensity. The response to rainfall mainly depended on its occurrence and then on its intensity (Worthington & Hoffmann, 2006). The minimum consumption level or threshold γ_w is highly significant and estimated at 4.48 (=4.4686/(1-0.0032) cubic metres per month per

[6] Rank test was conducted for all IV estimation techniques and the null hypothesis was rejected suggesting that the models are identified.

household without autocorrelation. Across different estimation techniques, the threshold values range from 2.72 to 4.48 cubic metres per month per household.

Table 4.5: Residential Water Demand Model Estimates – Stone-Geary Model

	Heteroskedastic and no autocorrelation	Heteroskedastic and common $AR(1)$	Heteroskedastic and panel specific $AR(1)$
Constant	4.4686 (1.3584)***	4.2585 (2.2470)**	2.7169 (2.1068)
Income/price	0.0032 (0.0002)***	0.0029 (0.0003)***	0.0024 (0.0003)***
Household size	0.3889 (0.3184)	0.2599 (0.5267)	0.5403 (0.4793)
Rainfall	-0.0018 (0.0004)***	-0.0002 (0.0003)	-0.0001 (0.0003)
Temperature	0.3127 (0.0195)***	0.3408 (0.0313)***	0.3649 (0.0302)***

Notes: *** Significant at α = 0.01, ** Significant at α = 0.05 and * Significant at α = 0.10; Standard error values (robust) in parentheses below estimates, Dependant variable is monthly residential quantity of water

Price and income elasticities can be derived from the estimates for β_w and in this particular case the two elasticities have the same magnitude but the opposite signs $(\xi_P = \beta(I/PQ) = -\xi_I)$. This is equivalent to assuming that income and price affect water consumption through their relative levels only (Nauges & Martinez-Espineira, 2004). This feature of Stone-Geary model should not be too strong for residential water as previous estimates of price and income elasticity of residential water demand are often found to be of similar magnitude (between 0.10 and 0.30) and opposite signs (Hoglund, 1999; Nauges & Thomas, 2000; Renwick & Archibald, 1998). In addition, the Cobb-Douglas estimates reported in Tables 4.3 and 4.4 yielded price and income elasticity of residential water demand for Sri Lanka between -0.06 and -0.58 and 0.04 and 0.12 respectively.

Table 4.6 shows the values of the estimated income and price elasticities at the sample mean, maximum and minimum price levels. Price elasticity lies in the range from -0.11 to -0.14, when computed at the sample mean. This is of similar magnitude to price elasticities obtained by the Cobb-Douglas model. The Stone-Geary gives estimates of price elasticities that increase with income but decrease with price and quantity.

Table 4.6: Residential Price Elasticities and Threshold Quantities – Stone-Geary Model

		Heteroskedastic and no autocorrelation	Heteroskedastic and common $AR(1)$	Heteroskedastic and panel specific $AR(1)$
Threshold (cubic metres)		4.48	4.27	2.72
Price elasticity	Mean	-0.14	-0.13	-0.11
	Min	-0.22	-0.21	-0.17
	Max	-0.08	-0.07	-0.06
Income elasticity	Mean	0.14	0.13	0.11
	Min	0.22	0.21	0.17
	max	0.08	0.07	0.06

Notes: price elasticities and income elasticities are calculated at the mean, minimum and maximum of instrumental real marginal price and real virtual income variables

The demand model using the Stone-Geary functional form proposes that households cannot reduce their water consumption to zero. The non-zero quantity corresponds to water consumed for the satisfaction of basic needs. These findings show the estimation of residential water demand provides consistent results and has important policy implications. Specifically, per month each household uses about 3 to 4.5 cubic metres for fulfilment of basic needs. Consumption at these volumes is highly insensitive to price changes. These findings conform with WHO (1997b) standards for subsistence level water use of 4 to 5 cubic metres per month, estimated to be sufficient for essential needs of a 5 member household. The threshold level reported herein is conditional. Ideally, the threshold parameter should be corrected by including some long-term determinants of the threshold water use. This is because increased water prices are expected to eventually affect the decision of buying water-intensive durable goods, which in turn will reduce the water use threshold.

These results provide water managers with important information about the threshold of the quantity of water below which consumption will not respond to price changes, assuming the household environment remains constant. The results suggest that household water demand is price responsive once the threshold is reached. Policies should explicitly recognize this in demand management efforts. The average household consumption in Sri Lanka according to the data set used in this chapter is 17 cubic metres per household per month. This implies that further price increases or temporary bans on water consumption would be effective in reducing consumption, although the latter may have other undesirable impacts.

Moreover, even with a price inelastic nature, water price increases may lead to some changes in water consumption patterns and income. If such a change takes place, then increasing the price of water may ultimately promote water conservation (Gunathilake, et al., 2001). However, to decrease the amount of water consumption, a mixture of instruments will be required in an environment with increasing incomes. Specifically, water price increases should be accompanied by activities such as consumer awareness and education on water leakage and wastage; investment on water efficient appliances and outdoor use of recycled water.

4.6 Conclusion

This chapter presents econometric analyses of residential water demand for pipe-borne water in Sri Lanka using monthly district data from January 2001 to December 2005. Using the instrumental variable techniques, for both the Cobb-Douglas and Stone-Geary forms, price elasticity of water demand is estimated to lie between -0.06 to -0.58. This is consistent with past findings for both developed and developing countries (Dalhuisen, et al., 2003; Espey, et al., 1997). Moreover, it confirms that Sri Lankan residential water demand is price inelastic.

The results show the estimated coefficients are fairly stable over the different techniques. However, the estimated coefficients on the difference variable across the models suggest instability. The income coefficient is relatively small and significant in Model B and Model A estimated with PCSE technique. The coefficient of the mean income variable ranges from 0.03 to 0.14 for both Cobb-Douglas and Stone-Geary functional forms.

The income inelasticity and smaller magnitude could be due to the fact that expenditure on water for residential consumption comprises a very small proportion of the household budget.

The number of household members was significant with Model A and PCSE technique and has a positive sign. As expected, larger households consume more water for bathing, laundry, toilet flushing and dish washing. Size of the coefficient is relatively larger and ranges from 0.21 to 0.86, implying that water use changes are less than proportional to the increase in household size. This is because of economies of scale in water usage including cooking, cleaning, car washing and gardening. The analysis provides a better approach to the investigation of climatic effects on water use by incorporating monthly and district differences. Both coefficients of monthly temperature and monthly rainfall are significant with expected signs.

The overall results suggest water consumption is not very responsive to price changes in Sri Lanka and this finding may be applicable for other developing countries. Moreover, the estimated price and income elasticities do not vary significantly from those estimated for developed countries. In the presence of inelastic responses to price changes, pricing policies have limited scope in changing water consumption. In addition, the scope of pricing policies to change water consumption depends on the range of prices that are employed in the empirical analysis. Political influence will play a major role in deciding the water prices and will be very difficult to prove empirically. However, continuous supply of water at the current subsidised rates may eventually lead to a collapse of the water supply system. Therefore, the inelastic nature of water consumption provides opportunities for the NWSDB to increase revenues by increasing water charges. Such price increases, however, should be accompanied by welfare measures to ensure adequate provision for poorer households.

The estimates reported herein will be useful to policy makers and water utility managers in assessing the likely impacts and prospects for residential water demand management through the pricing mechanism. The current available data does not take into account the differences in households within each district. Further panel data analysis using exact household specific characteristics such as household incomes, age and gender distribution within the household and sizes of the house would provide additional insights into the factors influencing residential water demand in Sri Lanka.

CHAPTER FIVE

PRICE RESPONSIVENESS OF INDUSTRIAL AND COMMERCIAL WATER DEMAND

5.1 Introduction

The economics of water demand in different sectors is a matter of interest for water resource planners and policy makers. Empirical studies on the demand for water, however, are substantially less abundant in developing countries. The NWSDB in Sri Lanka categorises water users into residential and non-residential (industrial, commercial, schools, religious institutions and shipping). Industrial and commercial classes constitute the major water consuming sectors of non-residential users and are considered for demand analyses in this chapter. Industrial and commercial water consumption accounted for approximately 10 per cent of the total water produced by the NWSDB and contributed 22 per cent of the total revenue in 2005 (NWSDB, 2005). The industrial and commercial water withdrawals are expected to increase in the future, both in terms of quantity and proportion of total water withdrawals due to increasing levels of economic development. Therefore, the analyses here provide necessary instruments for water authorities to assess variation in consumption of non-residential users and the resulting welfare effects of a price change.

This chapter presents the estimation of the industrial and commercial water demands using panel data on monthly observations of aggregate water use for all the NWSDB districts (14) for 60 months (January 2001 to December 2005) for Sri Lanka. The estimation in this chapter uses two separate models for commercial and industrial consumers, but separate demand models for different industry categories cannot be estimated because of data unavailability. The findings of this chapter reveal that the price elasticities of industrial and commercial demand are inelastic and industrial water users are relatively more elastic than the commercial users. However, the significance of the price of water in industrial and commercial water demand is not as conclusive as the results for residential water demand. Moreover, this chapter presents the analyses of the effects of climatic factors on industrial and commercial water consumption. An additional purpose of industrial and commercial water demand estimation is to use the parameter estimates, along with the findings of chapter 4 and 6 to evaluate the welfare effects of different water pricing scenarios undertaken in chapter 7.

The industrial and commercial water use can be a typical example of a producer's derived demand for an input (Renzetti, 1992b; Reynaud, 2003). However, data required for comprehensive assessment of water usage for commercial and industrial purposes are not available in Sri Lanka. Hussain et al., (2002) is the only published study that estimates commercial and industrial water demands using aggregate time-series data for Sri Lanka. The main reason for this is the difficulty in collecting appropriate data required for estimating industrial and commercial water demands. In addition, it is difficult to estimate industrial and commercial water demand representing the aggregate industry or commercial entity since the industrial firms and commercial units use water for different purposes with different intensities. Nevertheless, some researchers have proceeded to analyse such demands with a greater or lesser degree of success in spite of data unavailability (Reynaud, 2003).

The industrial and commercial sectors play a pivotal role in the country's economy. Shopping centres, health clubs, restaurants and boutiques are considered to be commercial consumers of water while the industrial sector comprises mainly of manufacturers. Manufacturing industries can be classified as food products, beverages, textiles, tanneries and leather, paper, industrial chemicals, petroleum, rubber products, iron and steel. The purpose and intensity of water use differs between and among commercial and industrial establishments (Malla & Gopalakrishnan, 1999). The sources and quantities of water for industries vary depending on the purpose of usage, products, magnitude of operations and desired quality. The sources of water could be pipe-borne water from the NWSDB, extractions from private dug wells and deep wells, or from rivers (Imbulana, et al., 2006).

The NWSDB charges commercial and industrial customers on a monthly basis and the monthly levels of consumption are likely to vary throughout the year. This requires the use of a monthly varying dependent variable, aggregated in some form. The advantage of aggregate models is, they are generally less sensitive to outliers and measurement errors compared to specifications based on observations corresponding to individual firms and billing periods (Moeltner & Stoddard, 2004). On the other hand, estimated parameters and price elasticities from such models generally will not reflect behaviour at the firm level. Therefore, if the consistent estimation of water price responsiveness at the firm level is the primary focus of a demand analysis, a panel data set of monthly consumption for a variety of establishments and sufficiently long time horizon is needed (Moeltner & Stoddard, 2004).

The structure of this chapter is set out as follows: a literature review in section 5.2. A description of data and variables used and the economic and econometric models are discussed in section 5.3 and 5.4 respectively. Section 5.5 discusses the results and section 5.6 ends the chapter with conclusions.

5.2 Literature Review

The literature concerning estimation of industrial and commercial water demands is significantly less developed than that of residential water demand. Previous studies that have conducted industrial and commercial water demand estimations have employed different types of data. For example, studies based on firm-level data used consumption figures that are aggregated over time, such as daily or monthly averages (Ziegler & Bell, 1984) or annual totals (Renzetti, 1988). Some studies combined temporal with cross-sectional aggregation. For example, Babin et al., (1982) used aggregate water demand over all firms within a given industry category and state for a given year and Williams and Suh (1986) used annual water demand for all commercial establishments within a given municipality as the dependent variable.

There is no consensus on the range of price elasticities for industrial and commercial water demand. In addition, sensitivity to economic factors such as input prices and the level of output of industrial and commercial demand is still being debated due to limited knowledge (Reynaud, 2003). Different researchers have estimated industrial and commercial water demand in different contexts, with different sets of variables. Table 5.1 summarizes the past studies for price elasticities of industrial water demand.

Rees (1969) applied regression analysis to manufacturing firms in England. This study used annual volume of purchased water by firms as the dependent variable and the average price of purchased water, employment and output levels as explanatory variables. The price elasticities of water with respect to different types of manufacturing firms are: Chemical -0.96, Food -3.29 to -6.17 and Beverage -1.3 to -4.1. Turnovsky (1969) conducted an empirical analysis to test whether increasing uncertainty in the supply of water increases the water consumption by using two cross-sectional data sets from Massachusetts towns for 1962 and 1965. He found that as uncertainty increases, consumers plan to purchase more of the commodity. Furthermore, he illustrated that industrial water consumer response to uncertainty decline when the consumer has already been subjected to uncertainty in the past. The average industrial price elasticity of demand was -0.50 to -0.63 (Turnovsky, 1969).

Table 5.1: Past Estimations of Industrial Water Demand

Authors	Area	Method	Price elasticity
Rees (1969)	England		-6.17/-0.96
Turnovsky (1969)	U.S.A.		-0.63/-0.50
Grebenstein and Field (1979)	U.S.A.	Trans-log	-0.80/-0.33
Babin et al., (1982)	U.S.A.	Trans-log	-0.66/-0.14
Williams and Suh (1986)	U.S.A.	Log-log	-0.97/-0.44
Schneider and Whitlach (1991)	Columbus, U.S.A.	Log-log	-1.16/-0.44
Renzetti (1988)	Canada	Log-log	-0.54/-0.12
Renzetti (1992a)	Canada	Trans-log	-0.59/-0.15
Malla and Gopalakrishnan (1999)	Honolulu, U.S.A.	Log-log	-0.40/-0.32
Reynaud (2003)	France	Trans-log	-0.79/-0.10
Hussain et al., (2002)	Sri Lanka	Log-log	-1.34

Grebenstein and Field (1979) analysed a cost function for industries in the U.S.A., using cross-sectional aggregate data of water use and input prices for 1973. They found the average cost share of water to be 1.9 per cent. Water was included as a standard input in their model and two price specifications were examined; average price computed by the American Water Works Association and the average price obtained by dividing total expenses for water by the volume bought. Own price conditional elasticity found by this study ranges from -0.326 to -0.801 and cross price elasticities were positive for water and labour (2.383) and negative for water and capital (-2.051). The admitted major weakness in their analysis was the use of a single production function for the entire U.S. manufacturing sector. A single production function for all manufacturing implies that all relevant industries will respond to a change in relative input prices in the same way.

Babin et al., (1982) estimated a trans-log cost function for several U.S. manufacturing industries using aggregate data at the standard industrial classification. They focussed on substitution possibilities between water and other productive inputs. They found that price elasticity of water ranges from zero to -0.66; -0.14 for food industry and -0.66 for paper and wood industry. Moreover, they concluded the average cost share of water exceeds 1 per cent only in four of the eight industry categories studied. Babin et al., (1982) showed that capital and labour were substitutes for every sector, but the substitution possibility with water and other inputs varied from one sector to another.

Williams and Suh (1986) estimated aggregate water demand equations for commercial and industrial sectors over 120 municipalities in the U.S.A. for 1973. The OLS technique was applied for the linear and log-linear forms. Explanatory variables were price, number of commercial connections, value of output and temperature (commercial sector) and price, value added in manufacturing and number of industry connections (industrial sector). The number of customers and the level of economic activity were found to be important determinants of water demand by the commercial sector. Price elasticities range from -0.141 to -0.36 (commercial) and -0.437 to -0.976 (industrial). The findings suggest the quantity of water demanded by the commercial sector was less responsive to price changes than residential and industrial customers. They argue that commercial water users were provided with water by the real estate owner as a part of the contractual obligations and separate meters were not provided to monitor the water use. Therefore, the level of water use is less likely to be affected by the price change.

Schneider and Whitlach (1991) analysed industrial and commercial water demand using data from Columbus, Ohio and suburban communities. They use GLS procedures to estimate eight regression equations with different combinations of explanatory variables. The significance of the price of water in commercial and industrial water demand was not conclusive. For commercial water demand, the price coefficient was found to be significantly less than zero only in four of the eight equations. Long-run price elasticity ranged from -0.179 to -1.136, while the estimate of short-run price elasticity was -0.236 (Schneider & Whitlach, 1991). The number of residents per commercial account and precipitation did not significantly influence the industrial and commercial water demand. Price had a very weak influence on industrial water demand and price elasticity of demand was found to be significantly less than zero in only one out of eight specifications at -1.162.

Renzetti (1988) was the first study to integrate the complexity of water use in the production process of a firm. Demands for four aspects of industrial water use (intake, treatment prior to use, recirculation, and treatment prior to discharge) were estimated as a system of simultaneous equations using Cobb-Douglas specification. He used a cross-section sample of 372 industrial firms of British Columbia, Canada in 1981. Four manufacturing subgroups were considered: petrochemicals, heavy industry, forest industry and light industry. Intake price elasticities ranged from -0.12 to -0.54 and the cross price elasticity between intake and recirculation was positive for all subgroups (indicating substitutability) and ranging from 0.14 to 0.26 (Renzetti, 1988). The average cost share of water was smallest in the heavy and petrochemical industries and the largest in the light industries. The absolute size of the intake price elasticities followed the same pattern.

Renzetti (1992a) estimated industrial demand for water using a similar model used in Renzetti (1988) for 2000 industrial firms in Canada. Seven industrial categories were studied and the cost functions were approximated as the trans-log form. The conditional factor demands were derived using Sheppard's Lemma. The price elasticities were significant for four of the seven industries considered: plastic and rubber -0.15, textile and clothing -0.33, paper and pulp -0.59 and minerals -0.32. The calculated own price elasticities were negative for all industry groups and the cross-price elasticity between intake and recirculation showed substitutability (Renzetti, 1992a). Dupoint and Renzetti (2001) estimated industrial water demand functions for Canadian manufacturing firms. They found that water intake was a substitute not only for water recirculation but for energy, labour and capital. The own price elasticity of intake water demand was estimated at -0.77 (Dupoint & Renzetti, 2001).

Malla and Gopalakrishnan (1999) estimated food and non-food industrial water demand functions for the county of Honolulu using the GLS technique. They estimated own price elasticity of water for food industry ranged from -0.32 to -0.39 and that for non-food industry and commercial sector ranged from -0.07 to -0.11. The coefficient of price for non-food industry and commercial sector were found to be negative but were statistically insignificant in all equations. They used number of employees as a proxy for the value of output.

Reynaud (2003) estimated industrial water demand for France using a trans-log cost function. Industrial water use was modelled for three components; quantity of water bought from water utility, quantity of autonomous water and quantity of water treated prior to use. Further, they included water effluents, which are considered as by-products of the production process. The model was estimated using a sample of 51 industrial plants in the Gironde district from 1994 to 1996. The network water elasticity was -0.29 and varied from -0.10 to -0.79 according to the type of industry considered. Autonomous water price elasticity was not significant and treated water elasticity was -1.42 (Reynaud, 2003).

Hussain et al.,(2002) estimated separate demand functions for industrial and commercial water consumption using aggregate monthly time-series data for 60 months from January 1994 to December 1998 for Sri Lanka. Both industrial and commercial water demands were estimated using the GLS technique. The average water quantity per commercial entity was regressed against price of water, number of commercial connections, rainfall and temperature and commercial price elasticity of demand was -0.17. The industrial water demand was estimated by regressing country average industrial water consumption against industrial water price, number of employees, temperature and rainfall. The price elasticity of industrial water use was -1.34. This value is larger than the price elasticity of commercial users (-0.17) (Hussain, et al., 2002). Most coefficients had expected signs and statistical significance. A positive sign on the rainfall coefficient in commercial demand equation and negative sign on the employment coefficient in industrial demand equation were unexpected but statistically insignificant.

Previous literature estimated industrial and commercial water demand using firm-level data and aggregate data. Past studies have derived industrial demand function using cost function and have estimated substitutability and complementarity between inputs. Some studies analysed industrial water demands for different phases of industrial activities (intake water, recirculation of water). The industrial and commercial water use can be a typical example of a producer's derived demand for an input (Renzetti, 1992b; Reynaud, 2003). However, data required for comprehensive assessment of water usage for commercial and industrial purposes are not available in Sri Lanka. The Cobb-Douglas functional form is more commonly used (Malla & Gopalakrishnan, 1999; Renzetti, 1988) and trans-log functional form is rarely used in the literature to estimate industrial and commercial water demands (Renzetti,

1992a). The present study assumes water is separable from other inputs in the production process and industrial and commercial water demands are estimated using the Cobb-Douglas functional form using price of water, total number of connections, rainfall and temperature as independent variables.

Due to the lack of firm-level data for industrial and commercial water consumption in Sri Lanka, industrial and commercial demands are estimated using aggregate data over all firms within a given district for sixty months. The use of aggregate data is expected to affect the magnitude and significance of the estimated coefficients. Use of aggregate data will not take into account the different intensities of water for different firms or industry category. For example, price elasticities of water for food and beverage industry are greater in magnitude than other sorts of manufacturing firms (Babin, et al., 1982; Turnovsky, 1969). However, this analysis provides important information for policy makers regarding the industrial and commercial water demand management using pricing policies. Moreover, industrial and commercial water withdrawals are expected to increase in the future, both in terms of quantity and proportion of total water withdrawals due to increasing levels of economic development (NWSDB, 2005).

5.2.1 Industrial and Commercial Water Pricing in Sri Lanka

In Sri Lanka, for non-residential users including industrial and commercial, water consumption charges are applied using uniform volumetric pricing. The monthly consumer bill is determined as:

$$B_I = [p_I * Q_I] \quad (5.1)$$

$$B_C = [p_C * Q_C] \quad (5.2)$$

In above equations, subscripts I and C represent industrial and commercial sectors; B represents monthly water bill; p is the volumetric charge and Q represents the average quantity of water consumption. The rates have generally been higher for commercial and industrial users than residential consumers. Although all consumers face fixed charges initially, significant changes in rate schedules have been implemented since the early 1990s. The NWSDB replaced the non-residential two-part tariff (a fixed charge and a volumetric charge) with a monthly volumetric charge from October 1997.

Appendix 1 Table 5 shows the three price structures during 2001 to 2005 which is the time period considered in this study. In 2001, industrial and commercial water were charged at the same rate of SLRS 35 per cubic metre and the charges gradually increased to SLRS 42 per cubic metre in mid-2002. The price structure underwent further revision in 2005, user charges increased to SLRS 50 and remain at this level to date.

5.3 Data

The panel data set used in this chapter contains information on monthly water consumption of industrial and commercial customers of the NWSDB for January 2001 to December 2005 covering 14 NWSDB districts. Unfortunately, relatively little data are collected on industrial water use in Sri Lanka, therefore, this study does not have disaggregate industrial or commercial water intake data. The price structures for industrial and commercial consumers for relevant years were obtained from the NWSDB. Price variables were adjusted for inflation using the Consumer Price Index. Aggregate data related to industrial and commercial water consumption and numbers of active industrial and commercial connections were obtained from the NWSDB. Weather data for the relevant period for the 14 districts were collected from the Department of Meteorology, Sri Lanka.

In the demand models the dependent variable, monthly district average water consumption is calculated by dividing monthly total industrial and commercial water quantity by total number of industrial and commercial connections respectively. Average price is obtained from the rate structure and measures the changes in the quantity of water purchased by the average industrial or commercial consumer with respect to changes in the price of water.[1] Assuming industrial and commercial users buy a lower amount of water when the price increases, the expected sign of the derivative of water use with respect to average price is negative. In addition, the expected sign on the derivative of water use with respect to number of connections is positive. It is expected that weather patterns influence water demand, that is, higher demand during the hot weather and lower demand during the rainy periods. Industrial and commercial activities may require more water for cooling of machinery, cleaning activities and for consumption by the employees during the hot weather.

---

[1] In case of the industrial and commercial water demand, average price is equal to the marginal price (uniform volumetric pricing).

5.3.1 Summary Statistics

Table 5.2 displays the minimum, maximum, mean and standard deviation of the variables used in estimations of industrial and commercial water consumption. The dependent variable, average monthly industrial water consumption ranges from a minimum of zero cubic metres to nearly 1527 cubic metres with a mean at 129 and a standard deviation of 206 cubic metres. There were no industrial connections or water use in some districts (Jaffna and Anuradhapura) for some months. Therefore, the standard deviation is very high and this is likely to affect the magnitude and the significance of the estimates. Similarly, monthly commercial water consumption ranges from 7.5 cubic metres to 85.8 cubic metres with a mean of 24 and a standard deviation 14.6 cubic metres.

Figures 5.1 and 5.2 represent the average industrial and commercial water consumption for each district for the period January 2001 to December 2005. On average, Trincomalee, Colombo and Ampara districts consume more industrial water than other districts. Trincomalee and Ampara districts show a wide monthly fluctuation in industrial water consumption over the time period being considered. Colombo and Trincomalee districts exhibit a wider fluctuation and the largest commercial water consumption for the period. Figure 4 and 5 in the Appendix 1 depict the seasonal consumption pattern for both industrial and commercial water users. However, both industrial and commercial consumption do not show a significant seasonal variation in water consumption.

Table 5.2: Summary of Variables in Industrial and Commercial Water Demand Analyses

Variable	Units	Mean	Std. Dev.	Min	Max
Monthly industrial water demand (per connection)	m^3	129.1	205.6	0.0	1527.3
Monthly commercial water demand (per connection)	m^3	24.3	14.6	7.5	85.8
Monthly industrial water demand (per district)	m^3	20899.1	62772.8	0.0	322022.0
Monthly commercial water demand (per district)	m^3	126711.5	343417.0	2286.0	1761797.0
Real average price for industrial	SLR S/m^3	51.2	2.5	47.2	57.6
Real average price for commercial	SLR S/m^3	51.2	2.5	47.2	57.6
No. of industrial connections	No.	117.0	254.0	0.0	1250.0
No. of commercial connections	No.	3139.0	5388.0	126.0	26667.0
Total employees in industrial	No.	94312.0	78392.0	15372.0	397063.0
Total employees in commercial	No.	57574.0	39953.0	14643.0	190332.0
Monthly temperature	^0C	27.2	2.2	18.9	31.7
Monthly rainfall	mm	158.0	140.3	0.0	1337.0

Figure 5.1: Average Monthly Industrial Water Consumption by District over Time

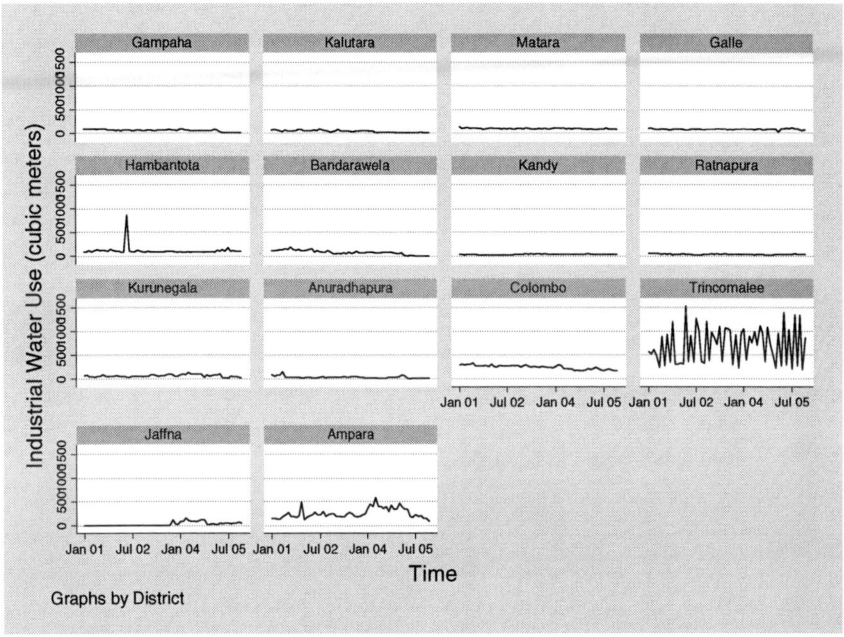

Figure 5.2: Average Monthly Commercial Water Consumption by District over Time

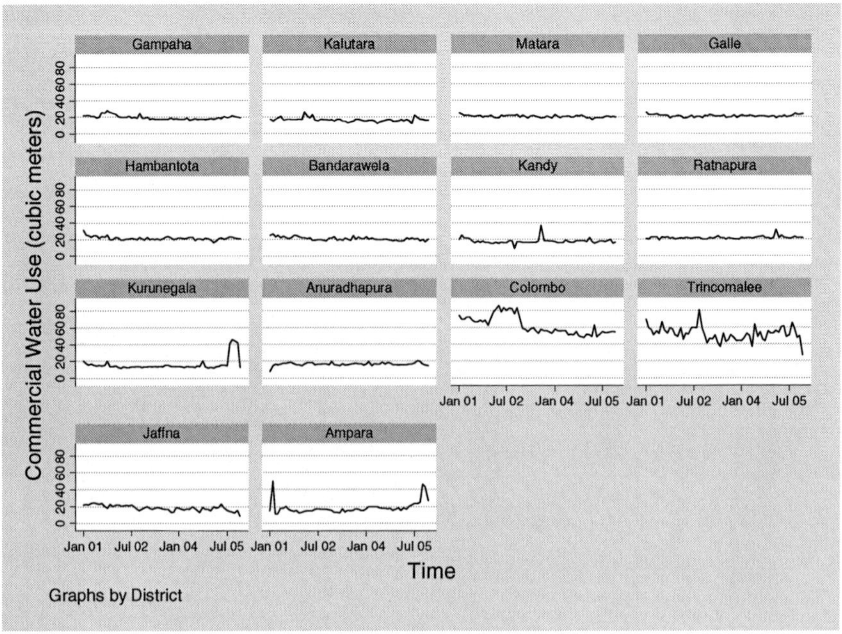

5.4 Methodology

Water can be considered an input in a commercial or industrial establishment's production process. Ideally, like any factor demand model, a model of water demand should be derived from an economic optimization process (Hanemann, 1997). Since output is subject to choice for most industrial and commercial customers, the appropriate economic framework would be profit maximization. However, this requires knowledge of prices of all other factor inputs and all outputs. Given the multitude of production inputs and end products associated with a single firm, this requirement far exceeds the scope of data traditionally available to public water utilities. In addition, very little is known about the way water enters as an input into the production function in both commercial and industrial firms (Reynaud, 2003).

This chapter focuses only on industrial and commercial water demand from connections located in the NWSDB districts. Firm's cost minimization enables the derivation of input demands (including water demand). This analysis assumes water is separable from other inputs. However, while this assumption cannot be tested here due to data limitations, there is some empirical evidence to support this view (Babin, et al., 1982; Reynaud, 2003). Although, it is assumed the commercial and industrial water demand is a function of output or sales level, sales or output data was hard to obtain (Malla & Gopalakrishnan, 1999).

5.4.1 Economic Model

Assuming that a representative firm chooses its input levels to minimize cost of production subject to the level of production, the models for industrial and commercial water demand are constructed. It is assumed that the production function is characterised by positive, strictly quasi-concave, monotonic and twice differentiable conditions.

$$C(p_1, p_2, \ldots\ldots\ldots\ldots\ldots p_N, Y) = \min \sum_{i=1}^{N} p_i X_i$$
$$s.t.\ f(X_i, \ldots\ldots\ldots X_N) \geq Y \tag{5.3}$$

Where, C is a total cost function, X_i and p_i are input quantities and prices respectively and Y is the exogenously determined level of output. $f(X_i, \ldots\ldots\ldots X_N)$ is the production function.

Partially differentiating the cost function with respect to input prices yield firm's conditional demand functions for respective inputs (Varian, 1984). For example, demand for water is a function of water price, other input prices and level of output.

$$X_w^* = \partial C(p_1, p_2, \ldots\ldots\ldots\ldots\ldots p_N, Y) / \partial p_w$$
$$= g(p_1, p_2, \ldots\ldots\ldots\ldots\ldots p_N, Y) \tag{5.4}$$

It is frequently the case that researchers have detailed information regarding water use but not on any other inputs. Therefore, it is necessary to assume the productive technology is separable in its inputs (Renzetti, 1992a). A firm's technology is said to be weakly separable if the cost function can be rewritten in the following way;

$$C(p_1, p_2, \ldots\ldots\ldots\ldots\ldots p_N, Y) = C(C_1(p_1, Y), C_w(p_w, Y), \ldots\ldots\ldots\ldots C_N(p_N, Y), Y) \tag{5.5}$$

The total cost function is composed of N sub-cost functions; the water use is separable from other inputs. Deriving sub-cost function

$(C_w(p_w,Y))$ with respect to input price leads to input demand function as given below (a function of own input price and level of output):

$$X_w^* = \partial C_w(p_w,Y)/\partial p_w$$
$$= g(p_w,Y) \quad (5.6)$$

For an average industrial firm, adopted demand function for water is specified as follows:

$$\ln W_I = \alpha + \beta_1 \ln p_I + \beta_2 \ln N_I + \beta_3 \ln T + \beta_4 \ln RF + \varepsilon \quad (5.7)$$

Where, W_I is quantity of water consumed by an average industrial connection in i^{th} district, p_I is average price of water for industrial connection, N_I is number of industrial connections in the ith district, T is average monthly temperature in the ith district, RF is average monthly rainfall in the ith district and ε is the error term.

For the average commercial entity, adopted demand function for water is given as follows:

$$\ln W_C = \alpha + \beta_1 \ln p_C + \beta_2 \ln N_C + \beta_3 \ln T + \beta_4 \ln RF + \varepsilon \quad (5.8)$$

Where, W_C is quantity of water consumed by an average commercial connection in i^{th} district, p_C is average price of water for commercial connection, N_C is number of commercial connections in the ith district, T is average monthly temperature in the ith district, RF is average monthly rainfall in the ith district and ε is the error term.

5.4.2 Estimation Techniques

The estimation of water demand for industrial and commercial entities over time poses several econometric challenges. Since water usage is presumably linked to some unobserved, time invariant firm characteristics, regression errors are expected to be correlated within a given unit for the entire time period under consideration (Moeltner & Stoddard, 2004). Ignoring this correlation will result in biased standard errors and unreliable t-values for estimated coefficients (Baltagi, 1995). The unobservable components driving consumption may exhibit time trends and seasonal patterns depending on market activities, economic conditions and the timing of exogenous price changes. If regressors correlated with time are included, parameter estimates will be affected by omitted variable bias.

The fixed effects regression model is used to control for omitted variables that differ between cases but are constant over time (Park, 2005). Fixed-effect models estimate industrial or commercial water use as a deviation from the firm's average use, based on the deviations of the explanatory variables from their averages. The fixed effects estimator uses only the variance in independent variables that vary over time; it ignores variation across groups. Therefore, the fixed effects estimator cannot be used to estimate the effects of time-invariant regressors (Greene, 2003).

A random-effects regression model is used if some omitted variables are constant over time but vary between cases and others are fixed between cases but vary over time. The random-effects model estimates variance components for districts and the error, assuming the same intercept and slopes (Park, 2005). In the random effects model, it is assumed that the unobserved effect is uncorrelated with each explanatory variable (Wooldridge, 2001). The random effects estimator assumes the intercept is a random outcome variable that is a function of a mean value plus a random error.

The standard error component of the above techniques assumes the regression disturbances are homoscedastic with the same variance across time and individuals. This is a restrictive assumption for panel data where the cross-sectional units may be varying in size and as a result may exhibit different variation. For example, in the data set used in this study, the size of the cross-sections is different and there is heteroscedasticity in the disturbance term. In order to correct for the possible presence of heteroscedasticity in the data, robust standard errors were computed.

The PCSE estimates expect different error variances for the different cross-sections. The PCSE model allows for correction for heteroscedasticity and serial correlation can also be adjusted using Prais-Winsten regression (Stata Press, 2003). The PCSE assumes the disturbances are, by default, heteroscedastic and contemporaneously correlated across panels. A GLS procedure is used to formulate estimates of the structural relationships since disturbance terms from the OLS model solution exhibited properties of autocorrelation, heteroscedasticity and mutual correlation. The GLS procedure is used to estimate the commercial and industrial water demand regression equation. The error term is assumed to be panel correlated (provide heteroskedastic error structure with cross-sectional correlation) and independent (independent autocorrelation structure) for GLS estimation.

5.5 Results and Discussion

Panel unit root tests provide an overall aggregate statistic to examine whether a unit root exists in the panel data and to judge the time series properties of the data accordingly (Wang, 2003). The test proposed by Levin, Lin and Chu, Im, Pesaran and Shin, ADF, PP and Breitung were carried out using Eviews statistical software and found none of the variables are non-stationary (Baltagi & Kao, 2000; Breitung, 2000; Im & Pesaran, 2003; Levin, et al., 2002). Panel unit root test results are given in the Appendix 1 Table 9.

The estimates of regression coefficients obtained for industrial water demand by employing OLS, PCSE and GLS techniques using STATA statistical software are presented in Table 5.3. Both fixed effect and random effect regressions are conducted along with the OLS technique. The Hausman test examines the null hypothesis that coefficients estimated by the efficient random effects estimator are the same as the ones estimated by the consistent fixed effects estimator (Hausman, 1978). In this estimation the null hypothesis is not rejected and hence, results of random effects estimator are presented.

Table 5.3 presents the estimated results of the industrial water demand. The estimates for the coefficients of the price variable for industrial consumers had the expected sign across all techniques but are not statistically significant at the 15 per cent level or better. However, PCSE technique presented a significant price coefficient at the 20 per cent significance level. Poor statistical significance results from the fact that the expenditure on water as a proportion of total cost by the firm is very small. In addition, the cross-section distribution of industrial types, coupled with a large variation in water usage per account may have led to the insignificance of the price variable. The magnitude of the price coefficient from random-effects technique and GLS technique is very small compared to PCSE. The price elasticity of demand is obtained directly from the regression coefficients (log-linear model) and varies widely between -0.03 and -0.76 indicating industrial water demand is price inelastic. These figures imply that a 10 per cent increase in the water price will result in a decline of industrial water consumption by 0.3 per cent to 7.5 per cent. Data used in this study is in aggregate form and failure to capture the industrial heterogeneity might have caused this large range of price elasticity.

Table 5.3: Industrial Water Demand Estimates

Variable		OLS – re (robust)	GLS (panels correlated)	PCSE (correlated)
Constant		0.5690	-3.6399	-1.3266
		(2.9992)	(3.2346)	(2.6103)
Average price		-0.0302	-0.0311	-0.7573
		(0.4317)	(0.2905)	(0.5971)^
No of connections		1.1353	0.4383	0.4406
		(0.0782)***	(0.0052)***	(0.0291)***
Temperature		-0.1293	1.9379	2.2163
		(0.8407)	(0.1627)***	(0.3877)***
Rainfall		-0.0245	-0.0411	-0.1176
		(0.0299)	(0.0112)***	(0.0378)***
Rho		0.7443		
R-sq	Within	0.3786		
	Between	0.1895		
	Overall	0.1949		0.2292

Notes: Column one: log-linear industrial water demand model is estimated using OLS technique; Column 2: log-linear industrial water demand model is estimated using GLS technique (panels correlated); Column 3: log-linear industrial water demand model is estimated using PCSE technique (correlated); *** Significant at $\alpha = 0.01$, ** Significant at $\alpha = 0.05$ and * Significant at $\alpha = 0.10$ ^ Significant at $\alpha = 0.20$ standard error values (robust) in parentheses below estimates, Dependant variable is natural log of monthly industrial quantity of water

The coefficient of the number of industrial connections is positive as expected and significant in all estimation techniques. One per cent increase in number of industry connections will increase the industrial water consumption by 0.44 per cent to 1.14 per cent. Both temperature and rainfall variables are significant in PCSE and GLS techniques with expected positive and negative signs respectively. The coefficients of temperature imply that a one per cent increase in temperature will increase the industrial water consumption by 1.94 to 2.22 per cent. The coefficient of the rainfall is negative, indicating that there is less demand for industrial water with more rainfall. One per cent increase in rainfall decreases the industry water consumption by 0.04 to 0.12 per cent.

The estimates of regression coefficients obtained for commercial water demand by employing OLS, PCSE and GLS are presented in Table 5.4. The Hausman test favours the random effects estimator; therefore, the results of the random effects estimator are presented. The coefficient of price is statistically significant at the 20 per cent level only in the GLS estimation technique. In all the other estimation techniques, price coefficients have the expected sign but are not statistically significant. The price elasticity estimates suggest commercial demand for water is relatively inelastic in the range -0.15 to -0.24. This implies a 10 per cent increase in the price of water will decrease the commercial consumption of water by 1.5 to 2.4 per cent. A significant part of the commercial sector is comprised of the informal sector such as home-based businesses or shops; therefore, this result is not surprising. The coefficient of number of commercial connections were significant with the expected sign implying a one per cent increase in the number of commercial connection will increase water consumption by 0.11 to 0.12 per cent.

Temperature and rainfall are significant determinants of water demand in the commercial sector. Coefficients of temperature and rainfall are statistically significant with expected signs. The coefficient of the temperature implies that one per cent increase in the temperature leads to a 0.2 to 0.88 per cent increase in water consumption while a one per cent increases in rainfall leads to a 0.01 to 0.03 per cent decrease in water consumption by commercial users.[2]

In addition to the above regressions, total industrial and commercial demand are estimated using total industrial and total commercial water quantity per district as the dependent variable. The results are given in the Appendix 1 Table 10 and 11 and the coefficient of the price variable is not significant in the commercial sector for all estimation techniques. However, the coefficient of the price variable is significant in the total industrial demand equation with the PCSE techniques, but insignificant with all other techniques. In the PCSE estimation, the magnitude of the coefficient of the price is large relative to other models and implies that industrial demand for water is price elastic. The price elasticity value is -1.37, implying a one per cent increase in price leads to a 1.37 per cent decrease in total district industrial water consumption. A higher price

[2] The number of employees for both industrial and commercial water demand was excluded from the analyses due to inconsistent results. This may be due to the fact that the number of employees was a poor proxy for industrial and commercial output or sales.

elasticity for industrial users are reasonable when it is considered that industrial customers are more likely to find alternative sources of supply or recycle water in the production process when adjusting to significant price increases (Williams & Suh, 1986). In Sri Lanka, a large number of industries such as textiles, food, beverages and milk are located close to rivers and there is an increasing trend to use alternative sources of water such as ground water and pumped river water (Hussain, et al., 2002).

Table 5.4: Commercial Water Demand Estimates

Variable		OLS – re (robust)	PCSE (correlated)	GLS (panels correlated)
Constant		4.2181 (1.0289)***	0.3636 (0.8703)	0.0450 (0.4442)
Average price		-0.1505 (0.1129)	-0.2367 (0.2095)	-0.1555 (0.0880)^
No. of connections		-0.1569 (0.0872)*	0.1206 (0.0062)***	0.1181 (0.0037)***
Temperature		0.1971 (0.1748)	0.8776 (0.0855)***	0.8625 (0.0375)***
Rainfall		-0.0107 (0.0060)*	-0.0315 (0.0111)***	-0.0177 (0.0034)***
Rho		0.8757		
R-sq	Within	0.0378		
	Between	0.0616		
	Overall	0.0461	0.0992	

Notes: Column one: log-linear industrial water demand model is estimated using OLS technique; Column 2: log-linear industrial water demand model is estimated using PCSE technique (correlated); Column 3: log-linear industrial water demand model is estimated using GLS technique (panels correlated); *** Significant at α = 0.01, ** Significant at α = 0.05 and * Significant at α = 0.10 ^ Significant at α = 0.15, standard error values (robust) in parentheses below estimates, Dependant variable is natural log of monthly commercial quantity of water

All the other variables such as number of industrial connections, temperature, rainfall and total number of employees in the industrial sector are significant in PCSE and GLS estimation procedures. The coefficient for the total number of employees is negative indicating the total district water consumption decreases with increasing employees in the industrial sector. This could be due to inconsistent data on number of employees or economies of scale on water usage with respect to industrial workers. The increase in total industrial water consumption in each district is less than proportional to the increase in number of industrial workers.

The total commercial demand estimation gives an insignificant price coefficient with the expected sign and in a similar range as the average commercial water demand (-0.16 to -0.24). The remaining variables such as number of connections, temperature and rainfall, are significant with expected signs in the PCSE estimation. Total number of employees in the commercial sector was included in the estimation, but is insignificant with a positive sign, implying more employees lead to more district total water consumption.

5.6 Conclusion

The economic characteristics of industrial and commercial water use have been unduly neglected. Despite the ubiquity of water use in industry and commercial entities, only a handful of studies have estimated industrial and commercial water demands. Industrial and commercial water use represents a smaller proportion of recorded total water use. The lack of information hampers the design of policy instruments aimed at efficiency in pipe-borne water supply system.

This chapter presented econometric analyses of demand functions for industrial and commercial water users of Sri Lanka for 14 NWSDB districts covering 60 months. This provides insights into the responses of commercial and industrial users to exogenous changes in price, temperature and rainfall. The sensitivity of water use in relation to the level of price was observed in the case of the commercial and industrial users albeit at a low significance level. Some of the past studies have indicated insensitivity to price in relation to water consumption by industrial and commercial users (Malla & Gopalakrishnan, 1999; Schneider & Whitlach, 1991). This insensitivity to price changes by industrial users may be because the expenditure on water accounts for only a small proportion of their total budget. Diversity of commercial and industrial water users analysed in this chapter could have contributed to the statistically insignificant results. However, industrial water use per connection as the dependent variable provided a significant price elasticity value which is much higher than the commercial sector. In addition, number of connections, temperature and rainfall are important determinants of commercial and industrial water demand.

The findings in the chapter are generally consistent with other studies; particularly the study by Hussain et al.,(2002) for Sri Lanka, which found that industrial water demand is highly responsive to price changes compared to commercial users. A 10 per cent increase in price of water will reduce the commercial water demand per connection by 1.6 per cent while a 10 per cent increase in price of water will reduce the industrial demand by 7.6 per cent. It is reasonable to expect industrial customers to adjust to significant price increases by altering the production process and accessing alternative water sources.

As evidenced herein, different user categories (industrial and commercial) respond differently to exogenous changes. These results suggest that raising the price of water may reduce industrial demand for water per connection; however, a substantial price change would be required to bring about the desired change in the commercial water demand per connection. According to these findings, pricing policy implemented to allocate scarce supplies among competing users is more likely to be effective if it is applied to industrial users.

The empirical evidence of this chapter provides important information for pipe-borne water planning and policies making, however, the findings are not conclusive since differences within districts and firms are not incorporated. This chapter does not have the data to take into account the differences in industrial and commercial units within each district. The lack of information on exact industrial and commercial water use may hamper the design of policy instruments aimed at efficiently managing water resources. Panel data analysis using exact industrial and commercial characteristics such as numbers of employees, value of output, type of industry and commercial unit and alternate sources of water would provide much greater insight into the factors influencing the industrial and commercial water demand. The findings of this chapter needs to be tested for robustness by, for example, conducting more disaggregated analyses with better quality data, when such data becomes available. In industrial and commercial setting, water quality and reliability are very important dimensions; however, these issues are not addressed in the estimations. More precise analysis of industrial and commercial water demand require information on water quality and data on number of supply or any interruptions to the water supply.

CHAPTER SIX

MARGINAL COST ANALYSIS

6.1 Introduction

There is a growing concern for the operations of water utilities responsible for supplying potable water (Renzetti, 1999). This trend has been encouraged by a variety of factors such as difficulties in maintaining aging capital stock, inability for cost recovery, water pollution and inefficiencies associated in allocating scarce water resources (Renzetti, 1992b). The NWSDB withdraws water to provide for the final use by the utility's residential, commercial, industrial and other customers and for various public functions. The NWSDB extracts raw water from sources such as aquifers, reservoirs, rivers and then treats it in various ways including filtration, chemical treatment to meet the public health standards and taste. This water is then distributed through a network of pipes to consumers. Production is measured in terms of the amount of water delivered to customers and generally this is not the same amount of water extracted from its sources as losses occur in the transmission (NWSDB, 2002).

An important feature of pipe-borne water facilities has been the level of subsidies and grants provided by the government (Renzetti, 1999). Revenues collected by the NWSDB directly from users account for only a portion of utilities total costs. The NWSDB recent annual report estimated that the average contribution of water user charges to operating, maintenance and capital costs was approximately 32 per cent (NWSDB, 2006b). It is interesting that a review of pipe-borne water supply systems in both developed and developing countries found that charges to consumers typically cover only an average of 35 per cent of the total cost of supply (Easter, et al., 1993; Renzetti, 1999). A major task for water utility operators is the determination of the appropriate rate structure for water services. While there are a number of water tariff reforms that are discussed in the literature, most of these focus on marginal-cost pricing (Kim, 1995). The goal of marginal-cost pricing for water is to provide the correct incentive to allocate and conserve water in an economically efficient manner. This efficiency serves to alert society about the cost of producing another unit so that usage can be adjusted accordingly (Hall, 2006).

Previous chapters have emphasized the importance of marginal-cost pricing by presenting the theoretical framework, institutional background and a literature review. This chapter is issued to introduce production cost models for short-run and long-run for pipe-borne water production in Sri Lanka. No previous study has been undertaken to estimate the marginal cost and other important cost variables for pipe-borne water for Sri Lanka. Apart from determining the marginal cost function, the cost models enable the estimations of economic parameters of production including cost-output elasticities, cost shares and economies of scale. An additional intention of the short-run and long-run marginal analyses is to employ the parameter estimates in a simulation model in chapter 7, along with the demand estimates in chapter 4 and 5 to evaluate the welfare effects of alternative pricing.

The application of dual theory to problems of economics has resulted in many useful outcomes in the past. The production and cost functions exhibit duality under given regularity conditions. The specification of the production function implies a cost function and vice versa (Christensen & Greene, 1976). The structure of the production can be studied empirically using either a production function or a cost function. Direct estimation of the production function is attractive when the level of output is endogenous whereas estimation of the cost function is attractive when the level of output is exogenous (Christensen & Greene, 1976).

In most of the situations, water utilities are not allowed to choose the level of production to maximize profits and they are required to supply all the pipe-borne water which is demanded at regulated prices. However, decisions are made with respect to the determination of the optimal levels of inputs. Furthermore, since water utilities compete with other industries for factors of production and since the water industry is small relative to the whole economy, the specification that input prices are exogenous variables is reasonable. Thus, the estimation of a cost function is more relevant than the direct estimation of the production function for studying the structure of water utility costs for Sri Lanka.

Marginal cost can be estimated from either a long-run or short-run perspective. The fundamental difference between SRMC and LRMC is the time frame under consideration and the implications for a firm's ability to adjust its production process to minimise costs (Turvey, 1976). From a theoretical perspective, the long-run is understood as the time horizon where all inputs are variable. When the demand for water reaches the production capacity, SRMCs rises steeply.[1] In the extreme case, additional supplies can only be secured for one customer by reducing the supplies to another customer. Therefore, SRMC can increase than that is being defined by the production costs to the customers who are not being served.

SRMC fluctuates with the capacity and demand and can be greater than pure operating and maintenance costs when demand exceeds the supply. It is difficult to estimate the opportunity cost of forgone demand for water, estimating SRMC in reference to operating and maintenance cost seems a reasonable proxy. In practice, SRMC may be estimated based on existing operating and maintenance costs or following a capacity expansion path (Marsden Jacob Associates, 2004). The variable cost (operating and maintenance cost) of supplying drinking water consists of expenses on production and distribution. Production cost includes cost of treatment, pumping and laboratory charges of raw and treated water. The distribution cost includes maintenance of pumping mains and distribution network, metering and allied activities. Replacement cost of capital and fixed capital cost should be considered in the long run and included in the total cost function. LRMC pricing is preferred over SRMC pricing due to the instability and implications of SRMC pricing in terms of pricing efficiency and equity (Garcia-Valinas, 2005).

Given the above considerations, this chapter is used to introduce the estimation of SRMC and LRMC and uses data from the NWSDB. The structure of this chapter is as follows: A review the literature of cost analysis is presented in section 6.2 and the data and variables used in the empirical analysis are discussed in the section 6.3. In section 6.4 models and estimation techniques are discussed. Estimation results are reported in section 6.5 and the final section, section 6.6, concludes the chapter.

6.2 Literature Review

There have been a few studies which empirically characterise the structure of water utility costs for developed countries (Garcia-Valinas, 2005; Garcia & Reynaud, 2004; Renzetti, 1992b). However, there is inadequate research in the context of developing countries and no study has been undertaken to research the structure of costs (short-run or long-run) for pipe-borne water in Sri Lanka. Past studies have primarily been concerned with either assessing the extent of scale economies in the technology of water delivery (Kim, 1987; Renzetti, 1992b) or identifying the efficiency differential that exists between the publicly administered

[1] Discussed in detail in chapter three

water departments and privately owned water utilities (Bhattacharyya, et al., 1994; Feigenbaum & Teeples, 1983; Gyler & Teeples, 1987; Renzetti, 1992b). The literature offers several methods of calculating marginal costs, such as econometric techniques of estimation (Bhattacharyya, et al., 1994; Feigenbaum & Teeples, 1983; Garcia-Valinas, 2005; Garcia & Reynaud, 2004; Kim, 1995; Renzetti, 1992b, 1999) or direct formulae (Turvey, 1976; Warford, 2003).

Kim (1987) estimated a trans-log cost function using cross-sectional data of sixty American water utilities and found scale economies decline with the size of the utility. A further study by Kim (1995) examined the pricing strategy of water services relative to marginal cost. He viewed the water utility as a multiproduct firm providing residential and non-residential services and a trans-log multiproduct cost function was estimated for a cross-section of sixty U.S. water utilities. The cost data from utility expenditures of labour, capital and energy was included. The price of labour was obtained by dividing the gross payroll by the number of yearly man-hours and the price of energy was estimated by dividing total power expenditure by yearly kilowatt-hour usage. The price of capital was computed by considering the interest rate on long-term debt and the depreciation rate. A trans-log multiproduct cost function and the share equations were estimated using the iterative Zellner efficient estimation method. At sample means of relevant variables, marginal cost values were estimated as US$ 0.16 per thousand gallons for residential service and US$ 0.14 per thousand gallons for non-residential service.

In the context of the debate concerning public verses private ownership of water utilities, Feigenbaum and Teeples (1983) estimated a hedonic model in trans-log form. They criticised the use of single output models and estimated a model with multiple output variables containing volume produced and a vector of service attributes. Teeples and Gyler (1987) replicated three cost models for water delivery systems as alternative specifications of a general form. They used a dual cost function methodology and used firm specific data and ownership proxies. They examined the effects on the efficiency of firms by ownership type. Their results showed that overall efficiency differences become insignificant as the specification improves and they used this finding to illustrate why past studies of overall efficiency of ownership forms have yielded mixed results.

Bhattacharyya et al., (1994) examined the behaviour of privately and publicly owned water utilities by estimating a generalized variable cost function. They used a trans-log form for the cost equation to estimate price and scale efficiencies based on a cross section of American water utilities.

They concluded that the public utilities were on average more efficient than the private utilities, but are more widely dispersed between the best and the worst practices (Bhattacharyya, et al., 1994). These studies have limited value in terms of providing a basis for water pricing study and fail to differentiate between short-run and long-run costs (Renzetti, 1992b).

Renzetti (1992b), in a case study of the Vancouver water works, used quarterly observations on input prices, output quantities and expenditure for the period 1975 to 1986. In the short-run model, an index of the capital stock constructed using the perpetual inventory method was included. The price or user cost of capital was included in the long-run cost model and constructed using Jorgenson's method and data on depreciation rates, interest rates and prices of investment projects. The price of raw water was obtained by estimating marginal cost of supply for the regional wholesaler and included in both short-run and long-run cost estimations. The long-run and short-run cost functions were estimated separately using an iterative three-stage procedure and a trans-log functional form. This study produced marginal cost that ranges from 0.53 to 0.85 per cubic metre (in 1986 Canadian dollars).

A similar study was conducted by Renzetti (1999) using cross-sectional data for Ontario municipal utilities that operated in 1991. The structure of the water and sewage long-run cost functions was approximated by a trans-log functional form. The price of labour, energy and capital were included in both cost functions. Each cost function and share equations were estimated using a seemingly unrelated regression procedure with linear homogeneity in prices and symmetry imposed. This study estimated the marginal cost as 0.87 per cubic metre (Canadian dollars) and found that scale economies were prevalent (Renzetti, 1999). In addition, he commented that this estimate was greater than those reported for U.S. and explained that this divergence may be due to higher labour and capital costs, greater temperature variability and lower population density in Ontario compared to U.S. cities.

Garcia and Thomas (2001) have modelled the structure of the cost for municipal water utilities with two outputs: water sold to final customers and water network losses. They proposed a measure of economies of scope to assess the benefits associated with joint production of water for final customers and water losses and several measures to evaluate potential gains in exploiting technological flexibility of water networks. They estimated the cost structure with a trans-log cost function using panel data of 55 water utilities for 3 years in South of France. Estimated results revealed a positive degree of economies of scope and significant economies of scale.[2]

Garcia and Reynaud (2004) estimated SRMC for French water utilities using trans-log approximation. They assumed that water utilities minimize their operating expenses, conditional on the length of network in kilometres and other technical variables such as number of customers and water volume. They used a panel data sample of 50 water utilities for period 1995 to 1998 corresponding to a total number of 200 observations. They produced marginal cost values between Euro 0.37 to 0.48 per cubic metre after imposing symmetry of the Hessian matrix as well as linear homogeneity in input prices (by dividing variable cost and input unit prices by the price of a given input) (Garcia & Reynaud, 2004). At the sample mean, they found the returns to scale are not significantly different from one and this result contradicted the general opinion of water production and distribution as a natural monopoly.

Garcia-Valinas (2005) proposed a Cobb-Douglas cost function in a case study for Seville, Spain for the period 1985 to 2000. This study used an index of capital stock; length of pipelines integrated in the supply network in kilometres in the short-run cost analysis and substituted with price of capital in the long-run analysis. The cost functions were estimated by an iterative seemingly unrelated regression procedure and the electric energy price had been eliminated in order to impose the constraint of homogeneity of degree one in prices. She reported LRMC value as Euro 0.97 per cubic metre and SRMC as Euro 0.52 per cubic metre for 2000 averages for relevant variables.

Past empirical results have shown that LRMC values are higher than SRMC values (Garcia-Valinas, 2005; Garcia & Reynaud, 2004; Renzetti, 1992b, 1999). This is because LRMCs include marginal capacity costs, that is the cost of extending capacity to accommodate an additional unit of consumption and are also affected by the different factors which influence the cost of reservoir construction such as technology and input prices. For example, technological advances will lower the cost but increases in input prices and increasing scarcity of suitable sites tend to raise the costs. It is also known that water services involve high capital investments, therefore, a lot of expenses are fixed costs and do not vary with the water quantity consumed in the short-run (Garcia & Reynaud, 2004). However, the

[2] Economies of scope exist if the average total cost of production decreases as a result of increasing the number of different goods produced. Economies of scale is defined as a decrease in average total cost of production as a result of increasing quantity of goods produced.

estimation of SRMC has ignored the opportunity cost of forgone demand which may result in a greater SRMC than the LRMC (Ng, 1987).[3]

Turvey (1976) defines the LRMC of water supply as the sum of marginal capacity costs, marginal operating costs, marginal distribution costs and per connection overhead costs. The U.K. Office of Water and Essential Services Commission in Australia have employed this concept of marginal capacity cost to estimate LRMCs (Altmann, 2007). Turvey (1976) estimated the LRMC using average incremental costs (AIC) or present worth incremental system cost (PWISC) method. The AIC is defined as the additional cost per unit of additional consumption when both additional annual costs and consumption are expressed as the present value of their flows (Warford, 2003). This is common to North American water suppliers since the AIC approach has the desirable property of producing a constant price over the period (Altmann, 2007). The difficulties of this approach for the regulator lie in the determination of discount rates and the possibility of a price discontinuity arising from a period in which no major investments are undertaken. However, the approach taken in this chapter is to empirically estimate the SRMC and LRMC by estimating the cost function for the NWSDB using data.

There have been inadequate studies to empirically characterise the structure of water utility costs for developing countries and no study has been undertaken to research the structure of costs (short-run or long-run) for pipe-borne water in Sri Lanka. Past studies have either assessed the extent of scale economies in the water delivery (Kim, 1987) or analysed the efficiency differential between the public and privately owned water utilities (Bhattacharyya, et al., 1994; Gyler & Teeples, 1987). The literature offers several models and econometric techniques of calculating marginal costs. The trans-log function form is being commonly used (Garcia & Reynaud, 2004; Kim, 1995; Renzetti, 1999) while the Cobb-Douglas functional form is rarely used (Garcia-Valinas, 2005). The trans-log function is a more flexible cost function and widely used in the estimation of production and cost functions in empirical economics (Christensen, et al., 1973). The trans-log cost function has the advantage of flexibility of specification and can be applied to multi-product and multi-factor production. It allows scale economies to vary with the level of output (Christensen & Greene, 1976). This chapter presents the analyses of marginal cost of water supply for short and long runs and scale economies for NWSDB Sri Lanka using aggregate data. Cost functions are estimated using general trans-log functional form and different model restrictions

[3] This is explained in detail in chapter 3.

(homotheticity, homogeneity, unitary elasticity of substitution and constant returns to scale) are imposed on the trans-log functional form to check for the appropriate functional form. The simultaneous analysis of a system of equations (cost function and input share equations) is preferable (Christensen & Greene, 1976).

The current study checks for concavity and monotonicity of the cost function and imposes theoretically derived conditions where appropriate. However, this approach is rarely used in the water utility cost studies. The data used for analysis are panel observations of the NWSDB districts compiled from several sources. Operating costs are used for short-run estimations and total costs (including cost of capital) are used in the long-run analysis. Input price variables for labour, chemical, electricity are calculated as unit costs. A price index was constructed for maintenance due to data limitations. Price of capital and the cost of capital were very difficult to compute and a number of proxy variables were used as described in the section 6.3. This analysis could not include the price of raw water since the NWSDB does not pay for ground or surface water extraction. However, a constant is added to the marginal cost estimates to account for raw water price.

6.3 Data

The data used for analysis are panel observations of NWSDB districts compiled from several sources. The monthly cost data was collected from the NWSDB for the period from January 2001 to December 2005 for 14 NWSDB districts. The operating cost is measured as the sum of monthly expenditures on labour, chemical, electricity, maintenance and other costs (for example, cost of stationary and miscellaneous expenses). Total cost is measured by including expenditure on capital in the operating costs. Operating costs are used for short-run estimations and total costs are used in the long-run analysis.

With regards to independent variables, the price of labour is obtained by dividing the total labour cost per month by the total number of employees per month. The price of electricity is represented by the average price of electricity charged to industrial customers by the Ceylon Electricity Board, Sri Lanka. The expenses on chemicals are composed of costs of different types of chemicals such as Lime, Chlorine gas and Alum. The price index is computed using the total cost of chemicals and the total quantity of chemicals used each month. Maintenance expenses consist of different categories of heterogeneous costs obtained by consolidating financial costs, such as stocking and different types of maintenance work involving subcontracting. Due to data limitations and the problem of heterogeneity; a price index is constructed for price of maintenance as unit cost per cubic metre delivered (Garcia & Reynaud, 2004; Garcia & Thomas, 2001).

In principle, the price of capital should reflect interest rates, depreciation rates and purchase price of capital equipment (Renzetti, 1999). Unfortunately, no data on costs of capital or other similar measures are available from the NWSDB. Therefore, the price of capital is constructed as long-term interest plus depreciation allowances on the plant in service; however, this may not represent the true capital price. It is considered as an approximate price of capital; data limitations force the adoption of this method. The total expenditure on capital was obtained from the data on capital fund utilization of each year published in the NWSDB annual reports. The stock of capital is unlikely to vary in the short run, therefore, the average price of capital has been excluded from short-run estimations (Garcia-Valinas, 2005; Renzetti, 1992b).

The analysis here assumes that prices of labour, electricity, capital and chemical do not vary substantially between districts. Factor shares of capital, labour, electricity, chemical and maintenance and other are calculated by dividing the expenditure of respective input by the total expenditure. In the short-run cost estimation, capital costs are excluded and the expenditure of respective inputs is divided by the operation and maintenance expenditure to obtain respective factor shares.

The raw water price is not included in the empirical estimation as the NWSDB does not pay for the water initially drawn from reservoirs or rivers (Billings, 1982; Garcia-Valinas, 2005; Garcia & Reynaud, 2004). In Sri Lanka, charges are not levied for the extraction of ground water for any purpose and are not restricted by any authority. However, not including raw water price is economically erroneous, regardless of whether the water utility is paying for raw water. Raw water is considered as a scarce resource, and hence it should have a shadow price. However, the NWSDB pays the Department of Irrigation for extracting water from irrigation tanks for drinking purposes. For example, NWSDB has signed an agreement with the Department of Irrigation to release a specific quantity of water from Thuruwila and Nilambe irrigation tanks and payment is made on a monthly basis. The payment, on average, is approximately SLRS 0.50 per cubic metre.[4] Since this is not a very accurate way of calculating the raw

[4] This information was obtained from email communication with the NWSDB officials (2008).

water price, this value is added to the marginal cost estimates as a constant.

The total number of cubic metres finally supplied is included in the long-run and short-run cost functions. Total number of cubic metres finally supplied is obtained as the difference between the total amount of cubic metres of initially supplied water and the distribution network losses (Garcia-Valinas, 2005). Non-revenue water in Sri Lanka accounts for 30 per cent on average and they must be taken into account when estimating the cost function for pipe-borne water.

6.3.1 Summary Statistics

Table 6.1 presents summary statistics of the variables used in cost estimations. The summary statistics show wide variations in the major variables such as total amount of consumption, real total cost of operation and maintenance and cost shares. The panel used in the study ranges from a very large NWSDB district treating 12.9 million cubic metres of water per month to a very small NWSDB district treating 18,558 cubic metres of water per month. This is evidenced by vast differences between minimum and maximum values of consumption level of output.

The input prices faced by the NWSDB districts are uniform, as shown by relatively small standard deviations. The share of chemicals in total costs (and in operation and maintenance costs) is small relative to those of labour, electricity and maintenance. Labour constitutes the largest proportion of the overall water board's operation while electricity and maintenance constitute about equal proportions. The cost share of labour and capital are increasingly important factors in the total cost of the water utility where the expenditure on capital is the largest item and expenditure on capital is the most challenging to estimate. Electricity and maintenance constitute about equal proportions in the overall utility's total cost.

6.4 Methodology

The NWSDB seeks to minimize the cost of supplying quantities of output. They are also constrained by exogenously determined input prices, production technologies and the operating environment characteristics. Long-run total cost is measured as the sum of monthly expenditures on labour, energy, chemical, capital and maintenance. Short-run operating cost excludes the cost of capital and assumes that stock of capital is fixed. It is assumed the production technology adapts slowly to the technological innovations and that, for a given network, the technology is the same for all production units. Major components of operating expenditure of NWSDB for 2004, 2005 and 2006 are given in the Appendix 1 Table 12.

The economically and statistically valid method for estimating marginal cost is the direct application of neoclassical economic theory through the estimation of a total cost function. The NWSDB sells to final consumers a water volume; often the volume of water sold to final customers and the volume of water injected into the distribution network are not the same. Water losses are a typical feature of water networks and should be taken into account when estimating the cost function (NWSDB, 2006a).[5] This is important as water utilities can use losses as an adjustment tool for production decisions (Garcia & Reynaud, 2004). Marginal cost is unlikely to vary for the various uses of delivered water services assuming the demand for water quality for various uses are similar. Water for different uses such as residential, industrial and commercial are produced under common costs and technology and cannot be properly segregated for different uses. Therefore, a single output model is estimated and secondary measures such as water quality or supply disruptions are not included.

The analysis in this chapter assumes that short-run and long-run cost functions of NWSDB are in the form of a trans-log approximation. The symmetry of the Hessian matrix and linear homogeneity in input prices are imposed. The more general specification of a trans-log cost function imposes no prior restriction on the production structure and it does not impose homotheticity, homogeneity, constant returns to scale and unitary elasticities of substitution restrictions. This chapter estimates the general specification of trans-log and cost functions along with other imposed restrictions such as homotheticity, homogeneity, constant returns to scale and unitary elasticities of substitution.

---

[5] Water losses mainly include non-revenue water.

Table 6.1: Summary of Variables in Short-run and Long-run Cost Analyses

Variable	Units	Mean	Std. Dev.	Min	Max
Real total cost of operation and maintenance	SLRS mn	31.20	42.90	4.22	373.00
Real total cost	SLRS mn	119.00	60.80	4.43	381.00
Total consumption	m^3 mn	1.41	2.83	0.02	12.90
Price of chemical	SLRS/ kg	29.79	12.09	10.02	81.06
Real wage for average employee ('000)	SLRS/ worker	23.50	12.54	13.47	96.09
Real average price of electricity	SLRS/ KWh	9.60	0.84	8.25	10.95
Real unit cost of maintenance and other	SLRS/ m^3	11.80	25.74	0.41	426.45
Price of capital	index	0.13	0.04	0.09	0.28
Short-run cost shares					
Share of wage cost	%	49.12	11.30	5.49	85.76
Share of electricity cost	%	24.97	10.54	0.05	54.32
Share of chemical cost	%	4.12	3.39	0.00	20.38
Share of maintenance and other cost	%	21.77	9.62	2.77	89.90
Long-run cost shares					
Share of capital cost	%	63.48	15.13	7.64	92.41
Share of wage cost	%	18.12	9.53	3.84	64.12
Share of electricity cost	%	8.51	3.80	0.01	24.73
Share of chemical cost	%	1.39	1.18	0.01	6.60
Share of maintenance and other cost	%	8.47	7.06	0.85	73.79

6.4.1 Cost Function

The cost function is the minimum cost of producing a given output level during a given time period expressed as a function of input prices and output (Chambers, 1988).

$$c(w, y) = \min_{x \geq 0} f\{w \cdot x : x \in V(y)\} \tag{6.1}$$

In equation (6.1), y is level of output, w is input price and x is an input quantity. This representation assumes that input prices are exogenous to the producer, it is presumed that producers are atomistic competitors in the sense that they take input and other prices as given (Chambers, 1988). The properties of the cost function $c(w, y)$ are;

1. $c(w, y) > 0 \; for \; w > 0 \; and \; y > 0$ (non-negativity) – Impossible to produce a positive output at zero cost.
2. If $w` \geq w, then \; c(w`, y) \geq c(w, y)$ (non-decreasing in w) – indicates that increasing any input price must not decrease cost.
3. Concave and continuous in w - when the cost function is concave, cost rises at a decreasing rate
4. $c(tw, y) = tc(w, y), t > 0$ (positively linearly homogenous) – If input prices vary proportionately, the cost minimizing choice of inputs will not vary.
5. If $y \geq y`, then \; c(w, y) \geq c(w, y`)$ (non-decreasing in y) – increasing output cannot decrease the costs
6. Shephard's lemma – if the cost function is differentiable in w, then there exists a unique vector of cost-minimizing demands that is equal to the gradient of the $c(w, y)$ in w. That is, if $x_i(w, y)$ is the ith unique cost-minimizing demand, then $x_i(w, y) = \partial c(w, y) / \partial w_i$ (Chambers, 1988).

6.4.2 Trans-log Cost Function

This chapter assumes the NWSDB cost function is in the form of well-known transcendental logarithmic (trans-log) approximation first introduced by Christensen et.al. (1973). The trans-log cost function could be considered as a second-order Taylor's series approximation in logarithms to an arbitrary cost function (Christensen, et al., 1973). It allows scale economies to vary with the level of output and this feature is essential to enable the unit cost curve to attain the classical U shape (Christensen & Greene, 1976).

The trans-log function is a more flexible cost function and widely used in the estimation of production and cost functions in empirical economics (Christensen, et al., 1973). The trans-log cost function has the advantage of flexibility of specification and can be applied to multi-product and multi-factor production. Unfortunately, it is impossible to mathematically provide an explicit solution to the underlying production function. The trans-log production function and the trans-log cost function do not generally correspond to the same technology, although they can be regarded as close approximations for the same technology. Thus, the trans-log is widely used in studies of factor demand and product supply (Christensen, et al., 1973).

SRMC and LRMC are derived from the estimated short-run and long-run cost functions. This analysis assumes the production technology adopts slowly to technological innovations and that, for a given network, the technology is the same for all production units (Garcia & Reynaud, 2004)

SRMC is estimated using the following equation to capture the short-run operation and maintenance costs. This analysis ignores the opportunity cost of forgone water demand and analyses the marginal cost of production only. Since the NWSDB does not pay for the raw water, a constant representing the raw water price is added to the marginal cost estimates.

$$C_{SR} = f(w_L, w_C, w_E, w_O, Q)$$

$$\ln C_{SR} = \alpha_0 + \sum_{i=1}^{4} \alpha_i \ln w_i + \frac{1}{2}\sum_{i=1}^{4}\sum_{j=1}^{4} \gamma_{ij} \ln w_i \ln w_j + \beta_Q \ln Q + \frac{1}{2}\beta_{QQ} \ln(Q)^2 + \sum_{i=1}^{4} \beta_{iQ} \ln w_i \ln Q$$

$$\omega_t t + \frac{1}{2}\omega_{tt}(t)^2 + \sum_{i=1}^{4} \omega_{it} \ln w_i t + \sum_{i=1}^{13} D_i + \varepsilon \qquad (6.2)$$

$i, j = L, E, C \text{ and } M$

The long-run total cost function is estimated to capture the long-run capital investments. Furthermore, LRMCs should include costs related to scarcity, negative externalities such as water pollution and the positive externalities arising from quality potable water. Much of the research in this area ignores these factors because these costs cannot be estimated to the same level of accuracy of operating and investment costs due to data limitations. Pollution of rivers by agricultural, industrial or human activities, poor quality and over-extraction of ground water may contribute to treatment costs. Due to limitations in valuing the externalities, this chapter only estimates the long-run operation and investment costs.

$$C_{LR} = f(w_L, w_C, w_E, w_M, w_K, Q)$$

$$\ln C_{LR} = \alpha_0 + \sum_{i=1}^{5} \alpha_i \ln w_i + \frac{1}{2}\sum_{i=1}^{5}\sum_{j=1}^{5} \gamma_{ij} \ln w_i \ln w_j + \beta_Q \ln Q + \frac{1}{2}\beta_{QQ} \ln(Q)^2 + \sum_{i=1}^{5} \beta_{iQ} \ln w_i \ln Q$$

$$\omega_t t + \frac{1}{2}\omega_{tt}(t)^2 + \sum_{i=1}^{5} \omega_{it} \ln w_i t + \sum_{i=1}^{13} D_i + \varepsilon \quad (6.3)$$

$i, j = L, E, C, K \ and \ M$

In equations (6.2) and (6.3), C_{SR} is cost in the short-run, C_{LR} is cost in the long-run, w_L is unit price of labour, w_C is unit price of chemicals, w_E is unit price of electricity, w_M is unit price for maintenance, w_K is average price of capital, Q is cubic metres of water supplied (residential + non-residential) at time t to final customers (quantity of water that reached the final consumers), t is time and D is district dummy variable, subscript L stands for labour, E stands for electricity, C stands for chemical, M stands for maintenance and K stands for capital.

For a cost function to be well behaved, it must be homogenous of degree one in prices, implying that for a fixed level of output, total cost must increase proportionally when all prices increase proportionally. Thus the following restrictions apply to equations (6.2) and (6.3):

$$\sum_{i=1}^{n} \alpha_i = 1 \quad (6.4)$$

$$\sum_{i=1}^{n} \beta_{iQ} = 0 \qquad \sum_{i=1}^{n} \omega_{it} = 0 \quad (6.5)$$

$$\sum_{i=1}^{n} \gamma_{ij} = \sum_{j=1}^{n} \gamma_{ji} = \sum_{i=1}^{n}\sum_{j=1}^{n} \gamma_{ij} = 0 \quad (6.6)$$

In addition, a well behaved cost structure should be monotonically increasing and concave in input prices. Therefore, monotonicity and concavity can be checked for each observation after the function has been estimated (Kohli, 1991). Monotonicity with respect to input prices can be given as follows;

$$\frac{\partial \ln C}{\partial \ln w_i} > 0 \quad (6.7)$$

Concavity in input prices are illustrated by the Hessian matrix with respect to factor prices to be negative semi-definite.

The trans-log cost function is an approximation to the general non-homothetic cost function, which is assumed to be homogenous in prices. Since the trans-log model is complicated, it is useful to look at other possible models that can be derived from it by imposing further restrictions.

Homotheticity means the cost function can be written as a separable function in output and factor prices.[6] For homotheticity, it is necessary and sufficient that (Berndt, 1991);

$$\beta_{iQ} = 0, \ \forall_i \tag{6.8}$$

Homothetic production functions generate cost functions with the property that elasticity of size and elasticity of scale are always equivalent (Chambers, 1988). Elasticity of size is a measure of how costs change when output changes, on the other hand elasticity of scale is a percentage measure of a change in output due to change in all inputs (Chambers, 1988; Christensen & Greene, 1976).

The cost function is homogenous in output if the elasticity of cost with respect to output is constant. This occurs with the following restrictions (Berndt, 1991):

$$\beta_{iQ} = 0, \qquad \beta_{QQ} = 0 \tag{6.9}$$

In this case, the degree of homogeneity equals to $1/\beta_Q$. The constant returns to scale of the dual production function can be imposed by forcing the restriction (6.10). In addition to the above restrictions, the cost functions satisfy (Berndt, 1991):

$$\beta_Q = 1 \tag{6.10}$$

Ultimately, the trans-log function becomes a constant returns to scale Cobb-Douglas function if, besides the previous restrictions each of the (Christensen & Greene, 1976).

---

[6] With non-homothetic cost functions ratios of cost minimizing inputs demands are allowed to depend on the level of output. By contrast, with homothetic functions relative input demands are independent of the level of output (Berndt, 1991).

$$\gamma_{ij} = 0, \forall_i \tag{6.11}$$

The elasticities of substitution can all be restricted to unity by the elimination of the second order term in the prices from the trans-log cost function and can be applied to the trans-log, homothetic, homogenous and CRS. Eight models are considered including the trans-log cost function (Model A). Model B imposes homotheticity; Model C imposes homogeneity and Model D with constant returns to scale. Models E, F, G and H corresponds to Models A, B, C and D respectively, with the additional restriction of unitary elasticities of substitution imposed on each case. The estimated cost models and the restrictions are summarised in the Table 6.2.

Table 6.2: Cost Models and Restrictions

Model	Cost function	Restrictions
A	Trans-log, non-unitary elasticities of substitution	None
B	Homothetic, non-unitary elasticities of substitution	$\beta_{iQ} = 0$
C	Homogenous, non-unitary elasticities of substitution	$\beta_{iQ} = 0 \;\; \beta_{QQ} = 0$
D	Constant returns to scale, non-unitary elasticities of substitution	$\beta_{iQ} = 0 \;\; \beta_{QQ} = 0 \; \beta_Q = 1$
E	Trans-log, unitary elasticities of substitution	$\gamma_{ij} = 0$
F	Homothetic, unitary elasticities of substitution	$\beta_{iQ} = 0 \; \gamma_{ij} = 0$
G	Homogenous, unitary elasticities of substitution	$\beta_{iQ} = 0 \;\; \beta_{QQ} = 0$ $\gamma_{ij} = 0$
H	Constant returns to scale, unitary elasticities of substitution	$\beta_{iQ} = 0 \;\; \beta_{QQ} = 0$ $\beta_Q = 1 \;\; \gamma_{ij} = 0$

Source: Christensen and Greene (1976), Chambers (1988) and Berndt (1991)

Direct estimation of the cost function can be carried out. However, gains in efficiency can be obtained if the optimal cost-minimising input demand equations or cost-share equations are estimated jointly with the cost equation (Christensen & Greene, 1976). Using Shephard's Lemma, the derived demand for an input is obtained by partially differentiating the cost function with respect to input prices.

$$\partial C_{SR}/\partial w_i = X_i \tag{6.12}$$

Where X_i is the conditional factor demand and this result is conveniently expressed in logarithmic form of the trans-log cost function as follows:

$$S_i = \frac{\partial \ln C_{SR}}{\partial \ln w_i} = \frac{w_i}{C_{SR}} \frac{\partial C_{SR}}{\partial w_i} = \frac{w_i X_i}{C_{SR}} = \alpha_i + \sum_{i=1}^{n} \gamma_{ij} \ln w_j + \beta_{iQ} \ln Q + v_i \tag{6.13}$$

$\sum_{i=1} w_i X_i = C_{SR}$, and if $S_i = \frac{w_i X_i}{C_{SR}}$, then $\sum_{i=1} S_i = 1$, which implies that $N-1$ of the share equations are linearly independent

One of the important objectives of cost analysis is the measure of marginal cost and this can be obtained by the partial derivative of the cost function with respect to output (Chambers, 1988). Because $C(w,Q)$ is non-decreasing in output, marginal cost is always non-negative. Often elasticity of cost with respect to output is measured and defined as the ratio of marginal cost and average cost. The cost elasticity of output for trans-log cost function is derived as follows:

$$\varepsilon_{CQ} = \frac{\partial \ln C_C}{\partial \ln Q} = \beta_Q + \sum_{i=1}^{n} \gamma_{iQ} \ln w_j + \beta_{QQ} \ln Q \tag{6.14}$$

The marginal cost equation is then obtained by the expression:

$$MC_C = \varepsilon_{CQ} \frac{C_C}{Q} \tag{6.15}$$

The marginal cost of output varies not only with the level of output but also with level of inputs prices. The effects of a change in these variables on the marginal cost of water services can be examined from the equation (6.15). The effect of input prices on marginal cost is examined as follows:

$$\frac{\partial \ln MC_C}{\partial \ln w_i} = \frac{\gamma_{iQ}}{\varepsilon_{CQ}} + S_i \tag{6.16}$$

Allen partial elasticities of substitution (σ_{ij}) between two factors i and j can be constructed using the estimated coefficients (Uzawa, 1962). These elasticities are useful in describing the pattern and degree of substitutability and complementarity amongst the factors of production. Basically, they measure the percentage change in factor proportions due to a one per cent change in their relative prices. Two inputs are Allen substitutes if $\sigma_{ij} \geq 0$ and Allen complements if the inequality is reversed. For the trans-log cost function, Allen partial elasticities of substitution can be defined as follows:

$$\sigma_{ij} = \frac{\gamma_{ij}}{S_i S_j} + 1 \quad for\ i \neq j \tag{6.17}$$

In addition, own-price and cross-price elasticities of factor demands can be computed. These measure how demand for input i responds with respect to changes in its own price or changes in the price of input j.

$$\eta_{ij} = \frac{\left(\gamma_{ij} + S_i \cdot S_j\right)}{S_i} \quad where \quad i \neq j \tag{6.18}$$

$$\eta_{ii} = \frac{\left(\gamma_{ii} + S_i^2 - S_i\right)}{S_i} \quad where \quad i = j \tag{6.19}$$

Economies of scale are defined in terms of the relative increase in output resulting from a proportional increase in all inputs. This is expressed as one minus the elasticity of total cost with respect to output (Christensen & Greene, 1976). The positive number indicates positive scale economies and negative numbers indicate scale diseconomies. Formulae for economies of scale for Models A to F are presented in the Table 6.3.

$$\Omega = 1 - \frac{\partial \ln C_C}{\partial \ln Q} \tag{6.20}$$

If economies of scale are present, then it may be rational for utility operators to accelerate investment and achieve higher levels of production. Economies of scale might arise because of the large fixed capital expenditure often required by the water utilities. The physical and technical relationships also can result in scale economies, for example, in the case of pipelines, costs are typically closely related to the surface area of the pipeline, yet output depends primarily on the potential volume.

The advantage of flexible functional forms like trans-log is that they do not constrain *a priori* the signs or the sizes of the elasticities of substitution (Kohli, 1991). Therefore, these functional forms are much more general than functional forms often used in the literature, such as the Cobb-Douglas and Constant Elasticity of Substitution (CES) functional forms (derivations of Cobb-Douglas and CES functional forms are given in the Appendix 2). However, flexible functional forms need not give a close approximation to the unknown technology. The second-order approximation holds at one point only and there is no guarantee the approximation is good for all other points (Kohli, 1991).

Table 6.3: Economies of Scale Formulae

Model	Economies of scale
A	$1-\left(\beta_Q+\beta_{QQ}\ln Q+\sum_{i=1}^{n}\beta_{iQ}\ln w_i\right)$
B	$1-\left(\beta_Q+\beta_{QQ}\ln Q\right)$
C	$1-\beta_Q$
D	1
E	$1-\left(\beta_Q+\beta_{QQ}\ln Q+\sum_{i=1}^{n}\beta_{iQ}\ln w_i\right)$
F	$1-\left(\beta_Q+\beta_{QQ}\ln Q\right)$
G	$1-\beta_Q$
H	1

Source: Christensen and Greene (1976), Chambers (1988) and Berndt (1991)

An important issue of estimation of a system of equations is the goodness of fit. In the context of a single equation, the goodness of fit is measured by R^2. Berndt (1991) explains the single equation measures of fit are not appropriate in system of equations, because a system of regressions does not minimise the sum of squared errors of each independent equation. Instead, the maximum likelihood estimator minimises the determinant of the residual cross-products matrix in estimations of equation systems. Therefore, the correct measure of goodness of fit for a system of equations proposed by Berndt (1991) is computed as

$$\tilde{R}^2 = 1 - \frac{|E`E|}{|y`y|} \tag{6.21}$$

In equation (6.21), E is the matrix of residuals and $y = (Y - \bar{Y})$. Y is the matrix of dependent variables and $\bar{Y}$ is the mean of variable Y. $\tilde{R}^2$ indicates the proportion of the generalized variance in Y explained by variation in the right-hand variables in the system of equations (Berndt, 1991).

6.4.3 Curvature Conditions

As is well known, a necessary and sufficient condition for concavity is that the Hessian matrix of the cost function be negative semidefinite. The curvature properties of the estimated functions can be checked either by computing the Eigenvalues of the matrix or by checking the principal minors of the matrix. Concavity requires the Eigenvalues be non-positive (Kohli, 1991). As noted by Diewert and Wales (1987), one of the most vexing problems confronting applied economists estimating flexible functional forms is that the estimates very often fail to satisfy required curvature conditions.[7]

Concavity of the estimated cost function with respect to input prices requires the matrix of estimated coefficients to be negative semi-definite.

$$[\gamma_{ij}] = \begin{bmatrix} \gamma_{KK} & \gamma_{KL} & \gamma_{KM} & \gamma_{KC} \\ \gamma_{LK} & \gamma_{LL} & \gamma_{LM} & \gamma_{LC} \\ \gamma_{MK} & \gamma_{ML} & \gamma_{MM} & \gamma_{MC} \\ \gamma_{CK} & \gamma_{CL} & \gamma_{CM} & \gamma_{CC} \end{bmatrix} \tag{6.22}$$

6.4.4 Imposing Local Concavity

The curvature property of the trans-log cost function is data dependant, hence concavity is not guaranteed if the usual estimation procedure is

[7] Curvature conditions are imposed assuming a perfect competitive industry; however, cost estimations in this chapter revealed that the NWSDB experience increasing returns to scale.

used. It is not possible to impose parametric restrictions to ensure concavity of the estimated trans-log cost function without affecting its flexibility (Chua, et al., 2005). In typical applied work, the trans-log cost function is estimated assuming that it satisfies the curvature condition. In this chapter, the estimated cost function satisfies the concavity condition only at 48.1 per cent of the observations.

There is no consensus as to what to do if the estimated cost function fails to satisfy concavity for a large number of data points. Therefore, most water cost studies do not report the extent to which the estimated cost function satisfies the concavity requirement. This chapter adopts a simple approach suggested by Ryan and Wales (1998, 2000), which involves imposing local concavity in the trans-log form. The main attraction of this approach is that, it preserves the flexibility of the trans-log specification. The disadvantage is that, it does not guarantee concavity for all observations (Chua, et al., 2005). Nevertheless, as demonstrated by Ryan and Wales (1998, 2000), this approach often results in a vast improvement in the curvature property of the estimated cost function.

The Hessian matrix of the trans-log cost function should be negative semidefinite to satisfy concavity requirements. The Hessian matrix depends on data and separate Hessian matrices are obtained for each observation. The parametric restrictions can be imposed at the reference point to ensure the Hessian matrix is negative semidefinite. This only guarantees that the function is concave at one observation or at the reference point (Chua, et al., 2005; Kohli, 1991; Ryan & Wales, 1998, 2000). However, this is often sufficient for the estimated function to satisfy the curvature conditions for all observations.

Let $TC^* = (Q^*, W^*)$ denote the chosen reference point. The input prices and output variable are scaled (but not the time and dummy variables) so that they are equal to one at TC^*. Let $\hat{W}$ denote $n \times n$ diagonal matrix where the diagonal elements are the input price vector W. Diewert and Wales (1987) show that

$$\hat{H} = \frac{\hat{W} H \hat{W}}{TC(W,Q)} \tag{6.23}$$

If $TC(W,Q) > 0$, H is negative semidefinite only and only if $\hat{H}$ is negative semidefinite. This transformation ensures that at TC^*, $\hat{H}$ is only a function of parameters;

$$\hat{H}_{ij} = \gamma_{ij} - \alpha_i \delta_{ij} + \alpha_i \alpha_j \quad (6.24)$$

$\hat{H}_{ij}$ denotes the ij^{th} element of $\hat{H}$ matrix, and $\delta_{ij} = 1$ if $i = j$ and 0 otherwise. To ensure that $\hat{H}$ is negative semidefinite, $\hat{H} = -DD'$. Let the D be a lower triangular matrix with elements d_{ij} rather than $\hat{H}_{ij}$ (Kohli, 1991). Let $(DD')_{ij}$ denote the ij^{th} element of DD' and substituting $(DD')_{ij}$ into equation (6.24) and rearranging will give;

$$\gamma_{ij} = -(DD')_{ij} + \alpha_i \delta_{ij} - \alpha_i \alpha_j \quad (6.25)$$

When γ_{ij}'s are replaced in the system of cost equations and cost-share equations, this amounts to parametric restrictions on the concavity of the trans-log cost function (details are given in the Appendix 2). Alternatively, instead of the Hessian matrix, the Allen partial matrix can be used to check whether concavity restrictions hold (Diewert & Wales, 1987; Mulik, et al., 2003). The Allen partial matrix can be defined as follows:

$$\Psi_{ij} = \frac{(\gamma_{ij} + S_i \cdot S_j)}{S_i S_j} \quad where \quad i \neq j \quad (6.26)$$

$$\Psi_{ii} = \frac{(\gamma_{ii} + S_i^2 - S_i)}{S_i^2} \quad where \quad i = j \quad (6.27)$$

If the Allen partial matrix is concave, then the Hessian matrix is also concave (Mulik, et al., 2003). The Allen partials are checked for each observation with predicted cost shares.

6.4.5 Estimation Techniques

It is feasible to estimate the parameters of each cost function using OLS. This technique is employed by several researchers because of simplicity (Christensen & Greene, 1976). However, it neglects the additional information contained in the cost-share equations, which are also easily computable. An alternative estimation procedure is to estimate cost shares as a multivariate regression system. This procedure is satisfactory with constant returns to scale ($\beta_{iQ} = 0,\ \beta_{QQ} = 0, \beta_Q = 1$). This approach is not satisfactory, when constant returns are not imposed, since the crucial parameters in the economies of scale and marginal cost estimates ($\beta_{QQ} = 0, \beta_Q = 1$) appear only in the cost function.

A direct estimation of the trans-log cost function is possible, however, this would neglect information contained in the cost-share equations. Therefore, it is preferable to employ a full-information method, by estimating the system of equations consisting of the cost equation and all except one share equation. Christensen and Greene (1976) conclude the optimal procedure is to jointly estimate the cost function and share equations as a multivariate regression system. Inclusion of cost-share equations in the estimation procedure includes many additional degrees of freedom without adding any unrestricted regression coefficients. This will result in more efficient parameter estimates than would be obtained applying OLS to the cost function alone (Christensen & Greene, 1976).

$$\begin{aligned} \ln C_{ht} &= \ln C(Q_{ht}, w_{ht}) + u_{C,ht} \\ S_{i,ht} &= S_i(Q_{ht}, w_{ht}) + u_{S_i,ht} \end{aligned} \tag{6.28}$$

$h = 1.........H$ denotes the NWSDB district, $t = 1........T$ is the time period and $u_{C,ht}$ is the residual associated with the trans-log cost equation and $u_{S_i,ht}$ is the residual entering cost-share equation i.

In panel data analysis, the error term for observation ht is decomposed as follows:

$$u_{m,ht} = \mu_{mh} + \varepsilon_{m,ht} \qquad (m = C, S_i) \tag{6.29}$$

In equation (6.29), μ_{mh} is the individual, NWSDB district specific effect and $\varepsilon_{m,ht}$ is an independent and identically distributed error term for equation m.

In the systems of M equations, m^{th} equation can be written in the following form:

$$Y_m = X_m \beta_m + u_m \tag{6.30}$$

Y_m the dependent variable, X_m is the $HT \times K_m$ matrix of explanatory variables, β_m is the $1 \times K_m$ vector of parameters to be estimated and u_m is the vector of residuals.

The cost function and the cost-share equations are estimated jointly in this chapter by iterated Zellner's seemingly unrelated regression method to obtain maximum likelihood estimates. The statistical software SHAZAM version 9 is used in conducting the empirical analysis. One cost share has to be dropped to avoid the problem of singularity of the disturbance covariance matrix when estimating the systems of equations. An assumption underlying this method of estimation is that the random error terms of the different equations are inter-related, but are independent of the exogenous variables entering the right hand side of the equations (Christensen & Greene, 1976). While estimating the parameters of the cost function and cost-share equations, appropriate restrictions on parameter estimates have been imposed both within and across equations. It has been shown that iteration of Zellner estimation procedure until convergence results in maximum-likelihood estimates. Iterating the Zellner procedure is a computationally efficient method for obtaining maximum-likelihood estimates (Christensen & Greene, 1976).

The maximum-likelihood estimates can be used to test the hypotheses such as homotheticity and homogeneity by using the likelihood ratio test (Christensen & Greene, 1976). Denoting the determinants of the unrestricted and restricted estimates of the disturbance covariance matrix by $\left|\hat{\Omega}_U\right|$ and $\left|\hat{\Omega}_R\right|$ respectively. The likelihood ratio can be written as

$$\lambda = \left(\left|\hat{\Omega}_U\right| / \left|\hat{\Omega}_R\right|\right)^{-N/2} \tag{6.31}$$

In equation (6.31), N is the number of observations. The hypothesis can be tested using the fact that $-2\ln\lambda$ is distributed asymptotically as Chi-squared with degrees of freedom equal to number of independent restrictions being imposed.

6.5 Results and Discussion

Common trends in costs, output and input data often lead to spurious correlation due to non-stationarity in data. In this chapter, a unit root test is performed to check for data stationarity.[8] As mentioned above, this data set consists of 14 cross sections and 60 time periods for each variable of

[8] The reasons for the performance of unit root tests are explained in detail in chapter 4.

interest. While a number of econometricians would argue that unit root tests may lack power in such small sample sizes, it is worth applying standard unit root test to check for non-stationarity. After transforming the data by taking natural logarithms, both common unit root and individual unit root processes were performed (results are given in the Appendix 1 Table 12).

This section presents the results of the short-run and long-run cost function estimation of the eight models (A to H). Capital, Labour, Electricity, Chemical and Maintenance are denoted by K, L, E, C and M subscripts respectively. The restriction of linear homogeneity of degree one in input prices and symmetry of Hessian matrix are imposed in all models to ensure the estimated cost functions represent well-behaved production structures. The majority of the parameters in the estimated cost functions are significant and have expected signs.[9]

The preliminary estimates of the short-run cost model, together with standard errors are reported in the Table 6.4. All the parameters are obtained by joint estimation of the cost function and input demand functions. For brevity, only selected parameters are included and a full set of parameter estimates are presented in Appendix 1 Table 13. Before proceeding with the calculation of marginal cost, scale economies and elasticities, it is important to ensure the estimated cost function satisfies regularity conditions of monotonicity and concavity for all observations. However, since the trans-log cost function does not satisfy the regularity conditions globally, it is necessary to check local properties at each data point. The monotonicity condition is satisfied since the fitted input shares are all non-negative at each data point. The curvature property of the trans-log function is data dependent, hence concavity is not guaranteed when the usual estimation procedure is used. In particular, no parametric restrictions can be imposed to ensure concavity of the estimated trans-log cost function without affecting its flexibility. The local concavity of the estimated trans-log cost function is checked by computing Eigenvalues of the Hessian matrix. The percentage of observations that satisfies concavity in the estimated cost function is 48.1 per cent.

[9] Breusch-Pagan test was conducted for all simultaneous equation estimations and the null hypothesis of the residuals from equations are independent was rejected.

Table 6.4: Trans-log Short-run Cost Function – Without Imposing Concavity

Variable	Para-meter	Trans-log Model A	Variable	Para-meter	Trans-log Model A
$\ln Q$	β_Q	0.9798 (0.1741) ***	$\ln W_c * \ln W_c$	γ_{CC}	0.0043 (0.0027)**
$\ln Q * \ln Q$	β_{QQ}	0.0123 (0.0158)	$\ln W_m * \ln W_m$	γ_{MM}	0.0917 (0.0015)***
$\ln W_l$	α_L	1.3367 (0.0563) ***	$\ln W_l * \ln W_e$	γ_{LE}	0.0537 (0.0070)***
$\ln W_e$	α_E	-0.0302 (0.0522)	$\ln W_l * \ln W_c$	γ_{LC}	0.0171 (0.0022)***
$\ln W_c$	α_C	-0.1809 (0.0203) ***	$\ln W_l * \ln W_m$	γ_{LM}	-0.0469 (0.0021)***
$\ln W_m$	α_M	0.1459 (0.0293) ***	$\ln W_e * \ln W_m$	γ_{EM}	-0.0374 (0.0030)***
$\ln W_l * \ln Q$	β_{LQ}	-0.0569 (0.0029) ***	$\ln W_c * \ln W_m$	γ_{CM}	-0.0074 (0.0012)**
$\ln W_e * \ln Q$	β_{EQ}	0.0153 (0.0028) ***	$\ln W_e * \ln W_c$	γ_{EC}	-0.0140 (0.0033)***
$\ln W_c * \ln Q$	β_{CQ}	0.0073 (0.0012) ***	Constant	α_0	-2.9142 (0.9736)***
$\ln W_m * \ln Q$	β_{MQ}	0.0343 (0.0015) ***	Berndt $\bar{R}^2$	$\bar{R}^2$	0.9958
$\ln W_l * \ln W_l$	γ_{LL}	-0.0238 (0.0072) ***			
$\ln W_e * \ln W_e$	γ_{EE}	-0.0022 (0.0071) ***			
$\ln W_c * \ln W_c$	γ_{CC}	0.0043 (0.0027) **			

Notes: *** Significant at α = 0.01, ** Significant at α = 0.05 and * Significant at α = 0.10 standard error values in parentheses below estimates, Dependant variable is natural log of monthly operation and maintenance cost of water

The failure of empirically estimated flexible functional forms to satisfy curvature conditions implies the estimated cost function is not consistent with underlying economic theory. Therefore, curvature conditions are imposed (as described in the section 6.4) and re-estimated the cost function and input share equations by checking for monotonicity and concavity at each data point. The resulting parameter estimates from the reparameterised model, together with the associated standard errors and Berndt adjusted generalized $\bar{R}^2$ are reported in the Table 6.5. In the re-estimated cost function, 97 per cent of observations satisfy concavity. Table 6.5 and Table 6.6 present the complete set of parameter estimates for short-run, the former with non-unitary elasticities of substitution (models A to D) and the latter with unitary elasticities of substitution imposed (models E to H).

The estimates point to statistically significant non-homotheticity involving labour (β_{LQ}), electricity (β_{EQ}) chemical (β_{CQ}) and maintenance (β_{MQ}). Moreover, all substitution parameters except γ_{EC} are statistically significant. This suggests neither the homotheticity nor the unitary elasticities of substitution hypotheses are consistent with the data.

Table 6.5: Short-run Cost Function Estimation for All Models with Non-unitary Elasticities of Substitution – Imposing Concavity

Parameter	Trans-log Model A	Homotheticity Model B	Homogeneity Model C	CRS Model D
β_Q	0.9105 (0.1811)***	1.4449 (0.1791)***	0.8251 (0.0253)***	1.0000
β_{QQ}	0.0065 (0.0162)	-0.0540 (0.0156)**		
α_L	0.7936 (0.0137)***	0.4626 (0.0125)***	0.4660 (0.0133)***	0.4333 (0.0124)***
α_E	0.0335 (0.0108)**	0.0681 (0.0117)***	0.0679 (0.0112)***	0.0650 (0.0097)***
α_C	0.0014 (0.0028)	-0.0050 (0.0023)**	-0.0045 (0.0022)**	-0.0051 (0.0023)**
α_M	0.1714 (0.0174)***	0.4743 (0.0176)***	0.4706 (0.0181)***	0.5067 (0.0157)***
β_{LQ}	-0.0366 (0.0028)***			
β_{EQ}	0.0068 (0.0028)***			

Parameter	Trans-log Model A	Homotheticity Model B	Homogeneity Model C	CRS Model D
β_{CQ}	-0.0020 (0.0008)***			
β_{MQ}	0.0318 (0.0014)***			
γ_{LL}	0.0119 (0.0052)**	-0.0089 (0.0016)***	-0.0089 (0.0017)***	-0.5892 (0.0016)***
γ_{EE}	0.0045 (0.0050)	0.0019 (0.0040)	0.0018 (0.0041)	-0.0002 (0.0039)
γ_{CC}	-0.0046 (0.0024)*	-0.0065 (0.0027)**	-0.0059 (0.0026)**	-0.0066 (0.0027)**
γ_{MM}	0.0870 (0.0013)***	0.0758 (0.0020)***	0.0753 (0.0019)***	0.0776 (0.0019)***
γ_{LE}	0.0228 (0.0048)***	0.0291 (0.0018)***	0.0293 (0.0018)***	0.0298 (0.0016)***
γ_{LC}	0.0111 (0.0017)***	0.0087 (0.0008)***	0.0085 (0.0008)***	0.0088 (0.0008)***
γ_{LM}	-0.0459 (0.0023)***	-0.0289 (0.0024)***	-0.0288 (0.0025)***	-0.0327 (0.0022)***
γ_{EM}	-0.0309 (0.0028)***	-0.0378 (0.0028)***	-0.0374 (0.0029)***	-0.0361 (0.0028)***
γ_{CM}	-0.0102 (0.0013)***	-0.0090 (0.0011)***	-0.0090 (0.0011)***	-0.0088 (0.0011)***
γ_{EC}	0.0036 (0.0024)	0.0069 (0.0020)***	0.0064 (0.0021)***	0.0065 (0.0019)***
α_0	-0.8053 (1.0116)	-3.0877 (1.0137)***	0.3199 (0.3257)	-1.8841 (0.0622)***
$\bar{R}^2$	0.9950	0.9931	0.9930	0.9925

Notes: *** Significant at α = 0.01, ** Significant at α = 0.05 and * Significant at α = 0.10 standard error values in parentheses below estimates, Dependant variable is natural log of monthly operation and maintenance cost of water

Table 6.6: Short-run Cost Function Estimation for All Models with Unitary Elasticities of Substitution – Imposing Concavity

Variable	Parameter	Trans-log Model E	Homotheticity Model F	Homogeneity Model G	CRS Model H
$\ln Q$	β_Q	-2.5629 (0.2747)***	-2.9939 (0.2687)***	0.1917 (0.0312)***	1.0000
$\ln Q * \ln Q$	β_{QQ}	0.2715 (0.0239)***	0.2793 (0.0234)***		
$\ln W_l$	α_L	1.0164 (0.0414)***	0.4868 (0.0042)***	0.4867 (0.0042)***	0.4861 (0.0043)***
$\ln W_e$	α_E	-0.2918 (0.0381)***	0.2452 (0.0041)***	0.2446 (0.0038)***	0.2441 (0.0038)***
$\ln W_c$	α_C	-0.1256 (0.0126)***	0.0408 (0.0012)***	0.0408 (0.0012)***	0.0407 (0.0013)***
$\ln W_m$	α_M	0.4010 (0.0396)***	0.2271 (0.0033)***	0.2278 (0.0033)***	0.2290 (0.0033)***
$\ln W_l * \ln Q$	β_{LQ}	-0.0395 (0.0031)***			
$\ln W_e * \ln Q$	β_{EQ}	0.0401 (0.0028)***			
$\ln W_c * \ln Q$	β_{CQ}	0.0124 (0.0009)***			
$\ln W_m * \ln Q$	β_{MQ}	-0.0130 (0.0029)***			
constant	α_0	20.601 (1.5678)***	25.6630 (1.5208)***	8.1634 (0.4177)***	-2.6775 (0.0468)***
Berndt $\bar{R}^2$	$\bar{R}^2$	0.9731	0.9626	0.9558	0.9188

Notes: *** Significant at α = 0.01, ** Significant at α = 0.05 and * Significant at α = 0.10 standard error values in parentheses below estimates, Dependant variable is natural log of monthly operation and maintenance cost of water

As explained, the validity of the restrictions imposed on Models B to H needs to be tested; Table 6.7 shows the likelihood ratio statistics. All the hypotheses on parameter restrictions can be rejected at the 5 per cent significance level. Therefore, Model A, which allows non-homotheticity and non-unitary elasticities of substitution, is the one that better represents the production structure of the Sri Lankan pipe-borne water sector and is used in further discussions.

Table 6.7: Test Statistics for Restrictions on Model A – Short-run

	Hypothesis (restriction on Model A)		
	No. of restrictions	Critical X^2 (5%)	Calculated X^2
Homotheticity Model B	2	5.99	262.92
Homogeneity Model C	3	7.82	275.21
CRS Model D	4	9.49	329.62
Unitary elasticities of substitution Model E	5	11.07	1409.50
Homotheticity and Unitary elasticities of substitution Model F	5	11.07	1686.35
Homogeneity and Unitary elasticities of substitution Model G	6	12.59	1827.27
CRS and Unitary elasticities of substitution Model H	6	12.59	2337.79

Notes: *** Significant at $\alpha = 0.01$, ** Significant at $\alpha = 0.05$ and * Significant at $\alpha = 0.10$ standard error values in parentheses below estimates

It is important to estimate input substitution possibilities in pipe-borne water generation. The elasticities of substitution and own and cross-price elasticities implicit in the cost function estimates are given in Table 6.8 and Table 6.9 (as an average over time and across districts). Table 6.8 presents the Allen-Uzawa partial elasticities of substitution and Table 6.9 presents the own and cross-price elasticities of Model A (non-homothetic and with non-unitary elasticities of substitution).

Table 6.8: Allen Uzawa's Elasticities of Substitution – Model A for Short-run

Parameter	Elasticity of substitution
σ_{LE}	1.1858 (0.0395)***
σ_{LC}	1.5488 (0.0840)***
σ_{LM}	0.5709 (0.0215)***
σ_{EC}	1.3512 (0.2381)***
σ_{EM}	0.4311 (0.0525)***
σ_{CM}	-0.1336 (0.1437)

Notes: *** Significant at $\alpha = 0.01$, ** Significant at $\alpha = 0.05$ and * Significant at $\alpha = 0.10$ standard error values in parentheses below estimates

The Allen-Uzawa partial elasticities of substitution provide a measure of the ease or difficulty with which one input can substitute for another. This is measured as the percentage change in factor proportions due to a one per cent change in their relative prices. The Allen-Uzawa partial elasticities of substitutions are computed at the mean of actual cost shares. All partial elasticities, except σ_{CM}, imply the existence of substitution possibilities amongst other inputs and are statistically significant at 1 per cent. Elasticities of substitution between chemical and maintenance signify to be Allen compliments but with statistical insignificance. The trans-log functional form does not constrain the partial Allen-Uzawa elasticities of substitution to be unitary or constant but rather permit them to vary from period to period and across inputs.

The own and cross-price elasticities for input demands are presented in Table 6.9, where each element is the elasticity of demand for input in the row associated with a price change of the input in the column. All the own-price elasticities of factor demand along the main diagonal are consistent with microeconomic theory of demand and have a negative sign in the short-run. In general, the demand for chemicals is unitary elastic, whilst the other inputs are price inelastic.

Table 6.9: Own and Cross Price Elasticities of Input Demands – Model A for Short-run

	Elasticity of Demand			
	Labour	Electricity	Chemical	Maintenance
Labour	-0.4844 (0.0105)***	0.2962 (0.0098)***	0.0638 (0.0034)***	0.1243 (0.0047)***
Electricity	0.5825 (0.0194)***	-0.7321 (0.0201)***	0.0557 (0.00998)***	0.0938 (0.0114)***
Chemical	0.7608 (0.0413)***	0.3375 (0.0595)***	-1.0692 (0.0599)***	-0.0291 (0.0312)
Maintenance	0.2804 (0.0106)***	0.1077 (0.0131)***	-0.0055 (0.0059)	-0.3573 (0.0101)***

Notes: Each element is the elasticity of demand for input in the row associated with a price change of the input in the column; *** Significant at $\alpha = 0.01$, ** Significant at $\alpha = 0.05$ and * Significant at $\alpha = 0.10$ standard error values in parentheses below estimates

Cross-price elasticities (reported in off-diagonal cells), contain the same information as the elasticities of substitution, but cross-section elasticities are not symmetric since they depend on the input shares. It can be observed that all cross-price elasticities are less than one and the positive signs verify the aforementioned results regarding input substitutability. All the estimations of cross and own-price elasticities are statistically significant except cross-price elasticity between chemical and maintenance. All the estimated cross-price elasticities indicate the inputs are substitutes; however, chemical and maintenance are complements. The estimation of cross-price elasticities is important to understand the magnitude of the changes on quantity of a specific input with respect to a price change in a different input used in the production process.

The substitutability between electricity and maintenance can be interpreted as empirical evidence of a possible trade-off between electricity for production of water and maintenance to reduce losses of water. A one per cent increase in electricity (maintenance) price leads to a

0.09 (0.11) per cent increase in demand for maintenance (electricity). Labour is also a substitute for electricity and maintenance, probably for the same reasons. Maintenance includes different input categories such as material, rcpairs and some heavily labour dependent components. But the substitutability between labour and maintenance implies water utilities either use their own labour or sub-contracted labour for maintenance activities. A one per cent increase in wages (maintenance price) leads to a 0.12 (0.28) per cent increase in demand for maintenance (labour).

The estimated output cost elasticities are all positive and significant as expected. For Model A, a one per cent increase in the level of output increases total costs by 0.7 per cent. An estimate of economies of scale can be derived for each model except for models D and H (when the restriction of constant returns to scale was imposed) by evaluating the formulae (equations (6.8), (6.9), (6.10) and (6.11)) at the mean level of output and factor prices. The estimates of scale economies are statistically significant for all models. As known, the estimates of scale economies for the homogenous models (C and G) are constant regardless of the level of output with respect to Models A to C and E to H. Scale economies can change with the level of output. It is observed that the scale economies diminish as the model restrictions increase (from Model A to C) with non-unitary elasticities of substitution. The scale economies increase as the restrictions increase (model E-G) with the unitary elasticities of substitution. In addition, the estimates are somehow similar between Models A and B and the estimates for Model C are considerably less than the estimates for Model A.

The marginal cost estimates for each model specification are given in Table 6.10 and estimated with the mean output, total operation and maintenance cost and input prices. All the estimated marginal cost values are significant and some estimates are similar across Model A and Model B. Therefore, in the short-run, the marginal cost of pipe-borne water varies from SLRS 16 to SLRS 18 per cubic metre. The estimates of all models specifications are presented, however, the likelihood ratio test favours the estimates from the non-homothetic, non-homogenous and non-unitary model specification (general trans-log cost function – Model A). Additional operation and maintenance cost of producing an additional cubic metre of water, including the raw water price (a constant of SLRS 0.50), is approximately SLRS 16.50.

Table 6.10: Short-run Output-cost Elasticity, Marginal Cost and Scale Economies

	Output-cost elasticity	SRMC	Scale economies
A	0.6994 (0.0412)***	15.959 (0.9101)***	0.3006 (0.0412)***
B	0.7216 (0.0406)***	15.915 (0.9027)***	0.2783 (0.0409)***
C	0.8251 (0.0259)***	18.196 (0.5725)***	0.1749 (0.0259)***
E	0.7833 (0.0552)***	17.275 (1.2175)***	0.2166 (0.0552)***
F	0.7433 (0.0557)***	16.392 (1.2284)***	0.2567 (0.0557)***
G	0.1917 (0.0309)***	4.2278 (0.6828)***	0.8083 (0.0309)***

Notes: *** Significant at $\alpha = 0.01$, ** Significant at $\alpha = 0.05$ and * Significant at $\alpha = 0.10$ standard error values in parentheses below estimates

It is also useful to estimate the effect of changing input prices on marginal cost. Table 6.11 shows SRMC elasticities with respect to input prices, evaluated at the sample means. The rows in Table 6.11 show the marginal-cost elasticities of output resulting from a one per cent change in the variable input prices. The elasticities of marginal-cost of output with respect to input prices are positive as expected, thus the marginal cost of output tends to increase when the prices of inputs increase. A one per cent rise in wages increase SRMC by 0.65 per cent while one per cent increase in chemical prices leads to 0.06 per cent increase in marginal cost.

Table 6.11: Short-run Elasticity of Marginal-cost of Output with Respect to Input Prices – Model A

Input variable	Elasticity of Marginal-cost of Output
Wages	0.6500 (0.0388)***
Electricity	0.3669 (0.0216)***
Chemical	0.0561 (0.0035)***
Maintenance	0.3568 (0.0211)***

Notes: *** Significant at α = 0.01, ** Significant at α = 0.05 and * Significant at α = 0.10 standard error values in parentheses below estimates

The LRMC is derived from the total cost function which includes expenditure on capital in addition to the operation and maintenance costs. The long-run cost function is positively linearly homogenous and monotonically increasing in input prices. Linear homogeneity is imposed and the positive fitted cost shares proved the monotonicity. Concavity in input prices is indicated by the Hessian matrix being negative semidefinite. A similar estimation procedure is followed as short-run cost estimation. Table 6.12 presents the preliminary estimates (without imposing concavity) of the long-run cost model, together with standard errors.[10]

[10] Detailed preliminary estimates for long-run cost estimations are presented in Appendix 1 Table 14.

Table 6.12: Long-run Cost Function Estimation – Without Imposing Concavity

Variable	Parameter	Trans-log Model A	Variable	Parameter	Trans-log Model A
$\ln Q$	β_Q	1.4884 (0.1650)***	$\ln W_c * \ln W_c$	γ_{CC}	0.0133 (0.0022)***
$\ln Q * \ln Q$	β_{QQ}	-0.0264 (0.0145)**	$\ln W_m * \ln W_m$	γ_{MM}	0.1107 (0.0017)***
$\ln W_k$	α_K	0.2893 (0.0466)***	$\ln W_l * \ln W_k$	γ_{LK}	-0.0151 (0.0048)***
$\ln W_l$	α_L	0.8176 (0.0625)***	$\ln W_l * \ln W_e$	γ_{LE}	0.0072 (0.0049)**
$\ln W_e$	α_E	0.1182 (0.0441)***	$\ln W_l * \ln W_c$	γ_{LC}	-0.0008 (0.0020)
$\ln W_c$	α_C	-0.1264 (0.0185)***	$\ln W_l * \ln W_m$	γ_{LM}	-0.0387 (0.0020)***
$\ln W_m$	α_M	-0.0987 (0.0272)***	$\ln W_e * \ln W_k$	γ_{EK}	0.0508 (0.0066)***
$\ln W_k * \ln Q$	β_{KQ}	0.0210 (0.0019)***	$\ln W_e * \ln W_m$	γ_{EM}	-0.0073 (0.0031)**
$\ln W_l * \ln Q$	β_{LQ}	-0.0705 (0.0023)***	$\ln W_e * \ln W_c$	γ_{EC}	0.0061 (0.0035)**
$\ln W_e * \ln Q$	β_{EQ}	0.0170 (0.0022)***	$\ln W_c * \ln W_k$	γ_{CK}	-0.0168 (0.0029)***
$\ln W_c * \ln Q$	β_{CQ}	0.0059 (0.0009)***	$\ln W_c * \ln W_m$	γ_{CM}	-0.0018 (0.0011)
$\ln W_m * \ln Q$	β_{MQ}	0.0264 (0.0015)***	$\ln W_k * \ln W_m$	γ_{MK}	-0.0630 (0.0020)***
$\ln W_k * \ln W_k$	γ_{KK}	0.0441 (0.0066)***	Constant	α_0	-1.7678 (0.9716)**
$\ln W_l * \ln W_l$	γ_{LL}	0.0474 (0.0077)***	Berndt $\bar{R}^2$	$\bar{R}^2$	0.9988
$\ln W_e * \ln W_e$	γ_{EE}	-0.0568 (0.0088)***			

Notes: *** Significant at α = 0.01, ** Significant at α = 0.05 and * Significant at α = 0.10 standard error values in parentheses below estimates, Dependant variable is natural log of monthly total cost of water

Following similar techniques described in the short-run cost analysis, curvature conditions are imposed and re-estimated parameters are given in the Table 6.13 and Table 6.14. All the eight models are estimated and the linear homogeneity in input prices is imposed throughout. Most of the parameter estimates are statistically significant with expected signs.

Table 6.13: Long-run Cost Function Estimation for All Models with Non-unitary Elasticities of Substitution – Imposing Concavity

Variable	Parameter	Trans-log Model A	Homotheticity Model B	Homogeneity Model C	CRS Model D
$\ln Q$	β_Q	1.9528 (0.1789)***	2.1851 (0.1405)***	0.7753 (0.0203)***	1.0000
$\ln Q * \ln Q$	β_{QQ}	-0.0622 (0.0158)**	-0.1226 (0.0121)***		
$\ln W_k$	α_K	0.2552 (0.0352)***	0.3574 (0.0184)***	0.4013 (0.0277)***	0.4027 (0.0281)***
$\ln W_l$	α_L	0.3936 (0.0410)***	0.1392 (0.0039)***	0.1080 (0.0363)***	0.0656 (0.0245)**
$\ln W_e$	α_E	0.2198 (0.0293)***	0.3659 (0.0189)***	0.3571 (0.0248)***	0.3818 (0.0223)***
$\ln W_c$	α_C	0.0061 (0.0032)**	0.0038 (0.0018)*	0.0049 (0.0017)*	0.0046 (0.0017)*
$\ln W_m$	α_M	0.1253 (0.0037)***	0.1336 (0.0049)***	0.1285 (0.0048)***	0.1452 (0.0071)***
$\ln W_k * \ln Q$	β_{KQ}	0.0241 (0.0017)***			
$\ln W_l * \ln Q$	β_{LQ}	-0.0604 (0.0029)***			
$\ln W_e * \ln Q$	β_{EQ}	0.0238 (0.0021)***			
$\ln W_c * \ln Q$	β_{CQ}	0.0170 (0.0007)***			
$\ln W_m * \ln Q$	β_{MQ}	0.0108 (0.0011)***			
$\ln W_k * \ln W_k$	γ_{KK}	0.0255 (0.0058)***	0.0125 (0.0042)***	0.0221 (0.0048)***	0.0160 (0.0049)***
$\ln W_l * \ln W_l$	γ_{LL}	0.0781 (0.0048)***	0.0137 (0.0011)***	0.0182 (0.0039)***	0.0210 (0.0027)***
$\ln W_e * \ln W_e$	γ_{EE}	-0.0805 (0.0078)***	-0.0767 (0.0069)***	0.0686 (0.0076)***	-0.0725 (0.0082)***

Variable	Parameter	Trans-log Model A	Homotheticity Model B	Homogeneity Model C	CRS Model D
$\ln W_c * \ln W_c$	γ_{CC}	0.0013 (0.0017)	0.0019 (0.0017)	0.0037 (0.0017)**	0.0033 (0.0017)**
$\ln W_m * \ln W_m$	γ_{MM}	0.1279 (0.0040)***	0.1513 (0.0021)***	0.1458 (0.0024)***	0.1567 (0.0024)***
$\ln W_l * \ln W_k$	γ_{LK}	-0.00286 (0.0035)***	-0.0057 (0.0019)***	-0.0065 (0.0029)**	-0.0095 (0.0026)**
$\ln W_l * \ln W_e$	γ_{LE}	-0.0073 (0.0033)**	0.0137 (0.0025)***	0.0114 (0.0032)***	0.0114 (0.0028)***
$\ln W_l * \ln W_c$	γ_{LC}	-0.0029 (0.0017)*	0.0014 (0.0013)	0.0003 (0.0013)	0.0012 (0.0014)
$\ln W_l * \ln W_m$	γ_{LM}	-0.0393 (0.0018)***	-0.0231 (0.0008)***	-0.0235 (0.0009)***	-0.0242 (0.0011)***
$\ln W_e * \ln W_k$	γ_{EK}	0.0707 (0.0063)***	0.0648 (0.0047)***	0.0575 (0.0052)***	0.0638 (0.0055)***
$\ln W_e * \ln W_m$	γ_{EM}	0.0056 (0.0024)**	-0.0068 (0.0024)***	-0.0051 (0.0024)**	-0.0061 (0.0027)**
$\ln W_e * \ln W_c$	γ_{EC}	0.0115 (0.0027)***	0.0050 (0.0025)**	0.0048 (0.0027)*	0.0033 (0.0028)
$\ln W_c * \ln W_k$	γ_{CK}	-0.0050 (0.0020)**	-0.0035 (0.0019)*	-0.0049 (0.0018)***	-0.0033 (0.0020)**
$\ln W_c * \ln W_m$	γ_{CM}	-0.0049 (0.0009)***	-0.0049 (0.0007)***	-0.0039 (0.0008)***	-0.0046 (0.0008)***
$\ln W_k * \ln W_m$	γ_{MK}	-0.0566 (0.0017)***	-0.0631 (0.0014)***	-0.0645 (0.0014)***	-0.0623 (0.0016)***
Constant	α_0	-3.8466 (0.1033)***	-3.8070 (0.8105)***	4.1814 (0.3104)***	1.3766 (0.1535)***
Berndt $\bar{R}^2$	$\bar{R}^2$	0.9987	0.9982	0.9980	0.9977

Notes: *** Significant at α = 0.01, ** Significant at α = 0.05 and * Significant at α = 0.10 standard error values in parentheses below estimates, Dependant variable is natural log of monthly total cost of water

Table 6.14: Long-run Cost Function Estimation for All Models with Unitary Elasticities of Substitution – Imposing Concavity

Variable	Parameter	Trans-log Model E	Homotheticity Model F	Homogeneity Model G	CRS Model H
$\ln Q$	β_Q	1.8152 (0.2032)***	1.4154 (0.2147)***	0.4076 (0.0324)***	1.0000
$\ln Q * \ln Q$	β_{QQ}	-0.0783 (0.0180)***	-0.0889 (0.0191)***		
$\ln W_k$	α_K	-0.3828 (0.0312)***	0.3021 (0.0058)***	0.3003 (0.0059)***	0.3121 (0.0059)***
$\ln W_l$	α_L	1.0229 (0.0343)***	0.3166 (0.0062)***	0.3177 (0.0062)***	0.3085 (0.0065)***
$\ln W_e$	α_E	-0.0384 (0.0274)***	0.2088 (0.0044)***	0.2094 (0.0046)***	0.2063 (0.0040)***
$\ln W_c$	α_C	-0.0564 (0.0095)***	0.0368 (0.0014)***	0.0368 (0.0015)***	0.0367 (0.0014)***
$\ln W_m$	α_M	0.4548 (0.0347)***	0.1356 (0.0048)***	0.1357 (0.0051)***	0.1362 (0.0054)***
$\ln W_k * \ln$	β_{KQ}	0.0506 (0.0022)***			
$\ln W_l * \ln$	β_{LQ}	-0.0522 (0.0024)***			
$\ln W_e * \ln$	β_{EQ}	0.0181 (0.0019)***			
$\ln W_c * \ln$	β_{CQ}	0.0068 (0.0006)***			
$\ln W_m * \ln$	β_{MQ}	-0.0234 (0.0025)***			
Constant	α_0	-3.8544 (1.1599)**	2.4964 (1.1955)**	7.9676 (0.43558)***	0.0953 (0.0619)**
Berndt $\bar{R}^2$	$\bar{R}^2$	0.9822	0.9645	0.9639	0.9482

Notes: *** Significant at α = 0.01, ** Significant at α = 0.05 and * Significant at α = 0.10 standard error values in parentheses below estimates, Dependant variable is natural log of monthly total cost of water

The significance of non-homotheticity parameters and substitution parameters for Model A suggest that neither homotheticity hypothesis nor unitary elasticity of substitution hypothesis is consistent with the data. This is confirmed by the likelihood ratio test statistics given in the Table 6.15. All of the restricted models are rejected at a reasonable level of significance. Thus, it is clear that a model which allows non-homotheticity and non-unitary elasticities of substitution (Model A) adequately represents the structure of production for pipe-borne water in Sri Lanka.

Table 6.15: Test Statistics for Restrictions on Model A for Long-run

	Hypothesis (restriction on Model A)		
	No. of restrictions	Critical X^2 (5%)	Calculated X^2
Homotheticity Model B	3	7.82	259.52
Homogeneity Model C	4	9.49	359.38
CRS Model D	4	9.49	479.59
Unitary elasticities of substitution Model E	3	7.82	2223.53
Homotheticity and Unitary elasticities of substitution Model F	1	3.84	2804.21
Homogeneity and Unitary elasticities of substitution Model G	2	5.99	2819.13
CRS and Unitary elasticities of substitution Model H	2	5.99	3121.67

Notes: *** Significant at $\alpha = 0.01$, ** Significant at $\alpha = 0.05$ and * Significant at $\alpha = 0.10$ standard error values in parentheses below estimates

The Allen-Uzawa partial elasticities of substitution values for Model A are given in the Table 6.16. Most Allen-Uzawa partial elasticities indicate the existence of substitution possibilities amongst the other inputs. The estimates indicate that (Allen partial) complementarity exists between chemical and maintenance and maintenance and capital, however, σ_{CM} estimate is statistically insignificant. The substitution possibility between chemical and capital is also statistically insignificant.

Table 6.16: Allen Uzawa's Elasticities of Substitution – Model A for Long-run

Parameter	Elasticity of substitution
σ_{LK}	0.7084 (0.0359)***
σ_{LE}	0.8841 (0.0533)***
σ_{LC}	0.7214 (0.1691)***
σ_{LM}	0.3241 (0.0312)***
σ_{EC}	3.2476 (0.5352)***
σ_{EM}	1.1950 (0.0852)***
σ_{EK}	2.4629 (0.1303)***
σ_{CM}	-0.0474 (0.2011)
σ_{CK}	0.3728 (0.2609)
σ_{MK}	-0.2722 (0.0377)***

Notes: *** Significant at $\alpha = 0.01$, ** Significant at $\alpha = 0.05$ and * Significant at $\alpha = 0.10$ standard error values in parentheses below estimates

The estimated own and cross-price elasticities for input demands in the long run are presented in the Table 6.17. All the own-price elasticities of factor demand have a negative sign indicating demand is downward sloping with respect to own-price. In general, the demands for all the inputs are price inelastic, however, demand for electricity is price elastic. A one per cent increase in price of electricity in the long-run leads to a 1.3 per cent decrease in the demand for electricity implying more energy efficient equipment is installed in the long-run. It is also observed that own-price elasticity values are greater in magnitude in the long-run than in the short-run indicating that water utilities respond more to input price changes in the long-run. All cross-price elasticities are less than one. Almost all the cross-price elasticities are positive indicating possible substitutability between the inputs. However, there is a complementarity relationship between chemical and maintenance and between capital and maintenance. A one per cent increase in price of capital (maintenance) leads to 0.04 (0.07) per cent decrease in demand for maintenance (capital). The complementarity between capital and maintenance can be interpreted as more capital is invested in the production of water; the more maintenance work is required.

Table 6.17: Own and Cross Price Elasticities of Input Demands – Model A for Long-run

	Elasticity of Demand				
	Capital	Labour	Electricity	Chemical	Maintenance
Capital	-0.6327 (0.0211)***	0.2536 (0.0128)***	0.4341 (0.0229)***	0.0108 (0.0075)	-0.0442 (0.0061)***
Labour	0.1944 (0.0098)***	-0.4238 (0.0134)***	0.1558 (0.0094)***	0.0209 (0.0049)***	0.0526 (0.0050)***
Electricity	0.6759 (0.0357)***	0.3165 (0.0191)***	-1.2807 (0.0444)***	0.0944 (0.0155)***	0.1939 (0.0138)***
Chemical	0.1023 (0.0716)	0.2583 (0.0605)***	0.5723 (0.0943)***	-0.9252 (0.0616)***	-0.0077 (0.0326)
Maintenance	-0.0747 (0.0103)***	0.1161 (0.0112)***	0.2106 (0.0150)***	-0.0014 (0.0058)	-0.0489 (0.0249)**

Notes: Each element is the elasticity of demand for input in the row after a price change of the input in the column; *** Significant at $\alpha = 0.01$, ** Significant at $\alpha = 0.05$ and * Significant at $\alpha = 0.10$ standard error values in parentheses below estimates

The estimated output-cost elasticities, scale economies and marginal cost values for Models A, B, C, E, F and G are given in the Table 6.18. Models A and B report similar scale economies values; estimate from Model E is the largest. The marginal-cost estimates for each model are estimated with the mean output, total cost and input prices. All the estimated marginal-cost values are significant and Model E shows the smallest estimate while Models C and A give the largest estimate. Therefore, the LRMC of pipe-borne water vary from SLRS 47 to SLRS 62 per cubic metre. However, the likelihood ratio test favours estimates from the general trans-log cost function. This implies, the additional total cost the water utility needs to incur to produce an additional cubic metre of water in the long run, including the raw water price (a constant of SLRS 0.50), is approximately SLRS 47.25.

Table 6.18: Long-run Output-cost Elasticity, Marginal Cost and Scale Economies

	Output-cost elasticity	LRMC	Scale economies
A	0.5468 (0.0385)***	46.735 (3.2458)***	0.4532 (0.0385)***
B	0.5441 (0.0302)***	45.767 (2.5371)***	0.4559 (0.0302)***
C	0.7753 (0.0203)***	65.215 (1.7046)***	0.2247 (0.0203)***
E	0.1632 (0.0519)***	13.728 (4.3683)***	0.8368 (0.0519)***
F	0.2255 (0.0537)***	18.972 (4.5196)***	0.7744 (0.0537)***
G	0.4076 (0.0324)***	34.284 (2.7286)***	0.5924 (0.0324)***

Notes: *** Significant at $\alpha = 0.01$, ** Significant at $\alpha = 0.05$ and * Significant at $\alpha = 0.10$ standard error values in parentheses below estimates

It is important to know the long-run elasticity of marginal-cost of output with respect to input prices. Estimates reported in Table 6.19 shows changes in the capital price and wages have the largest effect on the LRMC. A one per cent increase in the price of capital and wages leads LRMC to increase by 0.55 and 0.54 per cent respectively.

Table 6.19: Long-run Elasticity of Marginal-cost of Output with Respect to Input Prices – Model A for Long-run

Input variable	Elasticity of Marginal-cost of Output
Capital	0.5459 (0.0387)***
Wages	0.5442 (0.0386)***
Electricity	0.3658 (0.0259)***
Chemical	0.0562 (0.0043)***
Maintenance	0.3164 (0.0225)***

Notes: *** Significant at $\alpha = 0.01$, ** Significant at $\alpha = 0.05$ and * Significant at $\alpha = 0.10$ standard error values in parentheses below estimates

The main results from the above analyses are that the estimated SRMC and LRMC is SLRS 16 and SLRS 47 per cubic metre respectively (including a proxy for the raw water price). In order to provide a proper context for the interpretation of these estimates, it is important to investigate other studies that employ the cost function approach in the water sector. Since this is the first study to estimate SRMC and LRMC of pipe-borne water in the Sri Lankan context, the results obtained in the context of other countries are examined. However, it is difficult to compare and contrast the empirical estimates of SRMC and LRMC values from other studies as most of the studies were concentrated on a developed country context. However, broadly speaking, the findings here confirm that LRMC is larger than SRMC and scale economies are prevalent with the Sri Lankan water utility. These results are similar to past findings for other countries with respect to scale economies (Garcia & Thomas, 2001; Renzetti, 1999).

6.6 Conclusion

The production decision of water utilities is modelled using a trans-log cost function for the NWSDB in Sri Lanka. Parameter estimates of the trans-log cost function and cost-share equations allow the estimation of marginal cost and economies of scale for pipe-borne water in both short and long run. The average marginal cost in the short run is SLRS 16.50 and in the long run it rises to SLRS 47.25 per cubic metre. The LRMC estimates differ from short-run cost estimates by a substantial margin. This demonstrates the significance of capital costs to the utility, because the SRMC estimate represents only expenditures on variable inputs, while the LRMC also includes expenditure on capacity expansion (Renzetti, 1992b). Marginal costs reported by the cost data of the NWSDB do not fully account for marginal social or user costs, therefore, the marginal social cost of water is likely to be greater than the estimated marginal costs in this chapter. Further, all estimates of marginal cost are substantially higher than average volumetric charges supporting the generally accepted belief that water is under-priced. The results for both the short and long runs indicate there are scale economies in the technology of water supply. This finding corresponds to similar results by other researchers (Garcia & Thomas, 2001; Kim, 1987; Renzetti, 1992b, 1999).

The analyses presented in this chapter are significant because it is the first attempt to estimate SRMC and LRMC for Sri Lanka. Results of this analysis are of great practical importance to the regulators, policy makers and the NWSDB managers in the design of rate structures for water. There is no doubt that the findings of this chapter help to overcome the lack of marginal-cost analyses from developing countries perspective. The findings of this chapter will be used in chapter 7 for evaluation of different pricing policies for pipe-borne water in Sri Lanka.

A limitation in this kind of empirical work of cost estimations is the difficulty in measuring capital stock. Most water infrastructure assets in Sri Lanka were installed many decades ago. Accounting book values may differ from replacement value. The outstanding debt on assets might be used as a capital stock measure but this also may not reflect the replacement value. Additional and better quality data on capital costs and raw water will improve the estimates and the understanding of the underlying costs.

CHAPTER SEVEN

PRICE REFORMS AND WELFARE EFFECTS

7.1 Introduction

One of the most important tasks of regulatory authorities is to determine an appropriate pricing scheme for the services provided by the water utility. Water utilities are often criticized for inefficient pricing practices (Renzetti, 1992b, 1999). Yet, there is limited evidence regarding the extent and effect of divergences between prices and marginal cost of supply. It is important to analyse the economic gains or losses under different tariff structures such as marginal-cost pricing, average-cost pricing, two-part tariff and two-block tariffs.

The purpose of this chapter is to evaluate the potential for welfare gains obtained as a result of the NWSDB moving from the current pricing practices towards more efficient prices. This chapter brings together the NWSDB's costs of supply estimated in chapter 6 and the structure of residential, industrial and commercial water demands estimated in chapters 4 and 5. These estimated cost and demand coefficients are employed in a simulation program to compute the change in welfare achieved by replacing the NWDSB's current price structure with alternative prices. Moreover, estimated cost and demand equations are combined with the NWSDB prices to determine the extent to which current consumption levels deviate from those predicted under alternative pricing. The alternative pricing arrangements considered here include SRMC and LRMC pricing, average-cost pricing and two-block pricing. This chapter therefore, provides an addition to the very few studies estimating welfare changes of reforming water prices in developing countries and is the first study for Sri Lanka.

An extensive literature exists on welfare measurements. The Marshallian Consumer Surplus (CS) is the measure of choice in most studies, since it is measurable using data typically available (S. Brown & Sibley, 1986). Compensating Variation (CV) and Equivalent Variation (EV) are being increasingly used for welfare estimations. Deadweight loss, defined as the excess of benefits that society as a whole loses by failure to adopt a policy in question, is also a tool used in welfare analysis.

The analyses of welfare due to water price changes are reviewed in the section 7.2. Section 7.3 discusses a variety of welfare measures that are commonly used and section 7.4 explains the alternative pricing arrangements used for the welfare analysis in this chapter. In section 7.5, methods to measure welfare changes employed in this chapter are presented. Section 7.6 contains the estimation results for different welfare measures outlined above. Section 7.7 offers some concluding remarks.

7.2 Literature Review

Economic literature has been consistent in its criticism of water utilities' pricing practices, however, few studies have estimated the magnitude of the welfare gains expected from moving to efficient water pricing (Garcia-Valinas, 2005; Garcia & Reynaud, 2004; Renzetti, 1992b, 1999; Whittington, 2003). CS is used as the measurement tool for welfare analyses by Renzetti (1992b), Basani et al., (1999) and Garcia-Valinas (2005), assuming a zero profit constraint and negligible effects on producer surplus. They calculated welfare benefits and welfare losses derived by a change from actual to proposed tariffs. Renzetti (1999) and Hajispyrou et al., (2002) used deadweight loss calculations arising from under-pricing and over-consumption of pipe-borne water. Barkatullah (1999), Rietveld et al., (2000) and Ruijs (2007) used CV and EV to measure the welfare impacts of water pricing reform.

Swallow and Marin (1988) showed that moving towards efficient prices results in an increase in welfare (approximately 2 per cent of the actual surplus) by simulating the welfare gains using a hypothetical case study. They conducted a partial equilibrium analysis of water supply by defining a constant price for water as a weighted average of the annual marginal short-run and capacity expansion costs. Renzetti (1992b) found a move to seasonally differentiated pricing raises the aggregate surplus by approximately 4 per cent in Vancouver water district. This study included a micro simulation exercise comparing proposed tariffs with those in the respective survey years. A simulation program approximated the change in aggregate welfare by measuring the change in each user group's Marshallian CS. The Vancouver water works is assumed to be constrained by a zero-profit condition, the analysis of changes in the producer surplus was ignored. Renzetti (1992b) failed to account for the benefits arising from installation of flow meters that aid in leak detection and reduction of water loss between the supply centre and final users. This exercise consisted of a partial welfare analysis in which only welfare variations regarding water distribution service was considered without taking into account welfare consequences for other goods and services.

Renzetti (1999) also calculated the welfare loss brought about by consumption at current prices compared to consumption at marginal-cost pricing for a cross section of municipal water and waste water utilities in Ontario, Canada. Deadweight loss per unit of output of water was calculated as US$ 0.25 per cubic metre for residential consumers and US$ 0.31 per cubic metre for non-residential users. He estimated the deviation, that is, the difference between predicted and efficient consumption levels, for residential water users to be 47.5 per cent and 62.8 per cent for non-residential water users. His estimations combined the estimated costs and demand equations with the water utilities' prices to determine the extent to which the prevalent consumption quantities deviate from efficient consumption levels under marginal-cost pricing and measured the approximate welfare changes associated with these deviations.

Basani et al., (1999) found the welfare impacts of obtaining a connection to the pipe-borne water network to be approximately 17 per cent of the actual expenditure of the poor unconnected households in Cambodia. Furthermore, it was demonstrated that providing a network connection to all households in the sample would decrease the estimated Gini coefficient by 3 percentage points and poverty head-count ratio by 6 percentage points. Reitveld et al., (2000) estimated the social welfare consequences of a shift to uniform pricing from block rate pricing in Salatiga, Indonesia. They confirmed the principal beneficiaries are large households who are not necessarily wealthy. The replacement of the complex rate structure by a uniform marginal price had positive effects on average welfare and the equity consequences were small. Their analysis revealed there is no systematic pattern in which high-income households benefit from the introduction of uniform prices. The shares of households that benefit from uniform prices are in the lowest and the highest income quartiles.

Barkatullah (1999) conducted a welfare simulation for New South Wales water utilities in Australia. Her thesis evaluated the welfare effects of current and alternative pricing strategies for water. The simulation model was developed to analyse pricing reforms using results from both cost and demand models. The study analysed individual and aggregate efficiency gains under each pricing policy and found a movement from the multi-part tariff structure to a two-part tariff policy with SRMC pricing, lead to the highest efficiency gains.

Hajispyrou et al., (2002) evaluated welfare effects associated with changes in the water pricing system for Cyprus using individual household data. They found that the current regionally heterogeneous, increasing block pricing system introduced gross price distortions that are not justified either on efficiency or equity grounds. They concluded that a shift towards uniform marginal-cost pricing eliminates the deadweight loss of the current system. However, benefits are distributed in favour of the better-off households while households in the bottom 10 per cent of the distribution of the income are net losers.

Using aggregate data, Garcia and Reynaud (2004) estimated surplus variation using Marshallian demand functions for France. They found a significant difference between the observed marginal prices and marginal costs and that the new pricing rule based on marginal costs lead to an 8.5 per cent increase of the marginal price. This study showed that the optimal pricing scheme is characterised by higher marginal prices and a lower fixed charge. However, they concluded that moving towards efficient prices did not result in important direct welfare effects. On average, welfare gain equalled to Euro 0.33 per user which corresponds to less than 0.4 per cent of the initial net welfare (Garcia & Reynaud, 2004). Further, their findings indicate that the pricing reforms save up to 0.4 per cent of actual water consumption. This study revealed the distributional effects of the fixed charge were much more important than the effects of moving towards efficient pricing. A decrease in the fixed charge favours the poorest consumers, but a high level of fixed charges set by the water utilities is an easy way to capture users' surplus.

Garcia-Valinas (2005) showed that proposed tariffs based on the seasonal demands resulted in welfare improvements for all user groups in Seville, Spain. She also found that Feldstein's formula achieves distributional objectives without substantially reducing social welfare. Two global social welfare indexes were formulated to calculate welfare variations per cubic metre. The first measure considers the consumption that would take place under applicable tariffs. The second measure takes into account consumption that would be generated under the proposed tariffs. Both expressions are calculated by dividing the welfare variations associated with the proposed tariffs and the registered consumption and weighted by the marginal utility of income.

Ruijs (2007) evaluated the distributional and welfare effects of changes in block pricing systems. This analysis discussed a method to apply EV in the case of a block price system using the Marshallian demand curve. The results shown there is a trade-off between average welfare and income distribution for the metropolitan region of Sao Paulo. The findings suggest a pro-poor price system may result in lower average welfare than a flat price system, but higher individual welfare for the poor. Moreover, he found that there is a trade-off between revenucs for the water company and income distribution.

Past literature has used different welfare measures in the pipe-borne water sector; CS is used by Renzetti (1992b) and Garcia-Valinas (2005), assuming negligible effects on producer surplus, deadweight loss is used by Renzetti (1999) and Hajispyrou et al., (2002) and CV and EV by Barkatullah (1999), Rietveld et al., (2000) and Ruijs (2007). The magnitude of the welfare gains from moving to efficient water pricing is estimated in this chapter using CS, EV and deadweight loss. The estimates of this chapter adds to very few studies estimating welfare changes of reforming water prices in developing countries and is the first study for Sri Lanka.

The analysis presented in this chapter depends on the estimates from previous chapters (4, 5 and 6) and assumes negligible effects on producer surplus. Estimated cost (chapter 6) and demand equations (chapter 4 and 5) are combined with the NWSDB prices to determine the extent to which current consumption levels deviate from those predicted under alternative pricing. In the section 7.3, theory behind different welfare measures (CS, CV, EV and deadweight loss) are discussed in relevance to increasing block tariffs.

7.3 Welfare Measures

There have been several debates about the appropriate measure of welfare changes amongst Marshallian CS, CV and EV. Marshallian CS is the most widely used welfare measure in applied welfare economics, because it can be directly measured from the estimated demand function (Ruijs, 2007). However, there is considerable controversy over employing the Marshallian CS in welfare analysis. The correct measures for determining the welfare effects of price changes are Hicks' CV or EV; however, these are also not perfect (Ng, 1983).

Marshallian CS measures the consumer's willingness to pay for a price change on the basis of the Marshallian demand function instead of the Hicksian demand function (Ruijs, 2007). However, it does not compensate for income effects of price changes, which are taken into account in the Hicksian demand. Willig (1976) argued in most cases the differences between CS and CV welfare measures are small and therefore, use of CS is an appropriate approximation of welfare changes. However, others showed these differences may be substantial. Hausman (1981) and Vartia

(1983) illustrated the indirect utility function or expenditure function can be derived using the Marshallian demand curve and, therefore, both CV and EV can be determined on the basis of the Marshallian demand function.

Marshallian CS is given as the area under the Marshallian demand curve and the Hicksian measures (CV and EV) are the area under the compensated demand function. Assuming a two goods case (water and a numeraire composite of all other goods), the vertical axis in Figure 7.1 part (a) shows the income spent on the composite good and the horizontal axis measures the quantity of water. Figure 7.1 part (b) presents the impact of a price change in terms of water price (vertical axis) and water consumed (horizontal axis). Suppose the consumer faces a decrease in the price of water from p_0 to p_1, the initial income of the consumer is OY_0, the initial utility level is U_0, and the indifference curve is tangent to the budget constraint (Y_0G) at point D. The budget constraint rotates outwards from Y_0G to Y_0E with a decrease in price of water.

The change in the CS is shown as the area under the Marshallian demand curve, p_0trp_1. The Hicksian CV measure is shown as the area p_0tsp_1. The triangle trs is the difference associated with the CS and Hicksian measure. Direction of this difference depends on the sign of the income effect because the CS measure includes the overall effect of price changes (income and substitution effect), whereas the Hicksian measure considers the substitution effect alone. In the case of zero income elasticity of demand, the difference vanishes, the triangle trs disappears and the Marshallian curve coincides with the Hicksian curve.

Figure 7.1: Deriving Marshallian and Hicksian Demand Curves

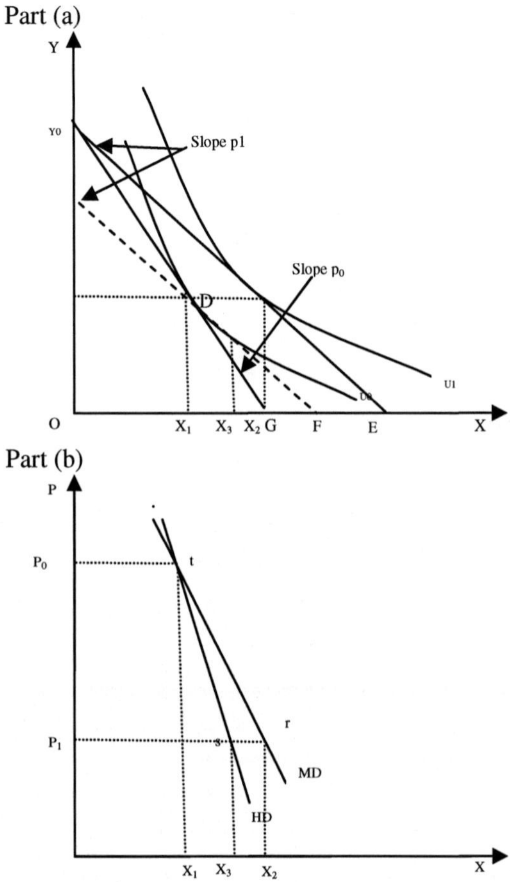

CV of a change in price is the amount of compensation that can be taken from an individual while leaving just as well off as before the change (Hausman, 1981; Ng, 1983). Alternatively, EV is the amount of compensation that has to be given to the individual in the absence of change, to make one as well off as one would be with the change (Mas-Colell, et al., 1995; Ng, 1983). CV is based on ex-ante utility and EV on ex-post utility (Ruijs, 2007). However, constant marginal utility of income is a sufficient condition for the Marshallian consumer's surplus to be equal to Hicks' consumer surplus (Hausman, 1981). Mas-Colell et al., (1995)

showed only EV can be used for ranking alternative policies with different price vectors. The reason is because equivalent measures are based on ex-post utility while the compensating measures are based on ex-ante utility. However, Ng (1983) showed CV possesses some properties EV does not and hence, neither EV or CV can be regarded as superior to the other. Both measures may be acceptable as approximate measures for changes whose effects are thinly spread (Ng, 1983).

Figure 7.2 and Figure 7.3, graphically represent the CV and EV. A two good situation is considered in which the second good (aggregate commodity), is a numeraire whose price is held constant. The price vector is defined as $p = (p,1)$. The price of the first commodity p and income y are normalized with respect to the price of the second commodity and both commodities are assumed to be separable. At price $p_0 = (p_0,1)$ and income level y_0, demand is equal to $x_0 = (x_0, x_0^{`})$ and utility u_0. If the price of the commodity 1 decreases to p_1, the budget line shifts outwards and becomes flatter.

Figure 7.2: Schematic Representation of Compensating Variation

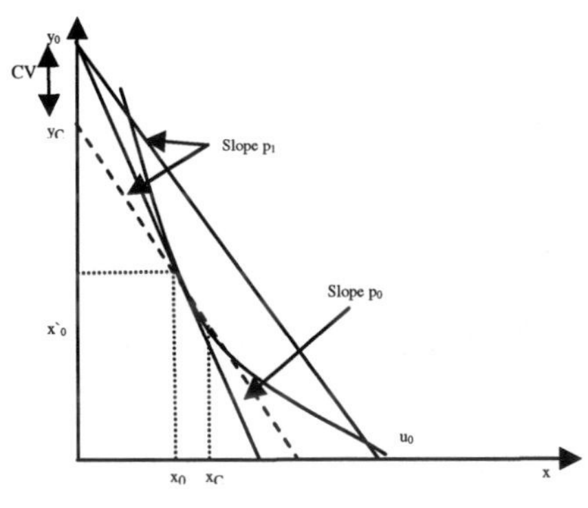

Compensating income, the income that the consumer would need to be as well off with as without the price change, is equal to y_C and the CV is measured by $y_0 - y_C$ in figure 7.2 (King, 1983). Equivalent income, the income the consumer would need to be as well off as with the price decrease, is equal to y_E in figure 7.3 (Ruijs, 2007). Therefore, the EV is measured by $y_E - y_0$ (King, 1983). In case of a price increase (decrease) EV and CV are equal to a welfare loss (gain).

Figure 7.3: Schematic Representation of Equivalent Variation

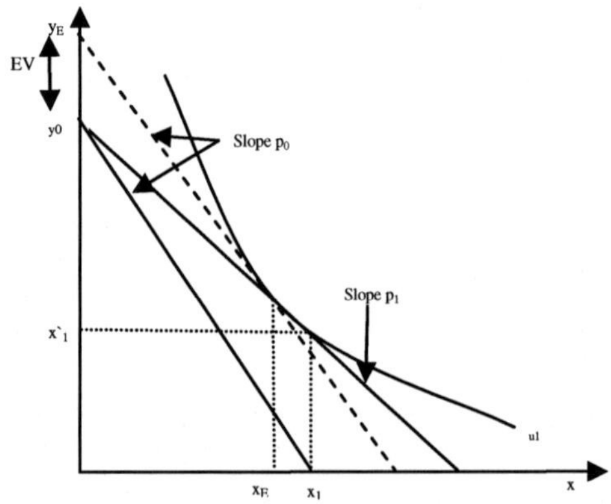

7.3.1 Equivalent Variation and Compensating Variation using Marshallian Demand Curve

The expenditure function of a given level of utility u_0 and price $p = (p,1)$ is defined as $e(p,u_0) = \min\{p \cdot x | u(x) \geq u_0\}$. EV and CV of a price change from p_0 to p_1 are

$$EV(p_0, p_1, y_0) = e(p_0, u_1) - e(p_1, u_1) = e(p_0, u_1) - y_1 \quad (7.1)$$
$$CV(p_0, p_1, y_0) = e(p_0, u_0) - e(p_1, u_0) = y_0 - e(p_1, u_0) \quad (7.2)$$

If $p_0 < p_1$, then $e(p_0,u_1) < e(p_1,u_1)$, therefore, a negative sign is expected for EV and CV. More money is needed to reach the same level of utility with p_1 than p_0, therefore, a change of p_0 to p_1 produces a negative welfare gain (welfare loss).

For most practical applications, it is likely the difference in the sum of CVs and sum of EVs is overwhelmed by inaccuracies in data collection. For each individual, the CV measure of a change equals the negative of the EV measure of the reverse change and vice versa (Ng, 1983).

For a log-linear Marshallian demand function, Hausman (1981) showed the expenditure function can be derived using Roy's Identity and the definition of the indirect utility function. The indirect utility function can be defined as:

$$V(p, y) = \max\{u(x) | p \cdot x \leq y\} \quad (7.3)$$

From Roy's identity

$$x(p, y) = -\frac{\partial V(p, y) / \partial p}{\partial V(p, y) / \partial y} \quad (7.4)$$

For a log-linear demand function

$$x(p, y) = e^{z\gamma} p^{\alpha} y^{\beta} \quad (7.5)$$

Hausman (1981) shows that the indirect utility function $V(p, y)$ has the following form:

$$V(p, y) = -e^{z\gamma} \frac{p^{1+\alpha}}{1+\alpha} + \frac{y^{1-\beta}}{1-\beta} \quad (7.6)$$

The corresponding expenditure function is:

$$e(p, u) = \left[(1-\beta)\left(u + e^{z\gamma} \frac{p^{1+\alpha}}{1+\alpha} \right) \right]^{1/1-\beta} \quad (7.7)$$

Equivalent income is defined as the level of income which, at the reference price vector affords the same level of utility as can be attained under the given budget constraint (King, 1983).

$$V(p_1, y_1) = V(p_0, y_0) \quad (7.8)$$

Therefore, equivalent income can be presented as:

$$y_1 = f(p_1, p_0, y_0) \quad (7.9)$$

For a log-linear demand function:

$$-e^{z\gamma}\frac{p_0^{1+\alpha}}{1+\alpha}+\frac{y_0^{1-\beta}}{1-\beta}=-e^{z\gamma}\frac{p_1^{1+\alpha}}{1+\alpha}+\frac{y_1^{1-\beta}}{1-\beta}$$

$$y_1=\left[\left(e^{z\gamma}\left(\frac{p_1^{1+\alpha}}{1+\alpha}-\frac{p_0^{1+\alpha}}{1+\alpha}\right)+\frac{y_0^{1-\beta}}{1-\beta}\right)(1-\beta)\right]^{1/1-\beta} \tag{7.10}$$

CV is given as:

$$CV(p_0,p_1,y_0)=e(p_0,u_0)-e(p_1,u_0)=y_0-e(p_1,u_0)$$

$$e(p_1,u_0)=\left[(1-\beta)\left(u_0+e^{z\gamma}\frac{p_1^{1+\alpha}}{1+\alpha}\right)\right]^{1/1-\beta}$$

$$u_0=-e^{z\gamma}\frac{p_0^{1+\alpha}}{1+\alpha}+\frac{y_0^{1-\beta}}{1-\beta}$$

$$e(p_1,u_0)=\left[(1-\beta)\left(-e^{z\gamma}\frac{p_0^{1+\alpha}}{1+\alpha}+\frac{y_0^{1-\beta}}{1-\beta}+e^{z\gamma}\frac{p_1^{1+\alpha}}{1+\alpha}\right)\right]^{1/1-\beta}$$

$$e(p_1,u_0)=\left[(1-\beta)\left(\frac{e^{z\gamma}}{1+\alpha}\left(p_1^{1+\alpha}-p_0^{1+\alpha}\right)\right)+y_0^{1-\beta}\right]^{1/1-\beta}$$

$$CV(p_0,p_1,y_0)=y_0-\left[(1-\beta)\left(\frac{e^{z\gamma}}{1+\alpha}\left(p_1^{1+\alpha}-p_0^{1+\alpha}\right)\right)+y_0^{1-\beta}\right]^{1/1-\beta} \tag{7.11}$$

EV is obtained as follows:

$$EV=e(p_0,u_1)-e(p_1,u_1)$$

$$e(p_0,u_1)=\left[(1-\beta)\left(u_1+e^{z\gamma}\frac{p_0^{1+\alpha}}{1+\alpha}\right)\right]^{1/1-\beta}$$

$$u_1=-e^{z\gamma}\frac{p_1^{1+\alpha}}{1+\alpha}+\frac{y_1^{1-\beta}}{1-\beta}$$

$$e(p_0,u_1)=\left[(1-\beta)\left(-e^{z\gamma}\frac{p_1^{1+\alpha}}{1+\alpha}+\frac{y_1^{1-\beta}}{1-\beta}+e^{z\gamma}\frac{p_0^{1+\alpha}}{1+\alpha}\right)\right]^{1/1-\beta}$$

$$EV = \left[\left((1-\beta)\frac{e^{z\gamma}}{1+\alpha}\left(p_0^{1+\alpha} - p_1^{1+\alpha}\right)\right) + y_1^{1-\beta}\right]^{1/1-\beta} - y_1$$

$$y_1 = \left[\left(e^{z\gamma}\left(\frac{p_1^{1+\alpha}}{1+\alpha} - \frac{p_0^{1+\alpha}}{1+\alpha}\right) + \frac{y_0^{1+\beta}}{1-\beta}\right)(1-\beta)\right]^{1/1-\beta}$$

$$e(p_0,u_1) = \left[\left((1-\beta)\frac{e^{z\gamma}}{1+\alpha}\left(p_0^{1+\alpha} - p_1^{1+\alpha}\right)\right) + \left((1-\beta)\frac{e^{z\gamma}}{1+\alpha}\left(p_1^{1+\alpha} - p_0^{1+\alpha}\right)\right) + y_0^{1-\beta}\right]^{1/1-\beta}$$

$$e(p_0,u_1) = \left[y_0^{1-\beta}\right]^{1/1-\beta}$$

$$EV = y_0 - \left[\left((1-\beta)\frac{e^{z\gamma}}{1+\alpha}\left(p_1^{1+\alpha} - p_0^{1+\alpha}\right)\right) + y_0^{1-\beta}\right]^{1/1-\beta} \quad (7.12)$$

7.3.2 Equivalent Variation with Kinked Budget Constraint

Commodity 1 has a two-block price system with block prices $p^b = (p^1, p^2)$ with p^i the price in block i and price jumps from p^1 to p^2 when demand exceeds $\bar{x}$ and $p^1 < p^2$. The price of the second commodity is equal to 1 and the price vector is $p = (p^b, 1)$. For this situation, EV for a price change from p_0^b to p_1^b is given as:

$$EV(p_0^b, p_1^b, y_0) = y_0 - e^b(p_0^b, u_1) \quad (7.13)$$

In equation (7.13), $e^b(p_0^b, u_1)$ is the expenditure in the case of a block price system and these expenditures reflect the income needed to reach a utility level u_1 if the price vector is $p = (p_0^b, 1)$.

x_e is the demand level at the tangency between the indifference curve $u_1 = V(p_o^b, y_0)$ and the kinked budget curve characterised by prices $(p_0^b, 1)$ and income $e^b(p_0^b, 1)$. The definition of $e^b(p_0^b, 1)$ depends on the segment of the budget line on which x_e is located (Ruijs, 2007).

Three different cases can be distinguished: x_e is at the first segment of the budget curve, at the second segment or at the kink. Hausman (1985) proved that in the case of a convex budget set and a quasi-concave utility function, there is a unique level of x_e, so that only one of the three cases will apply.

First, consider the situation if x_e is at the first segment of the budget curve. Figure 7.4 illustrates this and expenditures are $e(p,u)=\left[(1-\beta)\left(u+e^{z\gamma}\frac{p^{1+\alpha}}{1+\alpha}\right)\right]^{1/1-\beta}$ with price substituted by p_0^1. $e^b(p_0^b,u_1)=e(p_0^1,u_1)$ *if* $x(p_0^1,e(p_0^1,u_1))\leq \bar{x}$. In this case $EV(p_0^b,p_1^b,y_0)=y_0-e(p_0^1,u_1)$ for this situation $x_e=x\left(p_0^1,e(p_0^1,u_1)\right)$ (Ruijs, 2007).

Figure 7.4: Expenditure in the Case of Kinked Budget Curve if x_e and x_1 are at Segment 2 of the Budget Curve

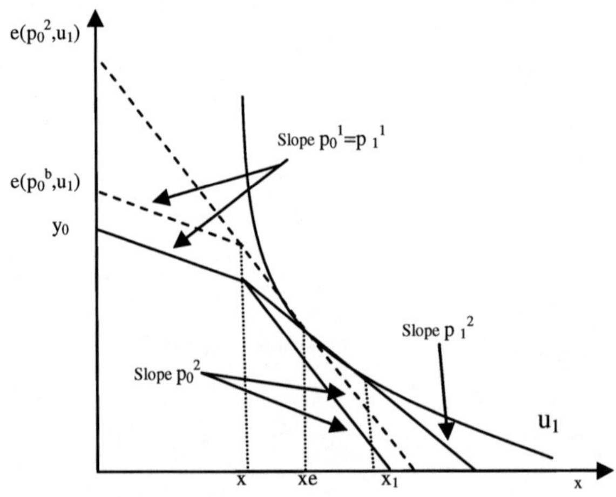

Second, if x_e is at the second segment as in Figure 7.5, the expenditure function is different. In that case expenditure $e^b(p_0^b,u_1)$ is not determined by substituting p_0^2 in $e(p,u)=\left[(1-\beta)\left(u+e^{z\gamma}\frac{p^{1+\alpha}}{1+\alpha}\right)\right]^{1/1-\beta}$, as an amount $(p_0^2-p_0^1)\bar{x}$ less is needed to purchase the quantity x_e. Expenditure $e(p_0^2,u_1)$ is called virtual expenditures which are expenditures necessary to purchase x_e if the price were p_0^2 throughout and the utility is u_1. Using this, for a block price system $p_0^b = (p_0^1, p_0^2)$, expenditures to purchase x_e are:

$$e^b(p_0^b, u_1) = e(p_0^2, u_1) - (p_0^2 - p_0^1)\bar{x} \tag{7.14}$$

In this definition $(p_0^2 - p_0^1)\bar{x}$ is the implicit subsidy for consumers in block 2 (the difference between expenditures if p_0^2 were the price and the actual expenditures in the block price system). It follows that if prices change from $p_0^b = (p_0^1, p_0^2)$ to $p_1^b = (p_1^1, p_1^2)$, expenditures are equal to

$e^b(p_0^b, u_1) = e(p_0^2, u_1) - (p_0^2 - p_0^1)\bar{x}$ if $x(p_0^2, e(p_0^2, u_1)) \geq \bar{x}$ and in that case:

$$EV(p_0^b, p_1^b, y_0) = y_0 - e(p_0^2, u_1) - (p_0^2 - p_0^1)\bar{x} \tag{7.15}$$

Figure 7.5: Expenditure in the Case of a Kinked Budget Curve if x_e and x_1 are at the Kink of the Budget Curve

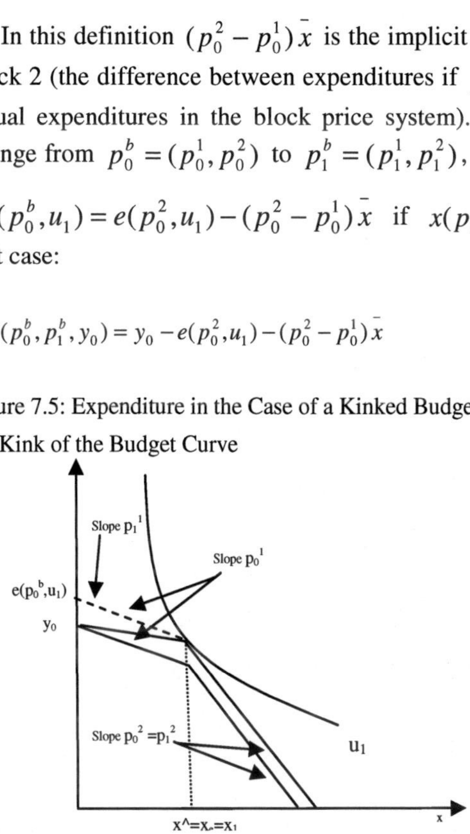

Third, if x_e is at the kink, ($x_e = \bar{x}$), the situation is more complex. The tangency of the indifference curve is at a point $x(p_0^1, e(p_0^1, u_1)) > \bar{x}$ for the budget line with slope p_0^1 and at a point $x(p_0^2, e(p_0^2, u_1)) < \bar{x}$ for the budget line with slope p_0^2. Price $\bar{p}$ *and* $e(\bar{p}, u_1)$ depends on the level of demand after the price change and the position of x_1 on the budget curve (Ruijs, 2007). If demand x_1 and x_e are at the kink, the method is simple (as shown in Figure 7.4). In that case, the demand for commodity 2, the numeraire, $\bar{x}` = y_0 - p_1^1 \bar{x} = e(p_0^b, u_1) - p_0^1 \bar{x}$. It directly follows that:

$$e^b(p_0^b, u_1) = y_0 + (p_0^1 - p_1^1)\bar{x}$$
$$EV(p_0^b, p_1^b, y_0) = (p_0^1 - p_1^1)\bar{x} \tag{7.16}$$

If demand level x_1 is in block i and demand level x_e is at the kink (Figures 7.6 and 7.7) the method is more complex. In that case virtual equivalent income $\bar{y} = e(\bar{p}, u_1)$ and price $\bar{p}$ for which demand would be $\bar{x}$ can be determined by using the demand functions $x(p, y) = e^{z\gamma}\bar{p}^{\alpha}\bar{y}^{\beta}$ and $x_1(p, y) = e^{z\gamma} p_1^{i\alpha} y_0^{i\beta}$ and by the fact that $V(p_1^i, \tilde{y}_0^i) = V(\bar{p}, \bar{y})$ has to hold with $y_0^1 = y_0$ (Ruijs, 2007). If demand $x_1 = x(p_1^1, y_0)$ is on segment 1 and $\tilde{y}_0^2 = y_0 + (p_1^2 - p_1^1)\bar{x}$ if demand in $x_1 = x(p_1^2, y_0 + (p_1^2 - p_1^1)\bar{x})$ is on segment 2. It follows that:

$$e^b(p_0^b, u_1) = e(\bar{p}, u_1) - (\bar{p} - p_0^1)\bar{x} \tag{7.17}$$

For n-tiered block price system, $p^b = (p^1, \text{K K}, p^n)$ with block frontier equal to $\bar{x} = (\bar{x}^0, \text{K K}, \bar{x}^n)$; so that for $\bar{x}^{i-1} < x < \bar{x}^i$, the price is equal to p^i. Note that $\bar{x}^0 = 0$ *and* $\bar{x}^n = \infty$. If demand is in block 1, the usual definition of expenditures is used. If demand is in block $i > 1$, EV for a change from p_0^b *to* p_1^b is defined as:

$$EV(p_0^b, p_1^b, y_0) = y_0 - \left[e(p_0^i, u_1) - \sum_{j=1}^{i-1} (p_0^{j+1} - p_0^j)\bar{x}^j \right] \tag{7.18}$$

If x_1 is at a kink or on segment l and x_e is at kink $i, x_e = \bar{x}^i$, EV is:

$$EV(p_0^b, p_1^b, y_0) = y_0 - \left[e(\bar{p}, u_1) - (\bar{p} - p_0^i) x^i - \sum_{j=1}^{i-1} (p_0^{j+1} - p_0^j) \bar{x}^j \right] \tag{7.19}$$

In equation (7.19), $\sum_{j=1}^{i-1} (p_0^{j+1} - p_0^j) \bar{x}^j$ and $(\bar{p} - p_0^i) x^i - \sum_{j=1}^{i-1} (p_0^{j+1} - p_0^j) \bar{x}^j$ are equal to the implicit subsidy the consumers receive (Ruijs, 2007). It is commonly known as the difference variable (explained in chapter 4).

Figure 7.6: Expenditure in the Case of a Kinked Budget Curve if x_e at the Kink and x_1 at Segment 1 of the Budget Curve

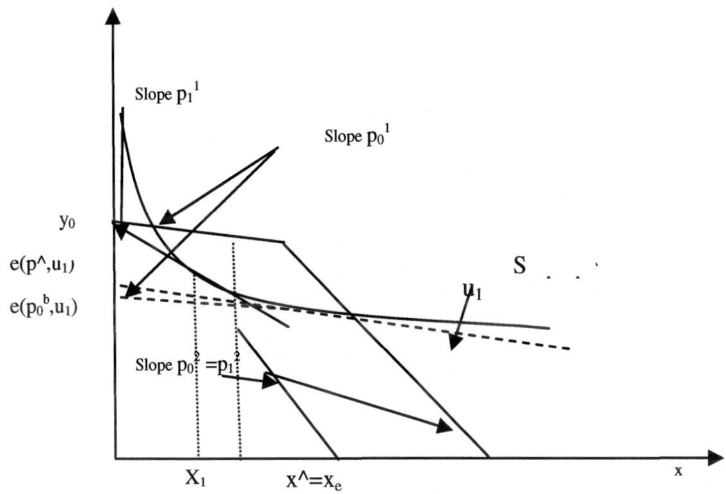

Figure 7.7: Expenditure in the Case of a Kinked Budget Curve if x_e at the Kink and x_1 at Segment 2 of the Budget Curve

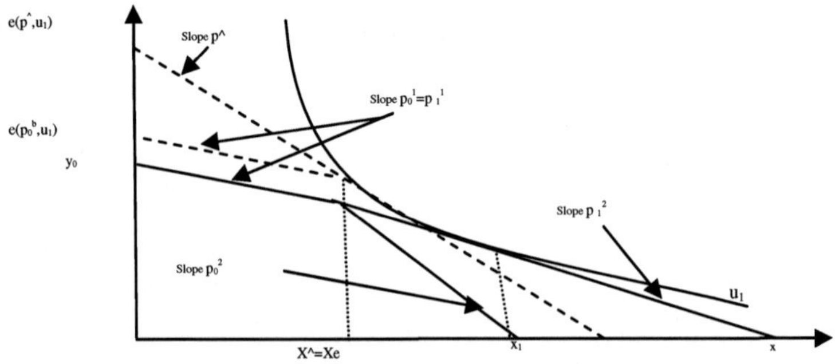

7.3.3 Deadweight Loss

The loss of welfare arising from water prices below marginal cost can be measured using deadweight loss. Deadweight loss is the loss of net benefit caused by inefficient pricing. This is illustrated as follows:

$$DWL = \int_{x^*}^{x^0} (MC(x) - MB(x,m))dx \tag{7.20}$$

x^0 is the inefficient level of output, x^* is the efficient level of output and $x^0 > x^*$. Figures 7.8, 7.9 and 7.10 depict deadweight losses associated with increasing, constant and decreasing marginal costs respectively.

Figure 7.8: Deadweight Loss with Increasing Marginal Cost

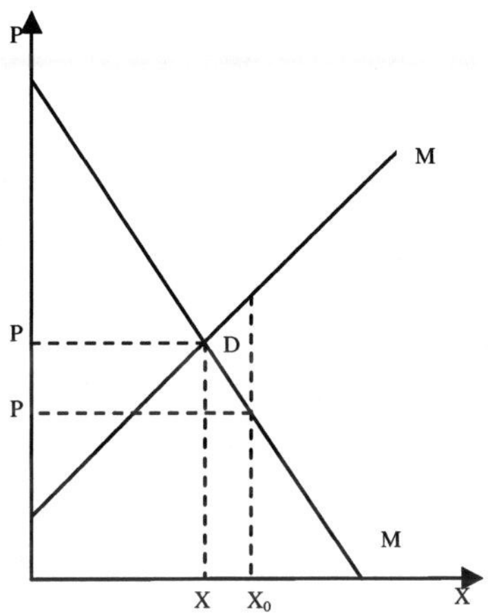

Figure 7.9: Deadweight Loss with Constant Marginal Cost

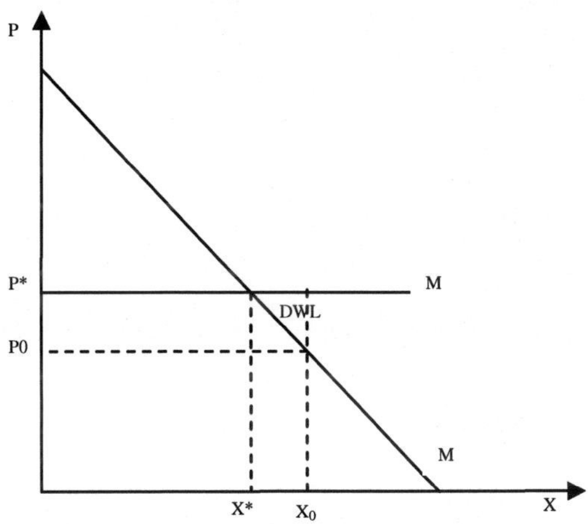

Figure 7.10: Deadweight Loss with Decreasing Marginal Cost

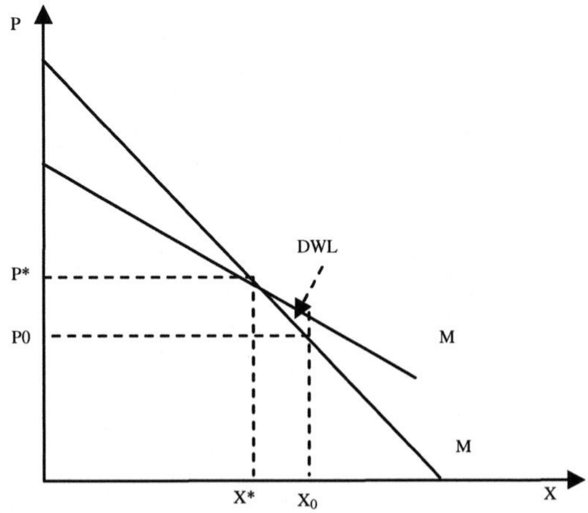

7.4 Pricing Rules for the Simulation Program

One justification water utilities provide for the block-rate pricing structure relates to equity. The system favours households with small budgets and presumably low water consumption, because the marginal price is relatively low for small consumption levels. Chapter 3 discussed advantages and disadvantages of increasing block tariffs. From the estimation results in chapter 4 it appears income has a small but significant effect on water consumption, whereas, household size has a more substantial influence. Therefore, with the current rate structure, larger households may pay a higher marginal price than small households, while income is an unimportant determinant of the marginal price.

The first best analysis where the $p = mc$ is based on very strong assumptions such as exogenously determined market price, homogenous product and perfect information. The violation of these assumptions in the case of public utilities is often observed. The water utility analysed in this book, rather than having a traditional U-shaped cost curve, has L-shaped cost curves because of economies of scale (estimated in Chapter 6). The lumpy or fixed capacity is present with the L-shaped marginal cost curves and is a fundamental characteristic of decreasing-cost industries. This production technology requires highly durable, fixed and inflexible inputs. The water utilities are often faced with the constraint of capital indivisibility and need to undertake lumpy investments.

The two-part tariffs are proposed as a means of achieving the break-even constraint for the decreasing-cost industries. Under two-part tariffs, consumers pay a fixed charge which does not vary with the level of usage, and usage charges in the form of a unit price. Assuming each consumer is faced with a unit price equal to SRMC or LRMC, for the utility to break-even it should recover the fixed cost (FC) by charging from each consumer FC/N (N is number of connections). Ng and Weisser (1974) suggested an appropriate balance needs to be considered between the fixed and usage charges to reduce any efficiency loss.

Table 7.1 shows the current pricing practices and alternative pricing practices considered for welfare evaluations in this chapter. In the first alternative (scenario 1) to current pricing practices, all users are charged with the SRMC of production and each user's monthly fixed charge is calculated as the total value of the deficit divided by the number of users connected to the system. The second option is similar to the first but LRMC of production is used instead of the SRMC. In the third and fourth scenarios of Table 7.1, all users are charged the short-run and LRAC of production respectively and monthly fixed charges are removed. This pricing option is used considering the revenue recovery of the NWSDB. Average-cost pricing can be a more appropriate policy in view of the substantial costs of the government subsidies to the NWSDB (Ng, 1987). There is no discrimination across different users in pricing scenarios 1, 2, 3 and 4.

Block tariffs consist of a sequence of prices with successive intervals of quantities demanded. This is an extension of the two-part tariff where the usage charge component has a number of steps. These block tariffs can be either increasing or decreasing: In an increasing block tariff succeeding units are sold at higher prices and in decreasing block tariffs, the succeeding blocks are sold at lower prices. Water suppliers employ block pricing systems as they are not only trying to promote efficiency but also have other objectives related to equity, cost recovery and local acceptability (Arbues & Villanua, 2006; Ruijs, 2007). In addition to the above mentioned objectives, governments insist on the use of block prices to achieve the political objectives.

Alternative pricing scenarios, five to ten as listed in the Table 7.1 include discrimination across residential and industrial and commercial users. Residential users are faced with block pricing with two-blocks, where the first block price is set at SRMC and the second block price is set at LRMC (for scenarios 5, 6 and 7) and vice versa (for scenarios 8, 9 and 10). The size of the first block is determined based on the findings of chapter 4, where 3, 4 and 5 cubic metres were considered. The size of the first block corresponds to the Stone-Geary findings of the threshold for a household with price insensitivity. In addition to block pricing for residential users, uniform LRMC pricing is considered for industrial and commercial users.

Table 7.1: Base Case and Alternative Pricing Rules for Water

Scenario	Pricing rule	Scenario	Pricing rule
Base	Current practice (base case) Residential: $p = p_R, A = A_R$ Commercial: $p = p_C, A = 0$ Industrial: $p = p_I, A = 0$	6	Two-block pricing 2 $p_R = p_1 = LRMC$ $q_1 = 4m^3$ $p_R = p_2 = SRMC$ $A = Deficit / N$ $p_I = p_C = LRMC$
1	SRMC pricing $p_R = p_I = p_C = SRMC$ $A = Deficit / N$	7	Two-block pricing 3 $p_R = p_1 = LRMC$ $q_1 = 5m^3$ $p_R = p_2 = SRMC$ $A = Deficit / N$ $p_I = p_C = LRMC$
2	LRMC pricing $p_R = p_I = p_C = LRMC$ $A = Deficit / N$	8	Two-block pricing 4 $p_R = p_1 = SRMC$ $q_1 = 3m^3$ $p_R = p_2 = LRMC$ $A = Deficit / N$ $p_I = p_C = LRMC$
3	Short-run Average-Cost (SRAC) pricing $p_R = p_I = p_C = SRTC / Q$ $A = 0$	9	Two-block pricing 5 $p_R = p_1 = SRMC$ $q_1 = 4m^3$ $p_R = p_2 = LRMC$ $A = Deficit / N$ $p_I = p_C = LRMC$
4	Long-run Average-Cost (LRAC) pricing $p_R = p_I = p_C = LRTC / Q$ $A = 0$	10	Two-block pricing 6 $p_R = p_1 = SRMC$ $q_1 = 5m^3$ $p_R = p_2 = LRMC$ $A = Deficit / N$ $p_I = p_C = LRMC$
5	Two-block pricing 1 $p_R = p_1 = LRMC$ $q_1 = 3m^3$ $p_R = p_2 = SRMC$ $A = Deficit / N$ $p_I = p_C = LRMC$		

7.5 Methodology

After estimating the parameters for residential, industrial and commercial water demand (chapter 4 and 5) and the marginal costs for the NWSDB (chapter 6), the current and alternative tariffs is evaluated from a welfare point of view. A common feature of the proposed tariffs used by this study is simplicity, which is one of the most important requirements of a water tariff structure (OECD, 1999). Marginal-cost pricing, average-cost pricing, two-part tariffs and two-step block pricing are proposed and the welfare implications of these will be compared with the current tariffs (base case). This chapter includes a micro simulation exercise comparing proposed tariffs with those in the respective survey years. In this analysis it is assumed that the NWSDB is trying to maximize the sum of CS over the years in which it operates while maintaining a balanced budget (Renzetti, 1992b). The simulation will permit an approximation of the change in aggregate welfare by measuring the change in each user group's Marshallian CS, deadweight loss and EV.[1]

7.5.1 Marshallian Consumer Surplus

Estimated demand model is illustrated as follows:

$$Q_i(p, y) = \alpha_i p_i^{-\varepsilon} y_i^{\rho} \tag{7.21}$$

Where, ε is price elasticity of demand, ρ is income elasticity of demand, p is price of water, y is average household monthly income and α_r is values of the other independent variables in the demand function

CS due to change in prices can be given by the following formula:

$$\Delta CS_i = \int_{p0}^{p1} Q_r(p_r, y_r)dp \tag{7.22}$$

The change in total CS as a result of altering the price regime can be computed as the difference between the total CS earned with proposed tariffs compared with current tariffs. Using the estimated (constant elasticity) demand function, the change in CS resulting from a change in price due to a reform can be calculated as (Maillebiau & Hansen, 1995)

---

[1] A measure of welfare changes would require Hicksian demand curves. However, Hausman (1981) showed that in the case of a single good it is possible to compute surplus variation using Marshallian demands.

$$\Delta CS_i = \int_{p0}^{p1} Q_r(p_r, y_r)dp = \alpha_i y_i \left(\frac{(p_1)^{-\varepsilon+1} - (p_0)^{-\varepsilon+1}}{-\varepsilon+1} \right) \tag{7.23}$$

Similarly, the surpluses earned by the industrial sector are computed as the area below the demand curve and above the prices.[2] The aggregate monthly surplus is computed as the sum of the CSs earned by each user group. Since the NWSDB is assumed to be constrained by zero-profit condition, changes in producer surplus are ignored. However, even if the water utility earns zero economic profit, producer surplus may appear in the form of rents. For simplicity, it is assumed the water utility does not have the ability to influence factor prices and therefore, the analysis of producer surplus is ignored.

7.5.2 Deadweight Loss Calculation

The approach here is to combine the estimated cost and demand equations with data on water prices to determine the extent to which current consumption levels deviate from that under predicted efficient pricing (marginal-cost pricing and other alternatives) and measure the approximate welfare changes associated with these deviations (Renzetti, 1999).

Deadweight loss is calculated separately for each user category. The difference between the predicted consumption levels (Q^0) at the observed prices and the efficient level of consumption (Q^*) at the marginal cost prices are determined. Q^0 is calculated by substituting the actual water supply prices and other variables into the estimated demand equation. The value of the Q^* is calculated by solving for the intersection of the estimated marginal cost and demand equations. $D_i(\cdot)$ represents the demand function for water.

The deviation of the ith output (residential, commercial and industrial) is the proportional difference between predicted and efficient consumption divided by the predicted level of output as shown below (Renzetti, 1999):

$$dev_i = \frac{Q_i^0 - Q_i^*}{Q_i^0} = \frac{Q_i^0 - D_i(\cdot)}{Q_i^0} \tag{7.24}$$

[2] Area under the demand curve is an acceptable approximation for welfare gain (Ng, 1984).

The deadweight loss associated with the deviation can be defined as the difference between the estimated marginal cost and estimated market valuation (inverse demand curve) integrated over the difference between predicted and efficient quantities. In this calculation, the absolute value of the deadweight loss is considered (Renzetti, 1999).

$$DWL_i = \int_{Q_i^0}^{Q_i^*} \left[mc(Q_i, Y) - D_i^{-1}(\cdot) \right] dQ_i \tag{7.25}$$

In equation (7.25), mc is the estimated marginal cost and the variable Y summarizes the other variables entering the marginal cost function.

$$Waste_i = (DWL_i / Q_i) \tag{7.26}$$

Thus, dev_i measures the proportional difference between predicted and efficient consumption levels, DWL_i measures the associated loss with under-pricing and $Waste_i$ measures the average deadweight loss per unit of output (Renzetti, 1999).

7.5.3 Equivalent Variation

The EV for an average household is calculated following King (1983) and Hausman (1981) methods. EV is the increment or adjustment made to the original income to keep the individual at the post reform utility level. The derived indirect function using estimated Marshallian demand can be given as $V(p, y) = -e^{z\gamma} \frac{p^{1+\alpha}}{1+\alpha} + \frac{y^{1-\beta}}{1-\beta}$ and the expenditure function can be given as $e(p,u) = \left[(1-\beta)\left(u + e^{z\gamma} \frac{p^{1+\alpha}}{1+\alpha} \right) \right]^{1/1-\beta}$ (Hausman, 1981). EV for an average household is derived as follows:

$$EV = y_0 - \left[\left((1-\beta) \frac{e^{z\gamma}}{1+\alpha} \left(p_1^{1+\alpha} - p_0^{1+\alpha} \right) \right) + y_0^{1-\beta} \right]^{1/1-\beta} \tag{7.27}$$

7.6 Results and Discussion

The simulation models generate predicted quantities of water for an average consumer under different pricing options while meeting the revenue constraint. The results are discussed in the following sections. First, the effect of price reforms on quantities consumed, CS changes, deadweight loss and EV are discussed separately under each pricing policy for residential, commercial and industrial user categories and then by income deciles of residential users. IBTS, the tariff structure in the period under consideration (January 2001 to December 2005) is treated as the base case against all other pricing options.

Table 7.2 summarizes the changes in average CS by residential, industrial and commercial user groups and total CS change for alternative pricing rules. All figures are monthly values and expressed in 2005 SLRS. It is observed that all of the alternative pricing rules lead to a decrease in average residential Marshallian CS because of rising residential water prices (compared to the base case). However, commercial and industrial water users exhibit an average CS gain with SRMC, short-run average and LRMC pricing and a CS loss with LRAC pricing. As a result, residential water users are worse off under the price reforms while commercial and industrial users are better off with SRMC, short-run average and LRMC pricing and worse off under LRAC pricing.

The fourth column adds the changes in surpluses of industrial and commercial water users to the second column (residential CS change). In terms of total average CS change, total surplus increases under SRMC and SRAC pricing while the total CS decreases for LRMC and LRAC pricing. The loss in CS for residential consumers has been more than offset by the CS gains by industrial and commercial users for SRMC and SRAC pricing rules. Different revenue constraints for the NWSDB are considered for the short-run and long-run, the short-run cost includes only operation and maintenance costs whereas, long-run includes capital costs in addition to operation and maintenance. Therefore, comparing change in CS of short-run and long-run is not sufficient and the differences in the revenues should be added for a complete comparison. However, comparison of pricing scenarios 1, 3, 5, 6 and 7 (cost of operation and maintenance is considered) and 2, 4, 8, 9 and 10 (total cost of operation and maintenance and capital cost is considered) is still possible.

Table 7.2: Average Consumer Surplus Changes under Alternative Pricing Rules

Scenario	ΔCS per connection (SLRS)			
	Residential	Industrial	Commercial	Total
1	-152.36	4768.70	819.57	5435.91
2	-682.41	423.01	96.88	-162.52
3	-264.22	3564.79	664.20	3964.77
4	-1276.80	-2497.09	-687.82	-3773.89
5	-203.38	423.01	96.88	316.51
6	-213.22	423.01	96.88	306.67
7	-219.53	423.01	96.88	300.36
8	-482.36	423.01	96.88	37.53
9	-423.57	423.01	96.88	96.32
10	-368.71	423.01	96.88	151.18

Note: scenario 1 – SRMC pricing, scenario 2 – LRMC pricing, scenario 3 – SRAC pricing, scenario 4 – LRAC pricing, scenario 5 – two-block pricing (LRMC, SRMC, $3m^3$), scenario 6 – two-block pricing (LRMC, SRMC, $4m^3$), scenario 7 – two-block pricing (LRMC, SRMC, $5m^3$), scenario 8 – two-block pricing (SRMC, LRMC, $3m^3$), scenario 9 – two-block pricing (SRMC, LRMC, $4m^3$) and scenario 10 – two-block pricing (SRMC, LRMC, $5m^3$).

Table 7.3 reports the equilibrium prices and quantities under each of the pricing rules. The predicted quantities given under each pricing policy and fixed charges are determined through the simulation process. The prices for residential consumers rise while prices for commercial and industrial consumers fall with SRMC, short-run average and LRMC pricing. Short-run cost pricing rules lead to substantial price decreases for industrial and commercial consumers.

Marginal-cost pricing and block pricing comprise a per cubic metre usage charge and a per month fixed charge. Results presented in Table 7.3

show a substantial divergence between the marginal cost (average cost) and the price of output. SRMC and SRAC and LRMC exceed the price of output for residential use and the price of output exceeds the short-run costs and LRMC for industrial and commercial water use. However, LRACs exceed the price of output for residential, industrial and commercial water use and reduce the average water use by all user categories.

Table 7.3: Equilibrium Prices and Average Quantities per Connection

Scenario	Fixed fee (SLRS)		p_R SLRS	Q_R (m^3)	p_I SLRS	Q_I (m^3)	p_C SLRS	Q_C (m^3)
Base case	50.00		8.00	19.99	51.19	91.76	51.19	21.59
1	101.00		15.96	18.73	15.96	239.43	15.96	26.33
2	476.00		46.74	14.98	46.74	98.31	46.74	21.90
3	0.00		22.13	17.99	22.13	182.88	22.13	24.91
4	0.00		84.40	13.99	84.39	35.83	84.39	18.06
5	81.00	Blk1	46.74	3.00	46.74	98.31	46.74	21.90
		Blk2	15.96	15.73				
6	52.00	Blk1	46.74	4.00	46.74	98.31	46.74	21.90
		Blk2	15.96	14.74				
7	23.00	Blk1	46.74	5.00	46.74	98.31	46.74	21.90
		Blk2	15.96	13.74				
8	563.00	Blk1	15.96	3.00	46.74	98.31	46.74	21.90
		Blk2	46.74	11.98				
9	592.00	Blk1	15.96	4.00	46.74	98.31	46.74	21.90
		Blk2	46.74	10.98				
10	621.00	Blk1	15.96	5.00	46.74	98.31	46.74	21.90
		Blk2	46.74	9.98				

Note: Base case – Current tariffs, scenario 1 – SRMC pricing, scenario 2 – LRMC pricing, scenario 3 – SRAC pricing, scenario 4 – LRAC pricing, scenario 5 – two-block pricing (LRMC, SRMC, 3m^3), scenario 6 – two-block pricing (LRMC, SRMC, 4m^3), scenario 7 – two-block pricing (LRMC, SRMC, 5m^3), scenario 8 – two-block pricing (SRMC, LRMC, 3m^3), scenario 9 – two-block pricing (SRMC, LRMC, 4m^3) and scenario 10 – two-block pricing (SRMC, LRMC, 5m^3).

The movement from the base tariff towards the SRMC pricing with a fixed charge decreases residential water consumption and increases consumption by the average industrial and commercial user. The residential consumption has also declined when moving towards the

SRAC pricing and long-run marginal and average-cost pricing. The lowest average consumption for residential, industrial and commercial is reached under LRAC pricing. The movement from base tariff to SRAC pricing policy approximately doubles the industrial average consumption. Under marginal-cost pricing, each user's monthly fixed fee is calculated as the total value of the deficit divided by the number of users connected to the system (Renzetti, 1992b, 1999). The proportional difference between LRMC and price (base case) is the smallest for commercial and industrial customers indicating that the current pricing is in line with the LRMC.

Table 7.4 presents the percentage deviation of quantity consumed from the current tariff structure to alternative pricing rules, deadweight loss and waste (deadweight loss per cubic metre of water used by each user group). The divergences from short-run and long-run marginal and average-cost pricing lead to significant deviations between predicted and efficient consumption levels. In the case of residential water use, under SRMC and LRMC pricing, the current average level of consumption exceeds the efficient level of consumption by 6 and 25 per cent respectively. In regard to industrial and commercial water use, the predicted consumption level is below the efficient consumption level. For example, under SRMC pricing, predicted consumption levels are below the efficient level of consumption by 161 per cent for industrial water use and 22 per cent for commercial water use. However, this deviation is less with the LRMC pricing. The predicted consumption levels lie below the consumption level with LRMC pricing by 7 per cent for industrial water use and 2 per cent for commercial water use.

It is interesting that the proportional difference between marginal cost and price is the smallest for industrial and commercial water use with LRMC pricing, however, the largest percentage deviation in consumption occurs with industrial water users. This is because industrial users' water demand exhibits a significantly larger average value of price elasticity than for residential and commercial demands. The industrial water use (-0.7573) exhibits a significantly larger average value of own price elasticity than for residential (-0.1131) and commercial (-0.1549) water use.

Table 7.4: Average Values for Deviation, Deadweight Loss and Waste

Scenario	Residential			Industrial			Commercial		
	DEV (%)	*DWL* SLRS	*WASTE* SLRS/ m^3	*DEV* (%)	*DWL* SLRS	*WASTE* SLRS $/m^3$	*DEV* (%)	*DWL* SLRS	*WASTE* SLRS $/m^3$
1	6.27	6.3	0.31	160.9	1753*	19.11	21.94	66.6*	3.08
2	25.20	332.1	16.62	7.14	277*	3.02	1.42	15.7*	0.72
3	9.98	14.4	0.72	99.30	1033*	11.26	15.38	42.3*	1.95
4	30.03	799.5	39.99	60.95	4429	48.27	18.06	319.5	14.79
5	6.27	33.2	1.66	7.14	277*	3.02	1.42	15.7*	0.72
6	6.27	45.5	2.28	7.14	277*	3.02	1.42	15.7*	0.72
7	6.27	58.3	2.93	7.14	277*	3.02	1.42	15.7*	0.72
8	25.20	627.4	31.40	7.14	277*	3.02	1.42	15.7*	0.72
9	25.20	729.5	36.51	7.14	277*	3.02	1.42	15.7*	0.72
10	25.20	832.7	41.67	7.14	277*	3.02	1.42	15.7*	0.72

Note: scenario 1 – SRMC pricing, scenario 2 – LRMC pricing, scenario 3 – SRAC pricing, scenario 4 – LRAC pricing, scenario 5 – two-block pricing (LRMC, SRMC, $3m^3$), scenario 6 – two-block pricing (LRMC, SRMC, $4m^3$), scenario 7 – two-block pricing (LRMC, SRMC, $5m^3$), scenario 8 – two-block pricing (SRMC, LRMC, $3m^3$), scenario 9 – two-block pricing (SRMC, LRMC, $4m^3$) and scenario 10 – two-block pricing (SRMC, LRMC, $5m^3$). *Deadweight loss is due to under consumption of water

The large differences between the SRMC and LRMC and average costs and price and between actual and efficient consumption levels combine to produce quite large deadweight loss estimates. In the case of residential water use, the absence of SRMC pricing, the average deadweight loss per unit of output is SLRS 0.40 per cubic metre, whereas in absence of LRMC the average deadweight loss per unit of output (SLRS 16.61 per cubic metre) is more than two times the current average price per unit of output (SLRS 8.00 per cubic metre). In the case of industrial water use without SRMC pricing, the deadweight loss per unit of output is greater as SLRS 19 per cubic metre due to under consumption; in absence of LRMC, deadweight loss per unit of output is SLRS 3 per cubic metre due to under-pricing. Overall, the deadweight loss per unit of output due to under and over-consumption is less for commercial water use than that shown by the industrial use. The minimum deadweight loss per unit of output for commercial users is observed in absence of LRMC pricing (SLRS 0.72) and the maximum is observed in absence of LRAC pricing (SLRS 14.8).

Another way to consider the deadweight loss estimates is to evaluate how social loss is distributed across income groups. However, this cannot be undertaken with the available data. In a study of Canada, Wasny (1986) indicated the expenditure on publicly supplied water decline as a proportion of household income when household income rises. Thus, the finding that the water supply is under-priced would suggest lower income households benefit more than higher income households. Nevertheless, someone in society must be paying for this under-pricing and the distribution of tax burden associated with the subsidies is not known (Renzetti, 1999).

To further explain the results, the data is divided into deciles by income.[3] Extrapolating the demand function to income deciles may result in biased estimates in welfare effects. The analysis could be more detailed if individual household data were available. However, these analyses will still give a good indication of the effects of alternative pricing policies on different income deciles. Tables 7.5 and 7.6 show the efficient quantities under different pricing alternatives for income deciles. The consumption is lower in every decile under each proposed pricing policy than the base case (with current pricing). Under the current tariff structure, the first income decile shows the lowest average water consumption whereas, the last income decile gives the highest average water consumption.

---

[3] The income decile classifications and price elasticities are presented in Table 15 in Appendix 1.

Table 7.5: Efficient Quantities for Each Pricing Reform for Each Residential Income Deciles – Base Case to Scenario 4

Income deciles	Base Case (m^3)	Scenario 1 (m^3)	Scenario 2 (m^3)	Scenario 3 (m^3)	Scenario 4 (m^3)
1	16.24	15.24	12.14	14.69	11.39
2	18.92	17.54	13.37	16.80	12.38
3	17.52	16.65	13.22	15.97	12.32
4	17.77	16.69	13.25	16.02	12.35
5	21.50	19.15	14.86	18.53	13.67
6	21.08	19.13	14.77	18.25	13.64
7	19.68	17.88	14.08	17.13	13.08
8	21.10	19.27	14.90	18.39	13.77
9	20.86	19.37	14.99	18.50	13.86
10	30.91	29.92	21.04	28.05	18.84
Average	19.99	18.73	14.98	17.99	13.98

Note: Base case – current tariffs, scenario 1 – SRMC pricing, scenario 2 – LRMC pricing, scenario 3 – SRAC pricing, scenario 4 – LRAC pricing.

Table 7.6: Efficient Quantities for Each Pricing Reform for Each Residential Income Deciles – Scenario 5 to Scenario 10

Income deciles	Scenario 5 (m^3)	Scenario 6 (m^3)	Scenario 7 (m^3)	Scenario 8 (m^3)	Scenario 9 (m^3)	Scenario 10 (m^3)
1	12.24	11.24	10.24	11.69	10.69	9.69
2	14.54	13.54	12.54	13.80	12.80	11.80
3	13.65	12.65	11.65	12.97	11.97	10.97
4	13.69	12.69	11.69	13.02	12.02	11.02
5	16.15	15.15	14.15	15.53	14.53	13.53
6	16.13	15.13	14.13	15.25	14.25	13.25
7	14.88	13.88	12.88	14.13	13.13	12.13
8	16.27	15.27	14.27	15.39	14.39	13.39
9	16.37	15.37	14.37	15.50	14.50	13.50
10	26.92	25.92	24.92	25.05	24.05	23.05
Average	15.73	14.73	13.73	14.99	13.99	12.99

Note: scenario 5 – two-block pricing (LRMC, SRMC, 3m^3), scenario 6 – two-block pricing (LRMC, SRMC, 4m^3), scenario 7 – two-block pricing (LRMC, SRMC, 5m^3), scenario 8 – two-block pricing (SRMC, LRMC, 3m^3), scenario 9 – two-block pricing (SRMC, LRMC, 4m^3) and scenario 10 – two-block pricing (SRMC, LRMC, 5m^3).

Figure 7.11 shows the average consumption per household per month by income decile, based on the information given in Table 7.5. Average consumption is given along the y-axis in cubic metres per month, and generally increases when moving to higher income groups. The average consumption is the highest for decile 10 and the second highest is for decile 5, after which it slightly drops for households belonging to decile 6.

Figure 7.11: Average Consumption per Household per Month by Income Deciles

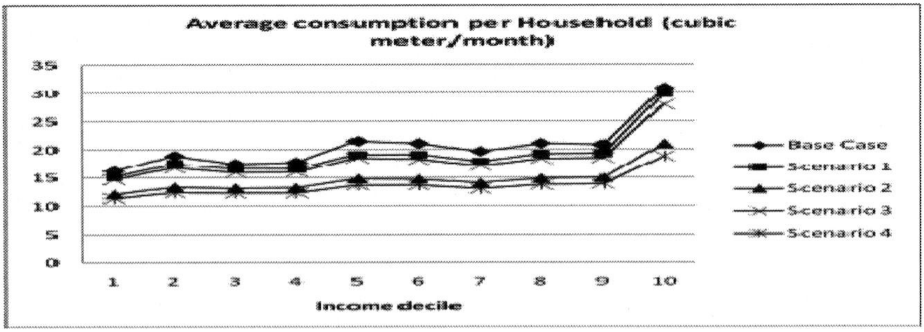

The results in Table 7.7 indicate the highest levels of deviation are observed in the middle income deciles (5 to 8) with SRMC pricing. The highest income decile shows the lowest deviation percentage with the SRMC pricing. Under the SRAC pricing the highest and the lowest income deciles show approximately similar magnitude of deviation. Consumption declines when moving towards the LRMC and LRAC pricing. The highest average deviation for all income deciles is reached under LRAC pricing and the highest deviation is observed in the last income decile.

A positive value for the EV represents a welfare increase whereas a negative value represents a welfare decrease. Almost all households lose when moving from current pricing to alternative pricing rules and the results are presented in Tables 7.8 and 7.9. Average loss is SLRS 155 per household per month with SRMC pricing. The main reason for the decrease in EV is an increase of the average price due to which a higher equivalent income is needed to reach the same utility level with the ex-ante price system. The households in decile 1 and decile 10 on an average, lose about SLRS 128 and SLRS 123 per household per month. The highest losses with SRMC pricing are attributed to decile 5 and 6, losing approximately SLRS 183 per month. Households located in all income deciles lose an average SLRS 694 per month under LRMC pricing. Households in decile 10 are the greatest losers and deciles 1 are the smallest losers with the LRAC pricing.

Table 7.7: Deviation between the Current and the Optimal Quantity for Each Pricing Rule for Residential Income Deciles

Income deciles	Scenario 1 (%)	Scenario 2 (%)	Scenario 3 (%)	Scenario 4 (%)
1	6.16	23.97	9.64	28.70
2	7.31	27.89	11.41	33.24
3	4.95	24.52	8.81	29.67
4	6.01	25.40	9.84	30.51
5	9.50	30.89	13.81	36.40
6	9.24	29.89	13.38	35.26
7	9.09	28.44	12.93	33.51
8	8.68	29.38	12.83	34.75
9	7.15	28.12	11.35	33.57
10	3.21	31.94	9.25	39.04
Average	6.27	25.20	9.98	30.03

Note: scenario 1 – SRMC pricing, scenario 2 – LRMC pricing, scenario 3 – SRAC pricing, scenario 4 – LRAC pricing.

Table 7.8: Equivalent Variation for Residential Users – Base Case to Scenario 4

Income deciles	Scenario 1 (SLRS)	Scenario 2 (SLRS)	Scenario 3 (SLRS)	Scenario 4 (SLRS)
1	-127.52	-562.07	-218.80	-1053.86
2	-147.08	-639.96	-251.57	-1189.12
3	-115.05	-586.15	-214.48	-1114.92
4	-130.07	-602.44	-229.79	-1132.39
5	-183.94	-726.69	-299.52	-1326.65
6	-182.06	-717.83	-295.87	-1312.52
7	-175.85	-680.15	-282.53	-1243.85
8	-176.97	-716.65	-291.60	-1315.73
9	-157.92	-700.60	-273.18	-1303.06
10	-122.70	-930.89	-298.21	-1794.40
Average	-154.85	-694.68	-268.64	-1301.99

Note: scenario 1 – SRMC pricing, scenario 2 – LRMC pricing, scenario 3 – SRAC pricing, scenario 4 – LRAC pricing.

In the presence of the block pricing systems, the average welfare reduction is larger in terms of first block size of 3 cubic metres and priced according to the SRMC and the rest of the water use is priced according to LRMC (scenario 8). Under scenario 5, 6 and 7 average welfare reduction increases with the increase of first block size (3, 4 and 5 cubic metres) and vice versa for scenario 8, 9 and 10 where average welfare reduction decreases with increase of first block size. The lowest welfare reduction is observed with income decile 3 and the largest welfare reduction is observed with income decile 5, when the first block is 3 cubic metres and charged according to the LRMC and the rest of the water use is charged at SRMC (scenario 5). Scenarios 8, 9 and 10 indicate the welfare effects for the richest are higher than in other scenarios and effects on welfare for the poor are small.

Table 7.9: Equivalent Variation for Residential Users – Scenario 5 to Scenario 10

Income deciles	Scenario 5 (SLRS)	Scenario 6 (SLRS)	Scenario 7 (SLRS)	Scenario 8 (SLRS)	Scenario 9 (SLRS)	Scenario 10 (SLRS)
1	-200.69	-224.62	-248.51	-477.72	-449.32	-420.77
2	-230.89	-258.20	-285.43	-545.03	-513.00	-480.76
3	-194.78	-220.81	-246.77	-495.07	-464.38	-433.49
4	-210.04	-236.14	-262.17	-511.14	-480.36	-449.40
5	-276.69	-306.85	-336.91	-622.56	-587.39	-551.98
6	-273.37	-303.10	-332.73	-614.83	-580.06	-545.05
7	-261.41	-289.31	-317.14	-582.85	-550.04	-517.02
8	-268.94	-298.88	-328.73	-612.88	-577.86	-542.59
9	-250.39	-280.49	-310.51	-596.25	-561.03	-525.57
10	-263.72	-309.26	-354.48	-778.45	-726.74	-674.54
Average	-246.09	-275.88	-305.61	-590.20	-554.99	-519.58

Note: scenario 5 – two-block pricing (LRMC, SRMC, $3m^3$), scenario 6 – two-block pricing (LRMC, SRMC, $4m^3$), scenario 7 – two-block pricing (LRMC, SRMC, $5m^3$), scenario 8 – two-block pricing (SRMC, LRMC, $3m^3$), scenario 9 – two-block pricing (SRMC, LRMC, $4m^3$) and scenario 10 – two-block pricing (SRMC, LRMC, $5m^3$).

Table 7.10 and 7.11 present the average expenses on water as a percentage of income for base case and alternative pricing rules by income deciles. Under the current pricing, the difference between poor and richer segments of the population are considerable, where the poorest 10 per cent of the consumers spend on average 0.8 per cent of their income on a consumption of 16 cubic metres of water per month compared with the richest part of the population that spends only about 0.4 per cent of their income on consumption of 31 cubic metres of water per month. The average expenses on water as a percentage of income are the largest with scenario 10 for the poorest and smallest for the richest groups (deciles 9 and 10) under scenario 1. Block pricing scenarios 8, 9 and 10 have a larger effect on the poorest income decile as the corresponding fixed costs are such a large part of the water bill, especially compared to the richer groups.

Table 7.10: Water Bill as a Percentage of Income for Each Pricing Reform for Each Residential Income Deciles – Base Case to Scenario 4

Income deciles	Base Case (%)	Scenario 1 (%)	Scenario 2 (%)	Scenario 3 (%)	Scenario 4 (%)
1	0.83	2.57	8.00	2.43	7.33
2	0.70	2.47	7.33	2.41	6.93
3	0.71	2.18	6.60	2.11	6.19
4	0.64	2.02	6.11	1.95	5.74
5	0.52	2.11	6.08	2.10	5.92
6	0.49	1.94	5.64	1.93	5.50
7	0.48	1.74	5.19	1.71	4.89
8	0.42	1.73	5.03	1.73	4.93
9	0.46	1.55	4.52	1.55	4.44
10	0.37	1.56	3.99	1.68	4.31
Average	0.53	1.87	5.59	1.87	5.54

Note: Base case – current tariffs, scenario 1 – SRMC pricing, scenario 2 – LRMC pricing, scenario 3 – SRAC pricing, scenario 4 – LRAC pricing.

Table 7.11: Water Bill as a Percentage of Income for Each Pricing Reform for Each Residential Income Deciles – Scenario 5 to Scenario 10

Income deciles	Scenario 5 (%)	Scenario 6 (%)	Scenario 7 (%)	Scenario 8 (%)	Scenario 9 (%)	Scenario 10 (%)
1	2.99	2.96	2.94	7.97	8.00	8.03
2	2.91	2.91	2.91	7.25	7.26	7.26
3	2.55	2.54	2.54	6.55	6.56	6.57
4	2.37	2.36	2.35	6.06	6.07	6.08
5	2.50	2.52	2.53	5.98	5.97	5.96
6	2.30	2.31	2.32	5.55	5.54	5.54
7	2.05	2.06	2.06	5.12	5.12	5.12
8	2.05	2.06	2.07	4.95	4.94	4.93
9	1.84	1.85	1.87	4.44	4.44	4.43
10	1.91	1.97	2.02	3.83	3.79	3.75
Average	2.22	2.23	2.23	5.49	5.48	5.47

Note: scenario 5 – two-block pricing (LRMC, SRMC, $3m^3$), scenario 6 – two-block pricing (LRMC, SRMC, $4m^3$), scenario 7 – two-block pricing (LRMC, SRMC, $5m^3$), scenario 8 – two-block pricing (SRMC, LRMC, $3m^3$), scenario 9 – two-block pricing (SRMC, LRMC, $4m^3$) and scenario 10 – two-block pricing (SRMC, LRMC, $5m^3$).

The pricing alternatives considered above are invariant to distance and time of use. However, there is some evidence that water supply costs vary with distance and peak loads of time (Renzetti, 1992b). Moreover, sewage treatment costs are not included in the analyses since it is not yet well established in Sri Lanka. In addition to the above issues in calculating the prices, the NWSDB's accounting of their costs is incomplete. Grants and subsidies lead to an underestimation of operating and capital costs. Further, water supply treatment facilities understate costs in several ways: for instance, they do not include depreciation of capital costs; do not assign a value for raw water input withdrawn from the natural environment; fail to impute the opportunity cost of the land holding and fail to account for the external costs associated with environmental damages caused by effluents (Renzetti, 1999).

7.7 Conclusion

In this chapter, the welfare effects of current and alternative pricing rules were evaluated. The estimated residential, industrial and commercial demand coefficients (chapters 4 and 5) and short-run and long-run cost coefficients (chapter 6) were used in the welfare evaluation. The demand relationships and estimated marginal costs are compared with current water prices and the gap between predicted consumption levels and those that would be predicted with alternative pricing rules are calculated. Then the welfare costs of observed divergences are estimated using CS change, deadweight loss and EV techniques.

The results here indicate water prices understate the marginal and average costs of providing water services by a wide margin. This chapter supports the theory discussed in chapter 3 regarding the marginal-cost pricing. If the water utility is concerned with maximizing social welfare, then moving to marginal-cost pricing (with an appropriately calculated monthly fixed fee to recoup any losses implied by marginal-cost pricing under increasing returns to scale) is necessary (Renzetti, 1999). The simulation results show the movement from the current tariff structure to a two-part tariff, where the volumetric charge is equal to the SRMC, leads to the highest welfare gains. In the presence of SRMC pricing, the deadweight loss per cubic metre of residential consumption is SLRS 0.30 as a result of over-consumption whereas, deadweight loss per cubic metre industrial and commercial consumption are SLRS 19 and SLRS 3 respectively, as a result of under consumption. Two explanations can be given for the small magnitude of the welfare gain for residential users. First, as the aggregated water demand function is very inelastic, changes in water prices only result in small modifications to water consumption. Second, the small efficiency gains could be related to return to scale of the water utilities (and utilities use average-cost pricing).

In terms of CS calculations, SRMC pricing provides the maximum aggregate CS gain even though residential users have lost CS as industrial and commercial users gain more. Almost all user groups lost CS under LRAC pricing and it needs to be borne in mind that this analysis ignores the changes to producer surplus. Considering welfare effects for different income groups gives greater insight into the effects of price changes. EV calculation for income deciles showed that all income deciles lose from alternative pricing rules. However, with SRMC pricing, EV for the poorest and the richest groups are comparable and with LRMC pricing richer groups lose more than poorer groups. A dollar must be treated as a dollar to achieve efficiency, and any desired level of equality can be achieved by general tax transfers (Ng, 1983).

The reformation of water prices does provide for the possibility of an improvement in aggregate welfare, however, carrying out these changes will not necessarily lead to a substantial decrease in aggregate water use (Renzetti, 1992b). The demand inelasticities show that it is difficult to reach a substantial reduction of water demand, especially with residential and commercial users, by only using pricing policies. Additional policies may be required to make people more aware of the pipe-borne water scarcity problems and if the water utility wishes to reduce water consumption. Since the water utility is currently employing some form of price discrimination, moving to efficient prices may imply price increases for some user groups and decreases for others. As a result, it is difficult to predict the direction of change for aggregate water use (Renzetti, 1992b).

Overall extent of welfare measures of water pricing reforms should be qualified because some welfare components that are affected by price reform have not been addressed in this chapter. For example, it will be important to examine the impact of changing water prices on all user groups. Measuring only the changes to the average consumer may neglect impacts on other user groups (Renzetti, 1992b). Specifically, with SRMC and average-cost pricing, residential CS decreases as a result of increasing water prices. However, this may have actually led to an increase in aggregate welfare with the benefits residential consumers may derive due to declining water prices to commercial and industrial users. Further, it is well understood that the change in the welfare of a heterogeneous population is not perfectly indexed by the change in aggregate Marshallian CS (Boadway, 1974; Renzetti, 1992b).

CHAPTER EIGHT

CONCLUSIONS

Water resources can be managed efficiently by using cost-reflective pricing. This book focused on the pipe-borne water sector in Sri Lanka and evaluated alternative pricing structures in terms of economic efficiency, equity and financial viability. This required an understanding of consumer behaviour and the cost structures of the NWSDB. The analyses reviewed the relevant theoretical and applied basis for water pricing and then empirically analysed the cost, demand and welfare implications of pipe-borne water in Sri Lanka. Very few studies have explored the efficient pricing policies and other related welfare aspects for developing countries. This is the only study to examine different pricing structures for water in a comprehensive framework involving demands, costs and welfare aspects for Sri Lanka. The findings presented here are important for policy makers and relevant authorities who are increasingly paying attention to efficiency and expansion of the pipe-borne water coverage.

This concluding chapter provides some concluding remarks of the book and the achievements of the book in section 8.1. Under this section, conclusions of the book are reported using various headings, which may relate to conclusions from more than one chapter. Policy implications are discussed in section 8.2 and the topics for future research are outlined in the final section, section 8.3.

8.1 Summary and Achievements of the Book

The water supply decisions for Sri Lanka in the past have been implemented with little regard for the links between demand, cost and pricing; therefore, this book links these components of optimal pricing problems. Most importantly, the approach undertaken here allows the measurement of parameters of water production and consumption including economies of scale, cost-output elasticities and price and income elasticities of demand. The results are of interest to scholars in applied research as well as those involved in public utilities and regulation.

The current pricing practices of the NWSDB promote inefficient levels of consumption. Current output prices do not reflect marginal costs and the value of raw water. This discourages technological innovation in water conservation and supply expansion. The perception of plentiful supplies of water has been artificially magnified by understating the cost of using that resource. The issue of inefficient water pricing is critically important for low-income countries, many of which have been fiercely criticised for failing to provide potable water to all citizens (J. J. Boland & Whittington, 1998; Whittington, 2003). It is often the case that the poorest citizens may purchase water from private vendors at prices many times those paid by households connected to the pipe-borne water supply system or poor people may secure water from unsafe sources. In situations such as these, reforming water prices combined with institutional reforms (to improve water utility performance) may provide the needed financial resources to improve system reliability and extend services to poor neighbourhoods. Further, policy makers can employ a mix of connection subsidies and information, education and communication campaigns to stimulate connecting to the pipe water network. In order to improve equity, water companies can reduce the installation fees, giving low-income households access to water connections and/or reinvest profits in network expansion to un-serviced areas.

Chapter 1 began with an introduction to the book and outlined the overall research purpose and research questions. The background for the analyses is explained in chapter 2 by explaining the institutional background and changes of pipe-borne water sector of Sri Lanka and the performances of the NWSDB over the years. Chapter 3 is used to introduce the theoretical framework for efficient water pricing. Chapters 4, 5, 6 and 7 are empirical chapters where, chapter 4 detailed the estimation of residential water demand model based on aggregate data. Similarly, chapter 5 presented the estimation of the industrial and commercial water demand models separately using aggregate data. In chapter 6 the estimations of the SRMC and LRMC were reported. Chapter 7 illustrated a number of welfare measures: CS, deadweight loss and Hicksian welfare measures – CV and EV by combining the results of chapter 4, 5, and 6 with the price structures. Conclusions from the four empirical chapters are now placed under broad headings. Some conclusions draw on findings in more than one chapter. This section, therefore, aims at drawing out conclusions across chapters, linking chapters together and placing them in context.

8.1.1 Importance of Price in Water Demand

The price responsiveness of residential, industrial and commercial water consumption were analysed in chapter 4 and 5. Demand for all major water users (residential, industrial and commercial) are price inelastic; however, industrial consumers are relatively more sensitive to water price changes than residential and commercial users. Residential water demand was estimated using both Cobb-Douglas and Stone-Geary specifications (chapter 4). The results from the residential water demand provides water utility managers with important information about the threshold of the quantity of water below which consumption will not respond to price changes. It is only after the threshold is reached that consumers have an incentive to reduce the quantity of water used if price increases. Estimating the minimum consumption threshold provides critical information to policy makers about the likely effectiveness of demand side management.

The sensitivity of water use in relation to the price was observed for both industrial and commercial water users (at a lower statistical significance level) (chapter 5). This insensitivity to price changes may be due to the fact that expenditure on water accounts for only a small proportion of their total budget. The magnitude of the price elasticity of commercial users is similar to that of residential users, but industrial users are relatively more elastic than residential or commercial users. This suggests raising the price of water may reduce industrial water demand per connection. However, a substantial price change would be required to reduce the average water consumption by commercial and residential users. The inelastic nature of water consumption by residential, industrial and commercial users provides opportunities for the NWSDB to increase revenues by increasing water prices.

8.1.2 Importance of Socio-demographic Factors in Water Demand

Price is not the only factor determining the household water consumption. The quantity of water consumed depends on household demographic factors. In order to capture demographics that influence residential water demand, chapter 4 included average household income and number of household members. Findings suggest residential water demand is inelastic with respect to income and small in magnitude. This was expected as water bills often represent a small proportion of total household expenditure. The number of household members affected the household water consumption positively and the effect is relatively larger in magnitude. However, an increase in household water use is less than proportional to the increase in household size.

The findings of chapter 4 and similar past studies have found the number of household members plays a more significant role than household income in water consumption decision. These findings are important to identify the limitations of IBTS. IBTSs are structured with the aim that high water volume users should cross-subsidize low water volume users. Therefore, IBTSs benefit low volume users, but these are not necessarily poor; rather, there are fewer household members.

8.1.3 Importance of Climatic Factors in Water Demand

The analyses of residential, industrial and commercial water demand provided a better approach to the investigation of climatic effects on water use by incorporating monthly and district differences. The average residential, industrial and commercial water consumption increases with temperature and decreases with rainfall. In all the findings, the coefficient of monthly temperature is relatively larger than the coefficient of monthly rainfall. The small magnitude of the coefficient indicates that rainfall does not have a significant impact on households', industrial or commercial establishments' water consumption decision. The extent of outdoor water using activities also can be captured by including the climatic variables in demand analyses. Increasing rainfall leads to decreasing outdoor water using activities while increasing temperatures leads to more outdoor water using activities (garden watering, outdoor recreational activities).

8.1.4 Economies of Scale and Marginal Costs of Water Production

Short-run and long-run cost functions and cost share equations for the NWSDB were estimated using trans-log functional form. The cost functions were re-estimated after imposing theoretical properties like monotonicity and concavity. It was found that pipe-borne water in Sri Lanka is produced under increasing returns to scale both in the short-run and the long-run. Estimated SRMC is approximately 12 times the average first block price over the period considered and the LRMC estimates differ from the short-run by a substantial margin.

The reported marginal cost values do not fully account for marginal social cost, therefore, the marginal social cost may be greater than the estimated marginal costs (chapter 6). However, a constant to the marginal costs estimates is added to represent values of raw water withdrawn from surface or ground water sources. In addition to estimates of marginal costs and scale economies, chapter 6 provided important findings for output-cost elasticities, substitutability and complementarity between the inputs in the pipe-borne water production and marginal cost elasticities with respect to input prices.

8.1.5 Welfare Implications of Different Price Reforms

Estimates of welfare effects of current and alternative pricing structures (SRMC, LRMC, SRAC, LRAC and two-block pricing) indicated the adoption of any one of the alternative pricing rules leads to significant price and welfare changes (chapter 7). This observation implies that the changes might meet with opposition from consumer groups that are adversely affected (Renzetti, 1992b). The current volumetric rate for Sri Lankan residential consumers was around 50 per cent less than the actual SRMC. The estimated SRMC is about 300 per cent more than the current volumetric charge for commercial and industrial water users. The findings suggest current pricing for industrial and commercial water users are in line with the estimated LRMC.

The highest aggregate welfare gains were obtained from two-part SRMC pricing, where a fixed charge is accompanied by a volumetric charge according to SRMC. The smallest deadweight loss for residential consumers compared with commercial and industrial users was found in the absence of SRMC pricing. The deadweight loss for residential users arises due to over-consumption whereas, for commercial and industrial, it is due to under-consumption of water.

8.2 Policy Implications

There are important policy implications arising from the findings presented here. The details of empirical findings upon which some of the remarks are based can be found at the end of each chapter. A broader water policy discussion is beyond the scope of this research as it would need to address the issues related to all of the uses of water including, agricultural, cultural, ecological and recreational. However, broadly the results reported here indicate pipe-borne water pricing in Sri Lanka is inefficient.

The present water tariff does not reflect costs of production and does not allow adequate profit for the NWSDB to maintain the pipeline network. Moreover, the Government of Sri Lanka intends to provide access to safe drinking water and adequate sanitation facilities for all by 2010. To achieve these targets, the government has estimated the required investments in the pipe-borne sector exceed their ability. Therefore, additional funding sources need to be tapped to fill this gap. In order to improve the NWSDB performance, it is important to pursue sector reforms to provide an appropriate institutional, legal and regulatory framework. These frameworks need to facilitate the decentralisation of service provision, introduction of private sector participation and creation of an independent regulatory framework. However, these are not empirically proven in this book.

The design of the water tariff structure is challenging with a number of objectives. IBTSs are popular, however, they have failed to deliver simultaneous meeting of competing objectives. More importantly, IBTS convey incorrect pricing signals to water users partly due the fact that low income households are not necessarily small consumers of water. It is important to evaluate whether pipe-borne water distribution networks are the best option for the delivery of subsidies to the poor. The relevant issue is to identify the subsidy mechanism that will reach the poor most efficiently and effectively, while allowing the water pricing structure to reflect the need and costs of the pipe-borne water sector. Uniform volumetric rates and two-part tariffs structure perform comparatively well in meeting different objectives of pricing. A simple two-block tariff aims to provide water in two blocks where it can be of DBTS or IBTS and combines cost, production information and responsiveness to price.

The existing pipe-borne water tariffs in Sri Lanka have a large subsidy segment. Ideally, the water tariffs should not be used to deliver subsidies to poor households as often subsides fail to reach the majority of these households. According to published statistics, only a few households in the rural areas have access to pipe-borne water and these pipe-borne water subsidies rarely reached the poor. At the same time, IBTSs are often designed for the heavy water users to cross-subsidise low water users. However, findings here confirm that number of household members is more important for household water consumption than household income.

This book presented important results of Stone-Geary specification by providing the quantity of water at which households are not responsive to price changes. The results suggest household water demand is price responsive once the threshold is reached. Policies should explicitly recognize this in demand management efforts. The continuous supply of water at the current subsidised rates may eventually lead to a collapse of the water supply system. Therefore, the inelastic nature of water consumption provides opportunities for the NWSDB to increase revenues by increasing water charges. Such price increases, however, should be accompanied by welfare measures to ensure adequate provision for poorer households and require political will.

Raising the price of water may reduce industrial demand for water per connection; however, a substantial price change would be required to bring about the desired change in the commercial water demand per connection. For regulators to set the water price and to influence the tariff design, an understanding of the marginal cost function and scale economies is essential. Understanding the relationship between marginal cost and existing price enables us to identify whether the utility has to subsidise the services to different users at different prices and whether the utility engages in monopoly pricing. The choice of water price and tariff design should be governed by efficiency, equity and financial viability of the water utility.

Both SRMC and LRMC were found to be higher than average volumetric charges supporting the belief that water is under-priced. The LRMC estimates differ from the SRMC estimates by a substantial margin demonstrating the significance of capital costs to the utility (Renzetti, 1992b). The results for both the short-run and long-run indicate there are scale economies in the technology of water supply. If the value of raw water (opportunity cost of raw water) is not taken into account, then regulators need to be cautious and add the estimated raw water value component to marginal cost. However, shadow price of raw water remains difficult to quantify, in particular with the pipe-borne water. SRMC pricing along with a fixed charge will therefore, increase revenues for the utility operating under increasing returns to scale production and distribution costs.

Simulation results supported theoretical models in chapter 3 that a move from the current tariff structure to a two-part tariff, with SRMC pricing leads to the highest welfare gains. In a broader sense, inefficiency in the pipe-borne water sector leads to an under-valuing and over-use of resources with the resultant loss to other competing uses. Continuation of this situation poses a very serious threat to the society when associated with decreasing inflows and increasing population growth. This and other studies have demonstrated welfare gains can be achieved by increasing pipe-borne water prices and adopting a marginal-cost approach to price determination. This is being practiced in countries like Australia. Nevertheless, while this approach is deemed welfare improving, it is important to address the additional problems that higher prices would create. In Australia, these issues are likely to be addressed through existing concession schemes for pensioners and welfare recipients. Another implication of an increase in water prices based on the LRMC and a fixed charge is that there may be periods when utilities make profits. These profits can be re-invested in water infra-structure and supply expansion.

A major constraint in moving to appropriate water pricing is the absence of meters in some areas. Meters should be installed as benefits exceed the cost. Sewage collection and treatment has not been well established in Sri Lanka. The cost accounting and pricing of sewage treatment also needs to be implemented. It is important to note that the structure of sewage treatment costs is a function of flow rates, treatment technology and input prices. Sewage costs should not be tied to water supply prices unless metering costs are very high (Renzetti, 1999).

The use of analytical and statistical approaches is dependent on the availability of quality data. Many studies have noted constraints on data availability are considerable in applied research, especially in developing countries. Pipe-borne water policy needs to address the data issue by making water accounting practice mandatory for water utilities.

8.3 Further Research

There are a number of limitations on the analyses brought about by lack of data. The current available data for residential water demand analysis does not take into account the differences in households within each district, further panel data analysis using exact household specific characteristics such as household incomes, age and gender distribution within the household and sizes of the house would provide further insights into the factors influencing residential water demand in Sri Lanka. Residential water demand was estimated assuming that household water consumption decisions are affected by only household size due to unavailability of data on other household characteristics. The aggregate data for all the NWSDB districts are matched with household demographics and climate data for each district and interpolation was used to derive monthly income and number of household members for the intervening periods. Aggregate marginal price and difference variables should be weighted by the proportion of households actually consuming in each block and unfortunately, this requires information beyond that was available at present. To capture the influence of climate, monthly and district average temperature and rainfall data are used in the models. Ideally number of rainy days or rain-free days should be used since the water consumption decisions may be influenced more by rainfall frequency than by the intensity.

It is difficult to estimate industrial and commercial water demand representing the aggregate industry or commercial entity since the industrial firms and commercial units use water for different purposes with different intensities. The estimated parameters and price elasticities from such models will not reflect behaviour at the firm level. Therefore, the consistent estimation of water price responsiveness at the firm level requires a panel data set of monthly consumption for a variety of establishments and sufficiently long time horizon. Unfortunately, relatively little data have been collected on industrial and commercial water use in Sri Lanka, therefore, this study does not have disaggregated industrial or commercial water intake data. However, while it is assumed the commercial and industrial water demand is a function of output or sales level, sales or output data could not be obtained, therefore, ignored in the analysis. Panel data analysis using exact industrial and commercial characteristics such as numbers of employees, values of output, types of industry and commercial unit and alternate sources of water would provide much greater insight into the factors influencing the industrial and commercial water demand. The industrial and commercial water demand estimations assumed water is separable from other inputs but data limitations meant this assumption could not be tested. The lack of information on exact industrial and commercial water use may hamper the design of policy instruments aimed at different industry and commercial categories.

It is difficult to estimate the opportunity cost of forgone demand for water; therefore, SRMC is estimated based on existing operating and maintenance costs. Due to data limitations and the problem of heterogeneity, a price index is constructed for price of maintenance as unit cost per cubic metre delivered for cost estimations. The price of capital should reflect interest rates, depreciation rates and purchase price of capital equipment and included in LRMC estimation. Unfortunately, no data on costs of capital or other similar measures are available from the NWSDB; therefore, the price of capital is constructed. The raw water price is not included in the empirical estimation as the NWSDB does not pay for the water initially drawn; however, a constant is added to the marginal cost estimates. But raw water price expects to vary with time across districts. In cost estimation, a single output model is estimated and secondary measures such as water quality or supply disruptions were not included. Additional and better quality data on capital costs and raw water will improve the estimates and hence, the understanding of the underlying costs.

The evaluation of welfare gains are calculated by employing estimated cost and demand coefficients in a simulation program. The estimated welfare effects are influenced by the limitations of data used for cost and demand analyses. The alternative pricing arrangements considered (SRMC and LRMC pricing, average-cost pricing and two-block pricing) are dependent on the cost estimations.

In applied work there is a need to more fully account for user cost and externalities of water use. However, the data set used in this book does not permit the estimation of the shadow price. It is important to compile a data set which can contribute to the understanding of above costs.

In terms of econometric method used, the use of non-linear models and multiple equation estimation are potentially useful in applied work, especially when data sets become more complex and seek for more complex relationships. The demand analysis can be further modified by using other techniques or methodologies like non-linear models and individual household survey data.

In terms of theory, the relationship between returns to scale, elasticity and welfare aspects are areas where more research is required. In addition, to explain capital adjustment in the cost model, a dynamic model is needed.

APPENDIX 1

Table 1: Percentage of Safe Drinking Water and Pipe-borne Water Coverage

District	Safe dirking water (%)	Pipe-borne water (%)
Colombo	95.5	62.3
Gampaha	91.4	22.3
Kalutara	84.0	18.5
Kandy	81.5	38.4
Matale	80.5	22.4
Nuwaraeliya	67.9	50.5
Galle	81.2	19.0
Matara	77.4	28.0
Hambantota	83.4	33.4
Ampara	85.4	9.8
Kurunegala	85.0	3.9
Puttalam	90.2	11.3
Anuradhapura	83.1	9.6
Polonnaruwa	75.3	10.9
Badulla	70.2	37.7
Moneragala	63.4	13.9
Ratnapura	61.3	27.8
Kegalle	69.1	18.2

Source: Population and Housing Census (Department of Census and Statistics, 2001)

Table 2: Loans Provided by ADB and WB for Piped Water Schemes

Project	Amount (US$ million)	Year	Agency
Water supply project I	9.2	1977	WB
Water supply and sewerage project II	30.0	1980	WB
Water supply and sanitation rehabilitation project	37.0	1986	WB
Water services sector project	30.0	1986	ADB
Community water supply and sanitation project	24.3	1992	WB
Second water supply and sanitation project	40.0	1993	ADB
Private sector infra-structure development project	77.0	1996	WB
Third water supply and sanitation project	75.0	1997	ADB
Water resources management project	19.7	2000	ADB
Community water supply and sanitation project II	39.8	2003	WB
Secondary towns and rural community based water supply and sanitation project	60.3	2003	ADB
Jaffna water supply and waste water management project	50.0	2007	ADB
Secondary towns and rural community-based water supply and sanitation project	46.7	2007	ADB
National water management improvement project	66.0	2007	WB
Greater Colombo waste water management project	50.0	2007	ADB
Small towns and rural arid areas water supply and sanitation project	50.0	2008	ADB

Source: MONLAR (2006)

Table 3: NWSDB Residential Connection Charges

Diameter of connection	1997 Oct[a]	1998 Mar[a]	Change %[b]	1999 Aug[a]	Change %[b]	2001 Jan[a]	Change %[b]	2002 Jun[a]	Change %[b]	2005 Mar[a]	Change %[b]
1/2"	50	50	0	60	20	60	0	70	16	70	0
3/4"	100	100	0	120	20	120	0	140	16	140	0
1" – 2"	200	200	0	240	20	240	0	280	16	280	0
2" – 3"	500	500	0	600	20	600	0	700	16	700	0
Above 3"	1000	1000	0	1200	20	1200	0	1400	16	1400	0

Source: NWSDB

[a] tariff rates measured in SLRS per cubic metre, [b] percentage change from the previous tariff structure

Table 4: NWSDB Residential Water Rates

	1994 Jan [a]	1997 Jan [a]	% [b]	1997 Oct [a]	% [b]	1998 Mar [a]	% [b]	1999 Aug [a]	% [b]	2001 Jan [a]	% [b]	20 02	% [b]	2005 Mar [a]	% [b]
Fixed charge	6.00	14.0	140		-100					40		50.25 00		50.00	0
1-10	0.75	0.6	-20	2.5	316	3.0	20	3.50	17	1	-71	1.225 5		1.25	0
11-15	1.30	1.5	14	1.8	20	2.5	39	2.75	10	2	-28	2.525 0		2.50	0
16-20	1.30	1.5	14	1.8	20	2.5	39	2.75	10	5	82	6.530 0		8.50	31
21-25	4.80	5.0	4	6.0	20	7.5	25	9.50	27	13	37	20.54 00		30.00	50
26-30	4.80	9.6	100	12.0	25	14.0	25	18.00	20	24	33	45.88 00		50.00	11
31-40	9.40	12.5	33	14.0	20	18.0	20	20.00	11	30	50	45.50 00		60.00	33
41-50	12.00	18.0	50	20.0	111	20.0	0	25.00	25	40	60	45.12 00		70.00	56
51-75	25.00	32.5	30	35.0	8	35.0	0	38.00	9	45	18	45.0 00		75.00	67
>75	25.00	32.5	30	35.0	8	35.0	0	40.00	14	45	12	45.0 00		75.00	67

Source: NWSDB

[a] tariff rates measured in SLRS per cubic metre, [b] percentage change from the previous tariff structure

Table 5: NWSDB Non-residential Water Rates

User category	1994 Jan[a]	1997 Jan[a]	%[b]	1997 Oct[a]	%[b]	1998 Mar[a a]	%[b]	1999 Aug[a]	%[b]	2001 Jan[a]	%[b]	2002 Jun[a]	%[b]	2005 Mar[a a a]	%[b]
Stand post	2	3	71	4	33	5	25	5	0	6	20	7	17	7	0
Commercial	22	25	14	25	0	28	10	30	9	35	17	42	20	50	19
Tourist hotels	27	27	0	27	0	30	11	30	0	35	17	42	20	50	19
Industries	25	25	0	25	0	28	10	30	9	35	17	42	20	42	0
Shipping	80	80	0	100	25	110	10	120	9	125	4	140	12	250	79
Religious		2	0	2	25	3	20	3	0	3	0	4	33	4	0
BOI								22		24	9	28	17	42	50
Un-metere	140	250	67	300	20	400	33	400	0	400	0				
Un-metere	1400	2500	67	3000	20	3500	17	3500	0	3500	0				

Source: NWSDB

[a] tariff rates measured in SLRS per cubic metre, [b] percentage change from the previous tariff structure

Table 6: Breakdown of Cost of Production of NWSDB for 2004 and 2005 (Rs. Million)

Year	Labour cost	Electricity cost	Chemical cost	Maintenance cost	Other cost	New establish-ment cost	Total cost
2004	1919	1126	171	224	316	451	4207
2005	2541	1245	214	308	355	610	5273
% change	32	10.57	25	38	12	35	25
2006	2922	1392	244	362	402	615	5937
% change	15	12	14	18	13	1	13

Source: NWSDB (2005, 2006a)

Table 7: NWSDB Household Water Tariffs (from 2005 March)

Consumption Range (m^3/month)		Rate (Rs.) (Proposed)
1-10	1-10	1.25
11-15	1-10	1.25
	11-15	2.50
16-20	1-10	1.25
	11-15	2.50
	16-20	8.50
21-25	1-10	1.25
	11-15	2.50
	16-25	30.00
26-30	1-10	1.25
	11-15	2.50
	16-30	50.00
31-40	1-10	1.25
	11-15	2.50
	16-40	60.00
41-50	1-10	1.25
	11-15	2.50
	16-50	70.00
51-75	1-10	1.25
	11-15	2.50
	16-75	75.00
Over 75	1-10	1.25
	11-15	2.50
	16 -Over 75	75.00

Source: NWSDB

Table 8: Panel Unit Root Test Results for Residential Water Demand Estimation

Variable	Test for common unit root process	Test for individual unit root process
Natural log of water quantity	LLC	IPS, ADF-Fisher, PP-Fisher
Natural log of real marginal price	LLC	IPS, ADF-Fisher, PP-Fisher
Natural log of real difference	LLC	IPS, ADF-Fisher, PP-Fisher
Natural log of real mean income	LLC	PP - Fisher
Natural log of real household members	LLC, Breitung	IPS, ADF-Fisher, PP-Fisher
Natural log of temperature	Breitung	IPS, ADF-Fisher, PP-Fisher
Natural log of rainfall	LLC, Breitung	IPS, ADF-Fisher, PP-Fisher

Note: tests that reject the null hypothesis or non-stationarity are given in the table where, LLC – Levin, Lin and Chu t*, Breitung – Breitung t-stat, IPS – Im, Pesaran and Shin W- stat, ADF-Fisher Chi-square –Augmented Dicky Fuller and PP-Fisher Chi-square – Phillip-Perron

Table 9: Panel Unit Root Test Results for Industrial and Commercial Water Demand

Variable	Test for common unit root process	Test for individual unit root process
Natural log of water quantity per industry		ADF-Fisher, PP-Fisher
Natural log of total industry water quantity		PP-Fisher
Natural log of real average price	Breitung	IPS, ADF-Fisher, PP-Fisher
Natural log of total employment in industry	Breitung	PP-Fisher
Natural log of total industry connections		PP - Fisher
Natural log of water quantity per commercial entity	LLC	IPS, ADF-Fisher, PP-Fisher
Natural log of total commercial water quantity	LLC	IPS, ADF-Fisher, PP-Fisher
Natural log of real average price	Breitung	IPS,
Natural log of total employment in commercial entities	Breitung	IPS, ADF-Fisher, PP-Fisher
Natural log of total commercial connections	LLC	IPS, ADF-Fisher, PP-Fisher
Natural log of temperature	Breitung	IPS, ADF-Fisher, PP-Fisher
Natural log of rainfall	LLC, Breitung	IPS, ADF-Fisher, PP-Fisher

Note: tests that reject the null hypothesis or non-stationarity are given in the table where, LLC – Levin, Lin and Chu t*, Breitung – Breitung t-stat, IPS – Im, Pesaran and Shin W- stat, ADF-Fisher Chi-square –Augmented Dicky Fuller and PP-Fisher Chi-square – Phillip-Perron

Table 10: Total Industrial District Water Demand Model Estimates

Variable		OLS - fe	OLS - re	PCSE (correlated)	GLS (panels correlated)
Constant		0.8640	2.1076	7.3814	3.6439
		(3.1108)	(3.0922)	(3.2284)**	(1.2701)***
Average price		-0.1332	-0.2248	-1.3720	-0.2036
		(0.4138)	(0.4183)	(0.7684)*	(0.2923)
No of connections		2.2421	2.1649	1.6977	1.6931
		(0.0946)***	(0.0910)***	(0.0268)***	(0.0064)***
Employees		-0.0314	-0.1244	-0.9633	-0.9573
		(0.0860)	(0.0798)	(0.0383)***	(0.0143)***
Temperature		-0.1150	0.0158	3.3093	2.8251
		(0.8734)	(0.8591)	(0.4000)***	(0.1591)***
Rainfall		-0.0211	-0.0195	0.0176	0.0088
		(0.0303)	(0.0310)	(0.0380)	(0.0100)
Rho		0.8638	0.6781		
R-sq	Within	0.6804	0.6798		
	Between	0.7821	0.7909		
	Overall	0.7379	0.7463	0.8083	

Notes: *** Significant at α = 0.01, ** Significant at α = 0.05 and * Significant at α = 0.10 standard error values (robust) in parentheses below estimates, Dependant variable is natural log of monthly industrial district water demand

Table 11: Total Commercial District Water Demand Model Estimates

Variable		OLS – fe (robust)	OLS – re (robust)	PCSE (correlated)	GLS (panels correlated)
Constant		4.1678	4.0427	0.3538	0.0945
		(1.0447)***	(1.0624)***	(0.8349)	(0.4505)
Average price		-0.1597	-0.1535	-0.2390	-0.1429
		(0.1101)	(0.1148)	(0.2004)	(0.1067)
Employees		0.0671	0.0356	0.0133	0.0045
		(0.1531)	(0.1363)	(0.0132)	(0.0088)
No. of connections		0.7571	0.8189	1.1161	1.1163
		(0.1888)***	(0.1658)***	(0.0080)***	(0.0047)***
Temperature		0.1963	0.1918	0.8498	0.8254
		(0.2185)	(0.2130)	(0.0878)***	(0.0433)***
Rainfall		-0.0109	-0.0111	-0.0319	-0.0210
		(0.0061)*	(0.0062)*	(0.0112)***	(0.0034)***
Rho		0.9095	0.8797		
R-sq	Within	0.3137	0.3135		
	Between	0.9065	0.9067		
	Overall	0.8899	0.8902	0.8922	

Notes: *** Significant at α = 0.01, ** Significant at α = 0.05 and * Significant at α = 0.10 standard error values (robust) in parentheses below estimates, Dependant variable is natural log of monthly water demand

Table 12: Panel Unit Root Test Results for Short-run and Long-run Cost Analyses

Variable	Test for common unit root process	Test for individual unit root process
Natural log of total operating cost	Breitung	IPS, ADF-Fisher, PP-Fisher
Natural log of total cost (including capital)	Breitung	IPS, PP-Fisher
Natural log of total consumption	LLC, Breitung	IPS, ADF-Fisher, PP-Fisher
Natural log of price for chemicals	LLC, Breitung	IPS, ADF-Fisher, PP-Fisher
Natural log of average price of electricity	Breitung	
Natural log of real wage of labour	LLC, Breitung	IPS, ADF-Fisher, PP-Fisher
Natural log of real unit maintenance cost	LLC, Breitung	IPS, ADF-Fisher, PP-Fisher
Natural log of price of capital	LLC	
Short-run Share of labour	LLC, Breitung	IPS, ADF-Fisher, PP-Fisher
Share of electricity	LLC, Breitung	IPS, ADF-Fisher, PP-Fisher
Share of chemical	LLC, Breitung	IPS, ADF-Fisher, PP-Fisher
Share of maintenance	LLC, Breitung	IPS, ADF-Fisher, PP-Fisher
Long-run Share of capital	Breitung	IPS, ADF-Fisher, PP-Fisher
Share of labour	LLC, Breitung	IPS, ADF-Fisher, PP-Fisher
Share of electricity	LLC, Breitung	IPS, ADF-Fisher, PP-Fisher
Share of chemical	LLC, Breitung	IPS, ADF-Fisher, PP-Fisher
Share of maintenance	LLC, Breitung	IPS, ADF-Fisher, PP-Fisher

Note: tests that reject the null hypothesis or non-stationarity are given in the table where, LLC – Levin, Lin and Chu t*, Breitung – Breitung t-stat, IPS – Im, Pesaran and Shin W- stat, ADF-Fisher Chi-square –Augmented Dicky Fuller and PP-Fisher Chi-square – Phillip-Perron

Table 13: Short-run Cost Analysis – with and without Imposing Concavity

Variable	Parameter	Trans-log (without imposing concavity)	Trans-log (with imposing concavity)
$\ln Q$	β_Q	0.9798 (0.1741)***	0.9105 (0.1811)***
$\ln Q * \ln Q$	β_{QQ}	0.0123 (0.0158)	0.0065 (0.0162)
$\ln W_l$	α_L	1.3367 (0.0563)***	0.7936 (0.0137)***
$\ln W_e$	α_E	-0.0302 (0.0522)	0.0335 (0.0108)**
$\ln W_c$	α_C	-0.1809 (0.0203)***	0.0014 (0.0028)
$\ln W_m$	α_M	0.1459 (0.0293)***	0.1714 (0.0174)***
$\ln W_l * \ln Q$	β_{LQ}	-0.0569 (0.0029)***	-0.0366 (0.0028)***
$\ln W_e * \ln Q$	β_{EQ}	0.0153 (0.0028)***	0.0068 (0.0028)***
$\ln W_c * \ln Q$	β_{CQ}	0.0073 (0.0012)***	-0.0020 (0.0008)***
$\ln W_m * \ln Q$	β_{MQ}	0.0343 (0.0015)***	0.0318 (0.0014)***
$\ln W_l * \ln W_l$	γ_{LL}	-0.0238 (0.0072)***	0.0119 (0.0052)**
$\ln W_e * \ln W_e$	γ_{EE}	-0.0022 (0.0071)***	0.0045 (0.0050)
$\ln W_c * \ln W_c$	γ_{CC}	0.0043 (0.0027)**	-0.0046 (0.0024)*
$\ln W_m * \ln W_m$	γ_{MM}	0.0917 (0.0015)***	0.0870 (0.0013)***

Table 13 (contd.)

Variable	Parameter	Trans-log (without imposing concavity)	Trans-log (with imposing concavity)
$\ln W_l * \ln W_e$	γ_{LE}	0.0537 (0.0070)***	0.0228 (0.0048)***
$\ln W_l * \ln W_c$	γ_{LC}	0.0171 (0.0022)***	0.0111 (0.0017)***
$\ln W_l * \ln W_m$	γ_{LM}	-0.0469 (0.0021)***	-0.0459 (0.0023)***
$\ln W_e * \ln W_m$	γ_{EM}	-0.0374 (0.0030)***	-0.0309 (0.0028)***
$\ln W_c * \ln W_m$	γ_{CM}	-0.0074 (0.0012)**	-0.0102 (0.0013)***
$\ln W_e * \ln W_c$	γ_{EC}	-0.0140 (0.0033)***	0.0036 (0.0024)
t	ω_T	-0.0178 (0.0017)***	-0.0189 (0.0015)***
t * t	ω_{TT}	-0.0001 (0.0000)*	-0.0001 (0.0000)***
$\ln W_l * time$	ω_{LT}	0.0020 (0.0002)***	0.0019 (0.0001)***
$\ln W_e * t$	ω_{ET}	-0.0022 (0.0001)***	-0.0021 (0.0001)***
$\ln W_c * t$	ω_{CT}	-0.0005 (0.0001)***	-0.0006 (0.0001)***
$\ln W_m * t$	ω_{MT}	-0.0007 (0.0003)***	0.0008 (0.0001)***
District dummy	D_1	-0.0643 (0.0279)**	-0.0610 (0.0290)**

Table 13 (contd.)

Variable	Parameter	Trans-log (without imposing concavity)	Trans-log (with imposing concavity)
District dummy	D_2	0.0692 (0.0235)**	0.0660 (0.0209)**
District dummy	D_3	-0.0336 (0.0211)*	-0.0369 (0.0208)*
District dummy	D_4	0.0131 (0.0252)	0.0127 (0.0236)
District dummy	D_5	0.0531 (0.0230)**	0.0519 (0.0242)**
District dummy	D_6	0.0565 (0.0369)*	0.0551 (0.0350)**
District dummy	D_7	0.0945 (0.0242)***	0.0947 (0.0209)***
District dummy	D_8	-0.0274 (0.0300)	-0.0224 (0.0209)
District dummy	D_9	-0.0906 (0.0234)***	-0.0913 (0.0228)***
District dummy	D_{10}	0.2968 (0.1719)***	0.2907 (0.1720)***
District dummy	D_{11}	-0.1273 (0.0353)***	-0.1224 (0.0362)***
District dummy	D_{12}	-0.1863 (0.0793)***	-0.1620 (0.0764)***
District dummy	D_{13}	0.1365 (0.0405)***	-0.1321 (0.0399)***
Constant	α_0	-2.9142 (0.9736)***	-0.8053 (1.0116)
	$\bar{R}^2$	0.9958	0.9950

Notes: *** Significant at α = 0.01, ** Significant at α = 0.05 and * Significant at α = 0.10 standard error values in parentheses below estimates

Table 14: Long-run Cost Analysis – with and without Imposing Concavity

Variable	Parameter	Trans-log (without imposing concavity)	Trans-log (with imposing concavity)
$\ln Q$	β_Q	1.4884 (0.1650)***	1.9528 (0.1789)***
$\ln Q * \ln Q$	β_{QQ}	-0.0264 (0.0145)**	-0.0622 (0.0158)**
$\ln W_k$	α_K	0.2893 (0.0466)***	0.2552 (0.0352)***
$\ln W_l$	α_L	0.8176 (0.0625)***	0.3936 (0.0410)***
$\ln W_e$	α_E	0.1182 (0.0441)***	0.2198 (0.0293)***
$\ln W_c$	α_C	-0.1264 (0.0185)***	0.0061 (0.0032)**
$\ln W_m$	α_M	-0.0987 (0.0272)***	0.1253 (0.0037)***
$\ln W_k * \ln Q$	β_{KQ}	0.0210 (0.0019)***	0.0241 (0.0017)***
$\ln W_l * \ln Q$	β_{LQ}	-0.0705 (0.0023)***	-0.0604 (0.0029)***
$\ln W_e * \ln Q$	β_{EQ}	0.0170 (0.0022)***	0.0238 (0.0021)***
$\ln W_c * \ln Q$	β_{CQ}	0.0059 (0.0009)***	0.017 (0.0007)***
$\ln W_m * \ln Q$	β_{MQ}	0.0264 (0.0015)***	0.0108 (0.0011)***
$\ln W_k * \ln W_k$	γ_{KK}	0.0441 (0.0066)***	0.0255 (0.0058)***
$\ln W_l * \ln W_l$	γ_{LL}	0.0474 (0.0077)***	0.0781 (0.0048)***

Table 14 (contd.)

Variable	Parameter	Trans-log (without imposing concavity)	Trans-log (with imposing concavity)
$\ln W_e * \ln W_e$	γ_{EE}	-0.0568 (0.0088)***	-0.0805 (0.0078)***
$\ln W_c * \ln W_c$	γ_{CC}	0.0133 (0.0022)***	0.0013 (0.0017)
$\ln W_m * \ln W_m$	γ_{MM}	0.1107 (0.0017)***	0.1279 (0.0040)***
$\ln W_l * \ln W_k$	γ_{LK}	-0.0151 (0.0048)***	-0.0286 (0.0035)***
$\ln W_l * \ln W_e$	γ_{LE}	0.0072 (0.0049)**	-0.0073 (0.0033)**
$\ln W_l * \ln W_c$	γ_{LC}	-0.0008 (0.0020)	-0.0029 (0.0017)*
$\ln W_l * \ln W_m$	γ_{LM}	-0.0387 (0.0020)***	-0.0393 (0.0018)***
$\ln W_e * \ln W_k$	γ_{EK}	0.0508 (0.0066)***	0.0707 (0.0063)***
$\ln W_e * \ln W_m$	γ_{EM}	-0.0073 (0.0031)**	0.0056 (0.0024)**
$\ln W_e * \ln W_c$	γ_{EC}	0.0061 (0.0035)**	0.0115 (0.0027)***
$\ln W_c * \ln W_k$	γ_{CK}	-0.0168 (0.0029)***	-0.0050 (0.0020)**
$\ln W_c * \ln W_m$	γ_{CM}	-0.0018 (0.0011)	-0.0049 (0.0009)***
$\ln W_k * \ln W_m$	γ_{MK}	-0.0630 (0.0020)***	-0.0566 (0.0017)***
t	ω_T	0.0087 (0.0016)**	0.0077 (0.0013)**

Table 14 (contd.)

Variable	Parameter	Trans-log (without imposing concavity)	Trans-log (with imposing concavity)
t * t	ω_{TT}	-0.0002 (0.0000)***	-0.0002 (0.0000)***
$\ln W_k * time$	ω_{KT}	-0.0000 (0.0000)	0.0001 (0.0000)**
$\ln W_l * time$	ω_{LT}	0.0001 (0.0000)**	0.0001 (0.0000)**
$\ln W_e * t$	ω_{ET}	-0.0002 (0.0000)***	-0.0001 (0.0000)**
$\ln W_c * t$	ω_{CT}	-0.0001 (0.0000)**	-0.0001 (0.0000)**
$\ln W_m * t$	ω_{MT}	0.0002 (0.0001)**	-0.0000 (0.0001)
District dummy	D_1	-0.0423 (0.0272)**	-0.0425 (0.0273)**
District dummy	D_2	0.1589 (0.0210)***	0.1528 (0.0189)***
District dummy	D_3	0.0257 (0.0199)**	0.0236 (0.0196)*
District dummy	D_4	0.0625 (0.0211)**	0.0612 (0.0218)**
District dummy	D_5	0.0112 (0.0235)	0.0079 (0.0221)
District dummy	D_6	0.3366 (0.0337)***	0.3260 (0.0349)***
District dummy	D_7	0.1582 (0.0200)***	0.1442 (0.0194)***
District dummy	D_8	-0.1389 (0.0282)***	-0.1447 (0.0276)***

Table 14 (contd.)

Variable	Parameter	Trans-log (without imposing concavity)	Trans-log (with imposing concavity)
District dummy	D_9	-0.0937 (0.0223)**	-0.0797 (0.0212)**
District dummy	D_{10}	1.2315 (0.1574)***	1.2981 (0.1628)***
District dummy	D_{11}	-0.2638 (0.0344)***	-0.2499 (0.0336)***
District dummy	D_{12}	-0.5847 (0.0694)***	-0.5778 (0.0700)***
District dummy	D_{13}	-0.2358 (0.0373)***	-0.2133 (0.0373)***
Constant	α_0	-1.7678 (0.9716)**	-3.8466 (0.1033)***
Berndt $\bar{R}^2$	$\bar{R}^2$	0.9988	0.9987

Notes: *** Significant at α = 0.01, ** Significant at α = 0.05 and * Significant at α = 0.10 standard error values in parentheses below estimates, Dependant variable is natural log of monthly total cost of water

Table 15: Price Elasticity of Demand for Residential Users – Income Deciles

Income deciles	Income	Price elasticity
1	13565.09	0.11
2	15604.46	0.13
3	17051.78	0.12
4	18448.79	0.12
5	19787.15	0.14
6	21262.27	0.13
7	22535.37	0.12
8	24077.12	0.13
9	26773.80	0.13
10	37296.72	0.18
Average	21640.02	0.11

Figure 1: NWSDB Employees for Thousand Connections

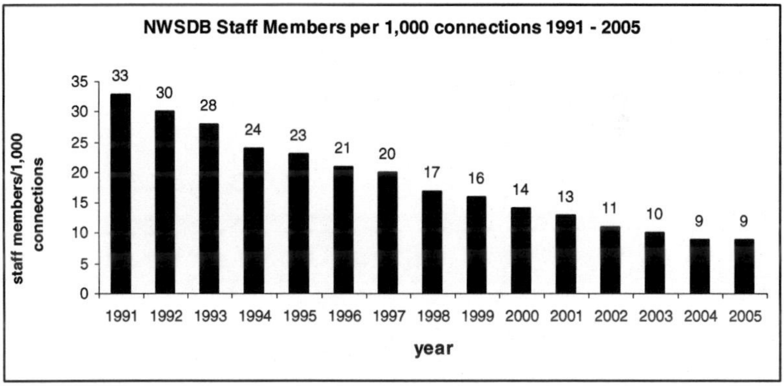

Source: NWSDB, 2005

Figure 2: NWSDB Bill Collection Efficiency

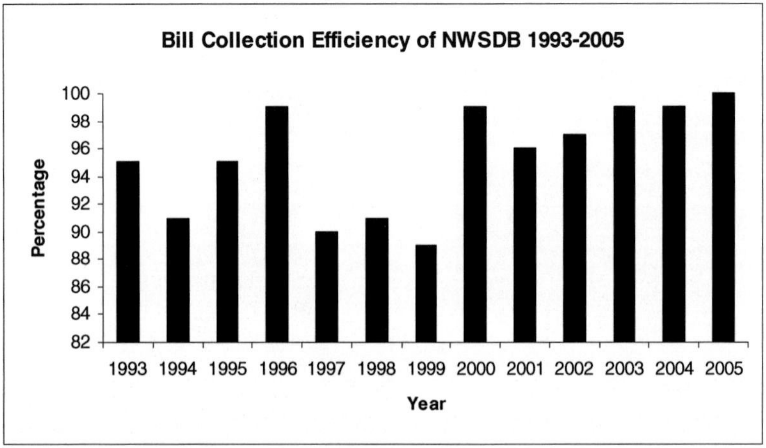

Source: NWSDB, 2005

Figure 3: Number of Pipe-born Water Connections

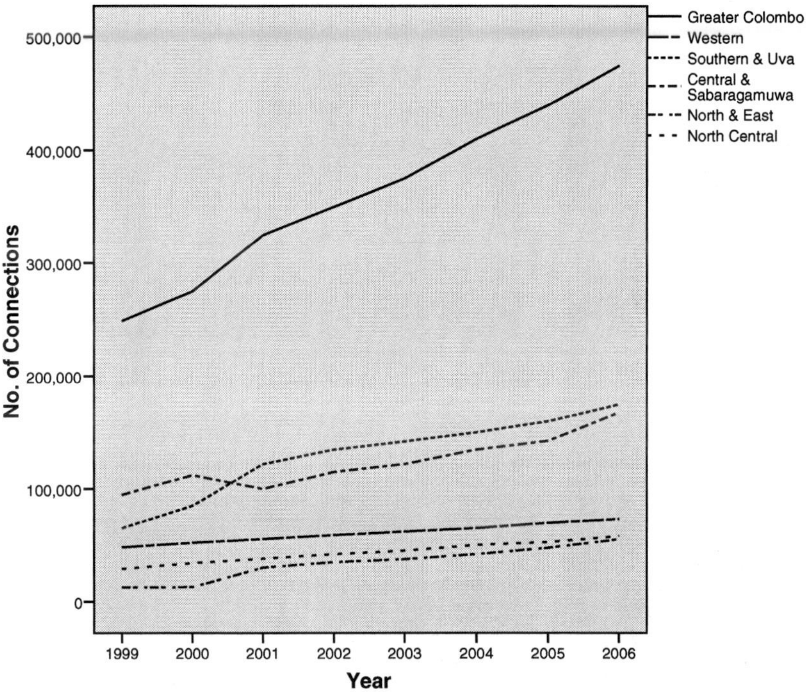

Source: NWSDB, 2005

Figure 4: Monthly Variation in Industrial Water Use

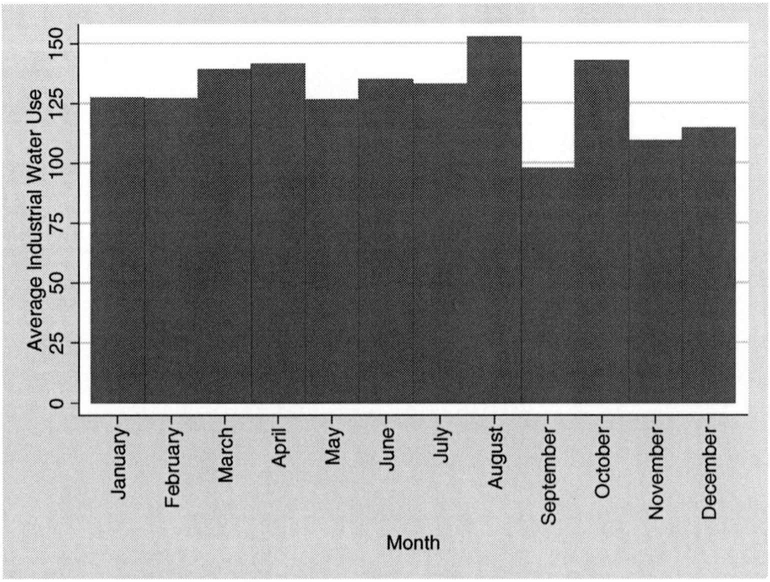

Figure 5: Monthly Variation in Commercial Water Use

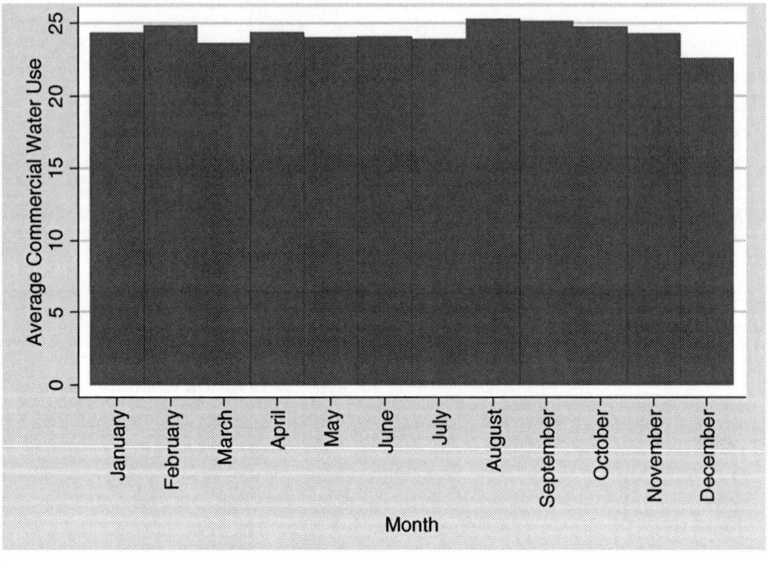

Appendix 2

Deriving Cost Function using Cobb-Douglas Function

Constant returns to scale

The Cobb-Douglas production function satisfies homogeneity of degree one in input prices, homogeneity of degree one in output, concavity in input prices and non-decreasing in input prices. Moreover, the homogeneity requirement means that this production technology exhibits constant returns to scale, a proportionate increase in both inputs results in the same proportionate increase in outputs.

$q = f(k,l) = k^{\alpha} l^{1-\alpha}$ where q- total cubic metres k-amount of fixed inputs, l - amount of variable inputs

$C = f(w,k,v,l) = vk + wl$ where w, v are prices of variable and fixed inputs

Deriving the long-run total cost

Minimize $C = f(w,k,v,l)$ subject to $q = f(k,l)$

$$L = vk + wl + \lambda(q - k^{\alpha} l^{1-\alpha})$$

$$foc\ \ L_k = v - \alpha\lambda k^{\alpha-1} l^{1-\alpha} = 0$$

$$L_l = w - (1-\alpha)\lambda k^{\alpha} l^{1-\alpha-1} = 0$$

$$L_\lambda = q - k^{\alpha} l^{1-\alpha} = 0$$

$$l^* = \left[\frac{v}{w}\frac{(1-\alpha)}{\alpha}\right]k \qquad and \qquad k^* = \left[\frac{w}{v}\frac{\alpha}{(1-\alpha)}\right]l$$

subsituting in prodcution function

$$l = \left[\left(\frac{w}{v}\frac{\alpha}{(1-\alpha)}\right)^{\alpha} q^{-1}\right]^{-1} = \left(\frac{1-\alpha}{\alpha}\right)^{\alpha}\left(\frac{v}{w}\right)^{\alpha}(q)$$

$$k = \left[\left(\frac{v}{w}\frac{(1-\alpha)}{\alpha}\right)^{1-\alpha} q^{-1}\right]^{-1} = \left(\frac{\alpha}{1-\alpha}\right)^{1-\alpha}\left(\frac{w}{v}\right)^{1-\alpha}(q)$$

substituting l and k back in the cost function

$$C = w\left[\left(\frac{1-\alpha}{\alpha}\right)^{\alpha}\left(\frac{v}{w}\right)^{\alpha}(q)\right] + v\left[\left(\frac{\alpha}{1-\alpha}\right)^{1-\alpha}\left(\frac{w}{v}\right)^{1-\alpha}(q)\right]$$

$$C = (q)v^{\alpha}w^{1-\alpha}\left[\left(\frac{\alpha}{1-\alpha}\right)^{1-\alpha}\left(\frac{1-\alpha}{\alpha}\right)^{\alpha}\right]$$

$$let\ D = \left(\frac{\alpha}{1-\alpha}\right)^{1-\alpha}\left(\frac{1-\alpha}{\alpha}\right)^{\alpha}$$

$$C = D(q)v^{\alpha}w^{1-\alpha}$$

Marginal cost can be defined as $MC = \frac{\partial C}{\partial q} = Dq^{-1}v^{\alpha}w^{1-\alpha}$

Taking the natural logarithm of TC

$$\ln C = \ln D + \ln q + \alpha \ln v + (1-\alpha)\ln w$$

$$\frac{\partial \ln C}{\partial \ln q} = 1$$

$$MC = \frac{C}{q}$$

Cost shares of each input:

$$\frac{wl}{C} = 1-\alpha \ \ and\ \ \frac{vk}{C} = \alpha$$

Non-constant returns to scale

There are situations where the constant-return-to-scale assumption is relaxed and a more flexible technology is sought. Water utilities and other industries may have barriers to entry that promote economies of scale. The following derivation presents a minimum cost function subject to a production constraint in a similar manner to the above constant returns to scale formulation but without the assumption about constant returns. Three factors of production are considered; capital, labour and energy.

Scale economies or returns to scale are usually defined in terms of the relative increase in output resulting from a proportionate increase in all inputs. It is more appropriate to represent scale economies by the relationship between cost and output along the expansion path, where input prices are held fixed and costs are minimized at every level of output

(L. Brown & Chachere, 1980; Hanoch, 1975). Formally, scale economies are measured by the relationship of average cost to marginal cost and can be given as $Scale\,economies(SE) = \frac{C}{Q*MC}$ where C is total cost, Q is level of output and MC is the marginal cost with respect to the output. If $SE > 1$, there exist economies of scale; if $SE = 1$, then constant returns to scale exist; and if $SE < 1$, diseconomies of scale exist.

$q = f(k,l) = l^{\alpha}k^{\beta}m^{\delta}$ where q - total cubic metres k - amount of fixed inputs, l and m - amount of variable inputs labour and energy

$C = f(w,k,v,l,s,m) = wl + vk + sm$ where $w, s\, and\, v$ are prices of variable and fixed inputs

Deriving the long-run total cost

Minimize $C = f(w,k,v,l,s,m)$ subject to $q = f(k,l,m)$

The sum of the exponents is the scale economies parameter $\Omega = \alpha + \beta + \delta; 0 \le \alpha \le 1, 0 \le \beta \le 1\, and\, 0 \le \delta \le 1$.

$$L = wl + vk + sm + \lambda(q - l^{\alpha}k^{\beta}m^{\delta})$$

$$foc\ L_l = w - \alpha\lambda l^{\alpha-1}k^{\beta}m^{\delta} = 0$$

$$L_k = v - \beta\lambda l^{\alpha}k^{\beta-1}m^{\delta} = 0$$

$$L_m = s - \delta\lambda l^{\alpha}k^{\beta}m^{\delta-1} = 0$$

$$L_{\lambda} = q - l^{\alpha}k^{\beta}m^{\delta} = 0$$

The first order condition yield three price ratios

$$\frac{w}{v} = \frac{\alpha}{\beta}\frac{k}{l}$$

$$\frac{w}{s} = \frac{\alpha}{\delta}\frac{m}{l}$$

$$\frac{v}{s} = \frac{\beta}{\delta}\frac{m}{k}$$

Using these equations, variable cost function can be decomposed into shares,

$$C = l\left(w + \frac{vk}{l} + \frac{sm}{l}\right), \text{ from above price ratios } \begin{array}{l} w\dfrac{\beta}{\alpha} = \dfrac{vk}{l} \\ w\dfrac{\delta}{\alpha} = \dfrac{sm}{l} \end{array}$$

$$C = l\left(w + w\frac{\beta}{\alpha} + w\frac{\delta}{\alpha}\right) = lw\left(1 + \frac{\beta}{\alpha} + \frac{\delta}{\alpha}\right) \text{ since } \Omega = \alpha + \beta + \delta$$

$$C = \frac{\Omega}{\alpha} wl$$

The cost shares are $\frac{wl}{C} = \frac{\alpha}{\Omega}$, $\frac{vk}{C} = \frac{\beta}{\Omega}$, $\frac{sm}{C} = \frac{\delta}{\Omega}$

The production function is used to derive the conditional factor demand for labour

$$l = \left[q\left(\frac{w}{v}\frac{\beta}{\alpha}\right)^{-\beta} \left(\frac{w}{s}\frac{\delta}{\alpha}\right)^{-\delta} \right]^{\frac{1}{\Omega}}$$

substituting l back in the cost function

$$C = \frac{\Omega}{\alpha} wl$$

$$C = \frac{\Omega}{\alpha} w\left[q\left(\frac{w}{v}\frac{\beta}{\alpha}\right)^{-\beta} \left(\frac{w}{s}\frac{\delta}{\alpha}\right)^{-\delta} \right]^{\frac{1}{\Omega}}$$

$$C(w,v,s,q) = \Omega\left(\frac{\alpha}{w}\right)^{\frac{-\alpha}{\Omega}} \left(\frac{\beta}{v}\right)^{\frac{-\beta}{\Omega}} \left(\frac{\delta}{s}\right)^{\frac{-\delta}{\Omega}} q^{\frac{1}{\Omega}}$$

$$let D = \Omega \alpha^{\frac{-\alpha}{\Omega}} \beta^{\frac{-\beta}{\Omega}} \delta^{\frac{-\delta}{\Omega}}$$

$$C(w,v,s,q) = D(w)^{\frac{\alpha}{\Omega}} (v)^{\frac{\beta}{\Omega}} (s)^{\frac{\delta}{\Omega}} q^{\frac{1}{\Omega}}$$

$$MC = \frac{1}{\Omega} D(w)^{\frac{\alpha}{\Omega}} (v)^{\frac{\beta}{\Omega}} (s)^{\frac{\delta}{\Omega}} q^{\frac{1}{\Omega}-1}$$

$$\ln C = \ln D + \frac{1}{\alpha+\beta+\delta}\ln q + \frac{\alpha}{\alpha+\beta+\delta}\ln w + \frac{\beta}{\alpha+\beta+\delta}\ln v + \frac{\delta}{\alpha+\beta+\delta}\ln s$$

$$\frac{\partial \ln C}{\partial \ln q} = \frac{1}{\alpha+\beta+\delta}$$

$$MC = \frac{1}{\alpha+\beta+\delta}\frac{C}{q}$$

$$\text{Scale economies} = \frac{1}{\cos t\, elasticity\, of\ output} = \frac{\partial \ln q}{\partial \ln C} = \alpha + \beta + \delta = \Omega$$

The measure of overall scale economies describes the behaviour of costs as all outputs increase by strictly the same proportion. However, since the input mixes rarely remain constant as output changes, the overall scale economies measure do not fully describe the behaviour of costs as the output changes (Kim, 1987).

Constant Elasticities of Substitution (CES) production function

The CES production function exhibits homogeneity of degree one in factor inputs, quasi-concavity and twice differentiability. The CES production function expresses a firm's output q as a function of its inputs, capital k and labour l:

$q = f(k,l) = \left(k^{\rho} + l^{\rho}\right)^{\frac{\gamma}{\rho}}$ where γ - returns to scale factor $\sigma = \frac{1}{1-\rho}$ - factor reflecting the elasticity of substitution

Deriving long-run total cost

Minimize $C = f(w,k,v,l)$ subject to $q = f(k,l)$

$$L = vk + wl + \lambda\left[q - \left(k^{\rho} + l^{\rho}\right)^{\frac{\gamma}{\rho}}\right]$$

$$foc\ \ L_k = v - \frac{\gamma}{\rho}\lambda\left(k^{\rho} + l^{\rho}\right)^{\frac{\gamma-\rho}{\rho}}\left(\rho k^{\rho-1}\right) = 0$$

$$L_l = w - \frac{\gamma}{\rho}\lambda\left(k^{\rho} + l^{\rho}\right)^{\frac{\gamma-\rho}{\rho}}\left(\rho l^{\rho-1}\right) = 0$$

$$L_{\lambda} = q - \left(k^{\rho} + l^{\rho}\right)^{\frac{\gamma}{\rho}} = 0$$

$$l^* = k\left(\frac{w}{v}\right)^{\frac{1}{\rho-1}} \quad and \quad k^* = l\left(\frac{v}{w}\right)^{\frac{1}{\rho-1}}$$

$$\textit{subsituting and simplify}\ \sigma = \frac{1}{1-\rho}$$

$$l = q^{\frac{1}{\gamma}}\left[\left(\frac{v}{w}\right)^{\frac{\rho}{\rho-1}} + 1\right]^{\frac{-1}{\rho}} = q^{\frac{1}{\gamma}}\left(v^{1-\sigma} + w^{1-\sigma}\right)^{\frac{\sigma}{1-\sigma}} w^{-\sigma}$$

$$k = q^{\frac{1}{\gamma}}\left[\left(\frac{w}{v}\right)^{\frac{\rho}{\rho-1}} + 1\right]^{\frac{-1}{\rho}} = q^{\frac{1}{\gamma}}\left(v^{1-\sigma} + w^{1-\sigma}\right)^{\frac{\sigma}{1-\sigma}} v^{-\sigma}$$

$$\textit{substituting l and k back in the}\ \cos t\ \textit{function}$$

$$C = w\left[q^{\frac{1}{\gamma}}\left(v^{1-\sigma} + w^{1-\sigma}\right)^{\frac{\sigma}{1-\sigma}} w^{-\sigma}\right] + v\left[q^{\frac{1}{\gamma}}\left(v^{1-\sigma} + w^{1-\sigma}\right)^{\frac{\sigma}{1-\sigma}} v^{-\sigma}\right]$$

$$C = q^{\frac{1}{\gamma}}\left(v^{1-\sigma} + w^{1-\sigma}\right)^{\frac{\sigma}{1-\sigma}}\left[v(v)^{-\sigma} + w(w)^{-\sigma}\right]$$

Marginal cost can be defined as

$$MC = \frac{\partial C}{\partial q} = \left(\frac{1}{\gamma}\right) q^{\frac{1}{\gamma}-1}\left(v^{1-\sigma} + w^{1-\sigma}\right)^{\frac{\sigma}{1-\sigma}}\left[v^{1-\sigma} + w^{1-\sigma}\right]$$

$$MC = \left(\frac{1}{\gamma}\right) q^{\frac{1-\gamma}{\gamma}}\left(v^{1-\sigma} + w^{1-\sigma}\right)^{\frac{\sigma}{1-\sigma}}\left[v^{1-\sigma} + w^{1-\sigma}\right]$$

Imposing Concavity for the Short-run Cost Function

Let the lower triangular element of D be

$$D = \begin{bmatrix} d_{11} & 0 & 0 & 0 \\ d_{21} & d_{22} & 0 & 0 \\ d_{31} & d_{32} & d_{33} & 0 \\ d_{41} & d_{42} & d_{43} & d_{44} \end{bmatrix}$$

Then DD' can be shown to be

$$DD'=\begin{bmatrix} d_{11}^2 & d_{11}d_{21} & d_{11}d_{31} & d_{11}d_{41} \\ d_{11}d_{21} & d_{21}^2+d_{22}^2 & d_{21}d_{31}+d_{22}d_{32} & d_{21}d_{41}+d_{22}d_{42} \\ d_{11}d_{31} & d_{21}d_{31}+d_{22}d_{32} & d_{31}^2+d_{32}^2+d_{33}^2 & d_{31}d_{41}+d_{32}d_{42}+d_{33}d_{43} \\ d_{11}d_{41} & d_{21}d_{41}+d_{22}d_{42} & d_{31}d_{41}+d_{32}d_{42}+d_{33}d_{43} & d_{41}^2+d_{42}^2+d_{43}^2+d_{44}^2 \end{bmatrix}$$

By replacing ijth element of the matrix DD' expressed above with $-(DD')_{ij}$, the parameters $\gamma_{11}, \gamma_{12}, \gamma_{13}, \gamma_{14}, \gamma_{22}, \gamma_{23}, \gamma_{24}, \gamma_{33}, \gamma_{34}$ *and* γ_{44} can be expressed as

$$\gamma_{11} = -d_{11}^2 + \alpha_1 - \alpha_1^2$$
$$\gamma_{12} = -d_{11}d_{21} - \alpha_1\alpha_2$$
$$\gamma_{13} = -d_{11}d_{31} - \alpha_1\alpha_3$$
$$\gamma_{14} = -d_{11}d_{41} - \alpha_1\alpha_4$$
$$\gamma_{22} = -d_{21}^2 - d_{22}^2 + \alpha_2 - \alpha_2^2$$
$$\gamma_{23} = -d_{21}d_{21} - d_{22}d_{32} - \alpha_2\alpha_3$$
$$\gamma_{24} = -d_{21}d_{41} - d_{22}d_{42} - \alpha_2\alpha_4$$
$$\gamma_{33} = -d_{31}^2 - d_{32}^2 - d_{33}^2 + \alpha_3 - \alpha_3^2$$
$$\gamma_{34} = -d_{31}d_{41} - d_{32}d_{42} - d_{33}d_{43} - \alpha_3\alpha_4$$
$$\gamma_{44} = -d_{41}^2 - d_{42}^2 - d_{43}^2 - d_{44}^2 + \alpha_4 - \alpha_4^2$$

The parameters $\gamma_{14}, \gamma_{24}, \gamma_{34}$ *and* γ_{44} are estimated imposing the constraint $\sum_{i=1}^{n}\gamma_{ij} = \sum_{j=1}^{n}\gamma_{ji} = \sum_{i=1}^{n}\sum_{j=1}^{n}\gamma_{ij} = 0$

Imposing Concavity for the Long-run Cost Function

Let the lower triangular element of D be

$$D=\begin{bmatrix} d_{11} & 0 & 0 & 0 & 0 \\ d_{21} & d_{22} & 0 & 0 & 0 \\ d_{31} & d_{32} & d_{33} & 0 & 0 \\ d_{41} & d_{42} & d_{43} & d_{44} & 0 \\ d_{51} & d_{52} & d_{53} & d_{54} & d_{55} \end{bmatrix}$$

Then DD' can be shown to be

$$DD'=\begin{bmatrix} d_{11}^2 & d_{11}d_{21} & d_{11}d_{31} & d_{11}d_{41} & d_{11}d_{51} \\ d_{11}d_{21} & d_{21}^2+d_{22}^2 & d_{21}d_{31}+d_{22}d_{32} & d_{21}d_{41}+d_{22}d_{42} & d_{21}d_{51}+d_{22}d_{52} \\ d_{11}d_{31} & d_{21}d_{31}+d_{22}d_{32} & d_{31}^2+d_{32}^2+d_{33}^2 & d_{31}d_{41}+d_{32}d_{42}+d_{33}d_{43} & d_{31}d_{51}+d_{32}d_{52}+d_{33}d_{53} \\ d_{11}d_{41} & d_{21}d_{41}+d_{22}d_{42} & d_{31}d_{41}+d_{32}d_{42}+d_{33}d_{43} & d_{41}^2+d_{42}^2+d_{43}^2+d_{44}^2 & d_{51}d_{41}+d_{52}d_{42}+d_{53}d_{43}+d_{44}d_{54} \\ d_{11}d_{51} & d_{21}d_{51}+d_{22}d_{52} & d_{31}d_{51}+d_{32}d_{52}+d_{33}d_{53} & d_{51}d_{41}+d_{52}d_{42}+d_{53}d_{43}+d_{44}d_{54} & d_{51}^2+d_{52}^2+d_{53}^2+d_{54}^2+d_{55}^2 \end{bmatrix}$$

By replacing ij^{th} element of the matrix DD' expressed above with $-(DD')_{ij}$, the parameters

$\gamma_{11}, \gamma_{12}, \gamma_{13}, \gamma_{14}, \gamma_{22}, \gamma_{23}, \gamma_{24}, \gamma_{33}, \gamma_{34}$ *and* γ_{44} can be expressed as

$$\gamma_{11}=-d_{11}^2+\alpha_1-\alpha_1^2$$
$$\gamma_{12}=-d_{11}d_{21}-\alpha_1\alpha_2$$
$$\gamma_{13}=-d_{11}d_{31}-\alpha_1\alpha_3$$
$$\gamma_{14}=-d_{11}d_{41}-\alpha_1\alpha_4$$
$$\gamma_{15}=-d_{11}d_{51}-\alpha_1\alpha_5$$
$$\gamma_{22}=-d_{21}^2-d_{22}^2+\alpha_2-\alpha_2^2$$
$$\gamma_{23}=-d_{21}d_{21}-d_{22}d_{32}-\alpha_2\alpha_3$$
$$\gamma_{24}=-d_{21}d_{41}-d_{22}d_{42}-\alpha_2\alpha_4$$
$$\gamma_{24}=-d_{21}d_{51}-d_{22}d_{52}-\alpha_2\alpha_5$$
$$\gamma_{33}=-d_{31}^2-d_{32}^2-d_{33}^2+\alpha_3-\alpha_3^2$$
$$\gamma_{34}=-d_{31}d_{41}-d_{32}d_{42}-d_{33}d_{43}-\alpha_3\alpha_4$$
$$\gamma_{34}=-d_{31}d_{51}-d_{32}d_{52}-d_{33}d_{53}-\alpha_3\alpha_5$$
$$\gamma_{44}=-d_{41}^2-d_{42}^2-d_{43}^2-d_{44}^2+\alpha_4-\alpha_4^2$$
$$\gamma_{45}=-d_{41}d_{51}-d_{42}d_{52}-d_{43}d_{53}-d_{44}d_{54}-\alpha_4\alpha_5$$
$$\gamma_{55}=-d_{51}^2-d_{52}^2-d_{53}^2-d_{54}^2-d_{55}^2+\alpha_5-\alpha_5^2$$

The parameters $\gamma_{15}, \gamma_{25}, \gamma_{35}, \gamma_{45}$ *and* γ_{55} are estimated imposing constraint $\sum_{i=1}^{n}\gamma_{ij} = \sum_{j=1}^{n}\gamma_{ji} = \sum_{i=1}^{n}\sum_{j=1}^{n}\gamma_{ij} = 0$

REFERENCES

ADB (1993). *Water Utilities Data Book: Asian and Pacific Region.* Manila: Asian Development Bank.

—. (1997). *Third water supply and sanitation project.* Colombo: Asian Development Bank.

—. (2000). *Second water supply and sanitation project* Colombo: Asian Development Bank.

—. (2001). *Water for All.* Manila: Water Policy of the Asian Development Bank.

—. (2007). *Sri Lanka Country Assistance Program Evaluation: Water Supply and Sanitation Sector Assistance Evaluation*: Operations Evaluation Department, Asian Development Bank.

Agthe, D., and Billings, B. (1987). Equity, Price Elasticity and household income under increasing block rates for water. *American Journal of Economics and Sociology, 46*(3), 273 - 286.

Agthe, D., Billings, B., Dobra, J., and Raffiee, K. (1986). A Simultaneous Equation Model for Block Rates. *Water Resources Research*(January), 1 - 4.

Al-Quanibet, M., and Johnston, R. (1985). Municipal Demand for Water in Kuwait: Methodological Issues and Empirical results. *Water Resources Research, 21*(4), 433 - 438.

Altmann, D. (2007). *marginal Cost Water Pricing: Welfare Effects and Policy Implications using Minimum Cost and Benchmarking Models, with Case Studies from Australia and Asia.* University of Adelaide, Adelaide.

Arbues, F., Garcia-Valinas, M., and Martinez-Espineira, R. (2003). Estimation of Residential Water Demand: A State-of-the-art-review. *Journal of Socio-Economics, 32*, 81 - 102.

Arbues, F., and Villanua, I. (2006). Potential for Pricing Policies in Water Resource Management: Estimation of Urban Residential Water Demand in Zaragoza, Spain. *Urban Studies, 43*(13), 2421 - 2442.

Ariyabandu, R. (2005, 11-02-2005). Gathering to collect one of the most precious natural resources. *Daily News.*

Babin, F., Wills, C., and Allen, P. (1982). Estimation of Substitution Possibilities between Water and Other Production Inputs. *American Journal of Agricultural Economics, 64*(1), 148 - 151.

Baltagi, B. H. (1995). *Econometric Analysis of Panel Data*. New York: John Wiley.

Baltagi, B. H., and Kao, C. (2000). Nonstationary Panels, Cointegration in Panels and Dynamic Panels: A Survey. *Advances in Econometrics, 15*, 7 - 51.

Barkatullah, N. (1996). *OLS and Instrumental Variable Price Elasticity Estimates for Water in Mixed-effects Model under Multiple Tariff Structure*. Sydney: Department of Economics, University of Sydney.

—. (1999). *Pricing, Demand Analysis and Simulation: An Application to a Water Utility*: Dissertation.com.

Basani, M., Jonathan, I., and Reilly, B. (1999). Water Demand and Welfare Effects of Connection: Empirical Evidence from Cambodia.

Baumol, W. J., and Bradford, D. F. (1970). Optimal Departures of Marginal Cost Pricing. *American Economic Review, 60*, 265 - 283.

Beattie, B., and Foster, H. (1979). Urban Residential Demand for Water in the United States. *Land Economics, 55*, 43 - 58.

Beattie, B., and Foster, H. (1981). on the specification of price in studies of consumer demand under block price scheduling. *Land Economics, 57*(4), 624 - 629.

Berndt, E. R. (1991). *The Practice of Econometrics Classic and Contemporary*: Addison-Wesley Inc.

Bhattacharyya, A., Parker, E., and Raffiee, K. (1994). An Examination of the effect of ownership on the relative efficiency of public and private water utilities. *Land Economics, 70*(2), 197 - 209.

Billings, B. (1982). Specification of Block Rate Price Variables in Demand Models. *Land Economics, 58*(3), 386 - 393.

—. (1987). Alternative Demand Model Estimators for Block Rate Pricing. *Water Resources Bulletin, 23*(2), 341 - 345.

Billings, B., and Agthe, D. (1980). Price Elasticity for Water: A Case of Increasing Block Rates. *Land Economics, 56*, 73 - 85.

Bishop, D. B., and Weber, J. A. (2001). Impacts of Demand Reduction on Water Utilities. American Water Works Association.

Biswas, A. K., and Tortajada, C. (Eds.). (2005). *Water Pricing and Public-Private Partnership*. Oxon: Routledge.

Boadway, R. (1974). The welfare foundations of cost-benefit analysis. *Economics Journal, 84*, 426 - 439.

Boland, J. J. (1997). *Pricing urban Water: Principles and Comromises*. Paper presented at the World Bank Seminar on Pricing of Sanitation and Water Services.

Boland, J. J., and Whittington, D. (1998). *The Political Economy of Increasing Block Tariffs in Developing Countries*. Washington DC: World Bank.

Bos, M. G. (1997). Performance Indicators for Irrigation and Drainage. *Irrigation and Drainage Systems, 11*(2), 119 - 137.

Breitung, J. (2000). The Local Power of Some Unit Root Tests for Panel Data. *Advances in Econometrics, 15*, 161 - 178.

Brown, L., and Chachere, G. (1980). A note on the cost elasticity - scale elasticity relation. *Econometrica, 48*(537 - 538).

Brown, S., and Sibley, D. (1986). *The Theory of Public Utility Pricing*. Cambridge: Cambridge University Press.

Cavanagh, S. M., Hanemann, W. M., and Stavins, R. N. (2002). Muffled Price Signals: Household Water Demand Under Increasing Block Prices. *FEEM Working Paper No. 40.2002*. Retrieved from http://ssrn.com/abstract=317924 or DOI: 10.2139/ssrn.317924

Central Bank of Sri Lanka (2001). *Annual Report, 2001*. Colombo, Sri Lanka: Central Bank.

—. (2002). *Annual Report 2002*. Colombo: Central Bank of Sri Lanka.

—. (2003). *Annual Report 2003*. Colombo: Central Bank of Sri Lanka.

—. (2004). *Annual Report 2004*. Colombo: Central Bank of Sri Lanka.

—. (2005). *Annual Report 2005*. Colombo, Sri Lanka: Central Bank.

—. (2006). *Annual Report 2006*. Colombo: Central Bank of Sri Lanka.

Chambers, R. (1988). *Applied Production Analysis: A Dual Approach*: Cambridge University Press.

Chicoine, D., and Ramamurthy, G. (1986). Evidence in the Specification of Price in the Study of Domestic Water Demand. *Land Economics, 62*(1), 26 - 32.

Christensen, L., and Greene, W. (1976). Economies of Scale in U.S. Electric Power Generation. *The Journal of Political Economy, 84*(4), 655 - 676.

Christensen, L., Jorgenson, D., and Lau, L. (1973). Transcendental Logarithmic Production Frontier. *The Review of Economics and Statistics, 55*(1), 28 - 45.

Chua, C. L., Kew, H., and Yong, J. (2005). airline code-share alliances and costs: imposing concavity on translog cost function estimation. *Review of Industrial Organizations, 26*, 461 - 487.

Coase, R. H. (1946). The Marginal Cost Controversy. *Economica, 13*, 169 - 189.

Cooper, B., and Crase, L. (2006). *Equity and Efficiency Tradeoffs in water: prospects for Choice Modelling*. Paper presented at the Australian Agricultural and Resource Economic Society.

Crase, L., O'Keefe, S., and Burston, J. (2007). Inclining Block Tariffs for Urban Water *Agenda, 14*(1), 69 - 80.

Dalhuisen, J. M., Florax, R. J., De-Groot, H., and Nijkamp, P. (2003). Price and Income Elasticities of Residential Water Demand: A Meta Analysis. *Land Economics, 79*(2), 292 - 308.

Danielson, L. E. (1979). An Analysis of Residential Demand for Water Using Micro Time-series Data. *Water Resources Research, 15*(4), 763 - 767.

David, C. C., and Inocencio, A. B. (1998). *Understanding Household Demand for Water: The Metro Manila Case*: EEPSEA.

Davidson, R., and MacKinnon, J. G. (1993). *Estimation and Inference in Econometrics*. New York: Oxford University Press.

Deaton, A., and Muellbauer, J. (1980). *Economics and Consumer Behaviour*. Cambridge: Cambridge University Press.

Deller, S., Chicooine, D., and Ramamurthy, G. (1986). Instrumental Variables Approach to Rural Water Service Demand. *Southern Economic Journal, 53*(2), 333 - 346.

Department of Census and Statistics (2001). *Population and housing census*. Colombo: Department of Census and Statistics.

Diewert, W. E., and Wales, T. J. (1987). Flexible Functional Forms and Global Curvature Conditions. *Econometrica, 55*(1), 43 - 68.

Dupoint, D., and Renzetti, S. (2001). The Role of Water in Manufacturing *Environmental and Resource Economics, 18*(4), 411 - 432.

Easter, K. W., Feder, G., Le-moigne, G., and Duda, A. (1993). *Water Resources Management*. Washington DC: World Bank.

Edwards, G. (2006). Whose Values Count? Demand Management for Melbourne's Water. *The Economic Record, 82*(special issue), 54 - 63.

Espey, M., Espey, J., and Shaw, W. D. (1997). Price Elasticity of Residential Demand for Water: A Meta-analysis. *Water Resources Research, 33*(6), 1369 - 1374.

Feigenbaum, S., and Teeples, R. (1983). Public versus private water delivery: a hedonic cost approach. *Review of Economics and Statistics*, 672 - 678.

Fernando Arbues, M.A., G.-V., and R., M.-E. (2003). Estimation of Residential Water Demand: A State-of-the-art-review. *Journal of Socio-Economics, 32*, 81 - 102.

Gandhi, V., Crase, L., and Herath, G. (2007). *Determinants of Institutional Success for Water in India: Results from a Study Across Three States*. Paper presented at the Annual Conference of the Australian Agricultural and Resource Economics Society.

Garcia-Valinas, M. A. (2005). Efficiency and Equity in Natural Resources Pricing: A Proposal for Urban Water Distribution Service. *Environmental and Resource Economics, 32*, 183 - 204.

Garcia, S., and Reynaud, A. (2004). Estimating Benefits of Efficient Water Pricing in France. *Resource and Energy Economics, 26*, 1 - 25.

Garcia, S., and Thomas, A. (2001). The Structure of Municipal Water Supply Cost: Application to a Panel of French Local Communities. *Journal of Productivity Analysis, 16*(1), 5 - 29.

Gaudin, S. (2005). *Using Water Bills to Reinforce Price Signals: Evidence from the U.S.* Paper presented at the IWA International Conference on Water Economics, Statistics and Finance.

Gaudin, S., Griffin, R., and Sickles, R. (2001). Demand Specification for Municipal Water Management: Evaluation of the Stone-Geary Form. *Land Economics, 77*(3), 399 - 422.

Gibbs, K. (1978). Price Variable in Residential Water Demand Models. *Water Resources Research, 14*(1), 15 - 18.

Grafton, R., and Kompas, T. (2006). *Sydney Water: Pricing for Sustainability*: Australian National University.

Grebenstein, C., and Field, B. (1979). Substituting for Water Inputs in U.S. Manufacturing. *Water Resources Research, 15*(2), 228 - 232.

Greene, W. H. (2003). *Econometric Analysis* (5th ed.). Upper Saddle River: Prentice Hall.

Griffin, R. C., and Chang, C. (1990). Pre-test Analyses of Water Demand in thirty Communities. *Water Resources Research, 26*(10), 2251 - 2255.

Gunathilake, H. M., Chandrasena, I., and Gopalakrishnan, C. (2001). The Economics of Household Demand for Water: The Case of Kandy Municipality, Sri Lanka. *Water Resources Development, 17*(3), 277 - 288.

Gunathilake, H. M., and Gopalakrishnan, C. (2002). Proposed Water Policy for Sri Lanka: The Policy verses the Policy Process. *Water Resources Development, 18*(4), 545 - 562.

Gyler, D., and Teeples, R. (1987). Cost of Water Delivery Systems: Specification and Ownership Effects. *Review of Economics and Statistics, 69*(3), 399 - 408.

Hajispyrou, S., Koundouri, P., and Pashardes, P. (2002). Household Demand and Welfare: Implications of Water Pricing in Cyprus. *Environmental and Development Economics, 7*, 659 - 685.

Hall, D. C. (2006). *Integrating Marginal Cost Water Pricing and Best Management Practices*. California: Metropolitan Water District of Southern California.

Hall, D. C., and Hanemann, W. M. (1996). *Urban Water Rate Design based on Marginal Cost Pricing, in Marginal Cost Rate Design and Wholesale Water markets*: JAI Press.

Hanemann, W. M. (1997). Price Rate and Structures. In D. D. Baumann, J.J. Boland and W.M. Hanemann (Ed.), *Urban Water Demand Management and Planning* (pp. 137 - 179). New York: McGraw-Hill.

Hanoch, G. (1975). the Elasticity of Scale and the shape of the average costs. *American Economic Review, 65*, 492 - 497.

Hansen, L. (1996). Water and Energy Price Impact on Residential Water Demand in Copenhagen. *Land Economics 72*(1), 66 - 79.

Hausman, J. A. (1978). Specification Tests on Econometrics. *Econometrica, 46*(6), 1251 - 1271.

—. (1981). Exact Consumer's Surplus and Deadweight loss. *American Economic Review, 71*, 662 - 676.

—. (1985). The econometrics of non-linear budget sets. *Econometrica, 53*(6), 1255 - 1282.

Hensen, S. (1984). Electricity Demand Estimates Under Increasing Block Rates. *Southern Economic Journal*(July), 147 - 156.

Hewitt, J. A., and Hanemann, W. M. (1995). A discrete/continuous choice approach to residential water demand under block rate pricing *Land Economics, 71*(2), 173 - 192.

Hoglund, L. (1999). Household Demand for Water in Sweden with Implications of Potential Tax on Water Use. *Water Resources Research, 35*(12), 3853 - 3863.

Howe, C. (2005). The functions, impacts and effectiveness of water pricing: evidence from the United states and Canada. In Biswas A.K. & C. Tortajada (Eds.), *Water Pricing and Public-Private Partnership*. Oxon: Routledge.

Howe, C. W., and Linaweaver, F. P. (1967). The Impact of Price on Residential Water Demand and Its Relation to System Design and Price Structure. *Water Resources Research, 3*(1), 13 - 32.

Hussain, I., Thrikawala, S., and R. Barker (2002). Economic Analysis of Residential, Commercial and Industrial Uses of Water in Sri Lanka. *Water International 27*(2), 183 - 193.

Im, K. S., and Pesaran, M. H. (2003). On the Panel Unit Root Tests using Nonlinear Instrumental Variables. University of Cambridge.

Imbulana, K. A., Wijesekera, N. T., and Neupane, B. R. (2006). *Sri Lanka National Water Development Report*: UNESCO.

Interim National Water Resources Authority of Sri Lanka (2002). *Outline of the Strategic Plan to Establish A National Water Resources*

Authority of Sri Lanka. Battaramulla, Sri Lanka: Interim National Water Resources Authority of Sri Lanka.

Jansen A., and Schultz, C. E. (2006). Water Demand and The Urban Poor: A Study of the Factors Influencing Water Consumption among Households in Cape Town, South Africa. *South African Journal of Economics, 74*(3), 593 - 609.

Jones, C. V., and Morris, J. R. (1984). Instrumental Price Estimates and Residential Water Demand. *Water Resources Research*(February), 197 - 202.

Just, E., Hueth, D. L., and Schmitz, A. (2004). *The welfare economics of public utility: A practical approach to project and policy evaluation*. Cheltenham, UK: Edward Elgar Publishing Limited.

Kim, H. Y. (1987). Economies of Scale in Multi Product Firms: An Empirical Analysis. *Economica, 54*(214), 185 - 206.

—. (1995). Marginal Cost and Second-Best Pricing for Water Services. *Review of Industrial Organizations, 10*, 323 - 338.

King, M. A. (1983). Welfare Analysis of Tax Reforms using Household Data. *Journal of Public Economics, 21*, 183 - 214.

Kleibergen, F., and Paap, R. (2006). Generalized Reduced Rank Tests Using the Singular Value Decomposition. *Journal of Econometrics, 133*, 97 - 126.

Kohli, U. (1991). *Technology, Duality and Foreign Trade: The GNP Function Approach to Modelling Imports and Exports*: Ann Arbor : University of Michigan Press.

Levin, A., Lin, C. F., and Chu, J. (2002). Unit Root Test in Panel Data: Asymptotic and Finite Sample Properties. *Journal of Econometrics, 108*, 1 - 24.

Livingston, M. L. (1995). Designing Water Institutions: Market Failure and Institutional Response. *Water Resources Management, 9*, 203 - 220.

Loehman, E. T. (2003). Water Utility Pricing and Local Collective Action. University of Colorado.

Maillebiau, E., and Hansen, M. (1995). Demand and Consumer Welfare Impacts of International Airline LIberalization: The Case of the North Atlantic. *Journal of Transport Economics and Policy, 29*, 115 - 136.

Malla, P. B., and Gopalakrishnan, C. (1999). The economics of Urban water demand: The case of Industrial and Commercial water use in Hawaii. *Water Resources Development, 15*(3), 367 - 374.

Marsden Jacob Associates (2004). *Estimating Long Run Marginal Cost*. Queensland: Queensland Competition Authority.

Martinez-Espeneira (2003a). Estimating Water Demand Under Increasing Block Tariffs Using Aggregate Data and Proportions of Users per Block. *Journal of Environmental Economics and Management, 26*, 5 - 23.

—. (2003b). Price Specification Issues Under Block Tariffs: A Spanish Case Study. *Water Policy, 5*, 237 - 256.

Mas-Colell, A., Whinston, M., and Green, J. (1995). *Microeconomic Theory*: Oxford University Press.

Mathur, O., and Thakur, S. (2003). *Urban water pricing: setting the stage for reforms*. New Delhi: National Institute of Public Finance and Policy.

Moeltner, K., and Stoddard, S. (2004). A Panel Data Analysis of Commercial Customers' Water Price Responsiveness Under Block Rates. *Water Resources Research, 40*(W01401), 1 - 9.

MONLAR (2006). *The authors of water policy in Sri Lanka*. Rajagiriya, Sri Lanka: Movement for National Land and Agriculture Reform.

Mulik, K., Featherstone, A., and Marsh, T. (2003). *Imposing Curvature Restrictions on a TRans-log Cost Function using Markov Chain Monte Carlo Simulation Approach*. Paper presented at the Annual Meeting of American Agricultural Economics Association

Munasinghe, M. (1992). *Water Supply and Environmental Management: Developing World Applications*. Boulder: Westview Press.

Nauges, C., and Martinez-Espineira (2004). Is All Domestic Water Consumption Sensitive to Price Control? *Applied Economics, 36*, 1697 - 1703.

Nauges, C., and Thomas, A. (2000). Privately Operated Water Utilities Municipal Price Negotiation, and Estimation of Residential Water Demand: The Case of France. *Land Economics, 76*(1), 68 - 85.

Nauges, C., and van-den Berg, C. (2006). *Water Markets, Demand and Cost Recovery for Piped Water Supply Services: Evidence from Southwest Sri Lanka*. Washington: World Bank.

Ng, Y. K. (1983). *Welfare Economics: Introduction and Development of Basic concepts, revised edition*. London: McMillan.

—. (1987). Equity, Efficiency and Financial Viability: Public-utility Pricing with Special Reference to Water Supply. *Australian Economic Review, 20*(3), 21 - 35.

Ng, Y. K., and Weisser, M. (1974). Optimal Pricing with a Budget Constraint - The Case of the Two-part Tariff. *The Review of Economic Studies, 41*(3), 337 - 345.

Nieswiadomy, M. (1992). Estimating Urban Residential Water Demand: Effects of Price Structure, Conservation and Education. *Water Resources Research, 28*(3), 609 - 615.

Nieswiadomy, M., and Molina, D. (1988). Urban Water Demand Estimates under Increasing Block Rates. *Growth and Change, 19*(1), 1 - 12.

Nieswiadomy, M., and Molina, D. (1989). Comparing Residential Water Estimates Under Decreasing and Increasing Block Rates Using Household Data. *Land Economics, 65*(3), 280 - 289.

Nieswiadomy, M., and Molina, D. (1991). A Note on Price Perception in Water Demand Models. *Land Economics, 67*, 352 - 359.

Nordin, J. A. (1976). A Proposed Modification on Taylor's Demand Supply Analysis: Comment. *The Bell journal of Economics, 7*(2), 719 - 721.

North, D. C. (1996). *Institutions, Institutional Change and Economic Performance*. Cambridge: Cambridge University Press.

North, D. C., and Thomas, P. R. (1973). *The Rise of the Western World: A New Economic History*. Cambridge MA: Cambridge University Press.

North, J. H., and Griffin, C. C. (1997). Water Source as a Housing Characteristic: Hedonic Property Valuation and Willingness to Pay for Water. *Water Resources Research, 29*(7), 1923 - 1929.

NWSDB (2002). National Policy on Water Supply and Sanitation. Retrieved 28-11-2006, from NWSDB: http://www.waterboard.lk

—. (2005). *Annual Report 2005*. Colombo: National Water Supply and Drainage Board.

—. (2006a). *Annual Report 2006*. Colombo: National Water Supply and Drainage Board.

—. (2006b). National Water Supply and Drainage Board Retrieved 27-08-2007: http://www.waterboard.lk

—. (2007). *Management Information Report*. Colombo: NWSDB.

Nygard, K., Wahl, E., Krogh, T., Tveit, O. A., Bøhleng, E., Tverdal, A., and Aavitsland, P. (2007). Breaks and maintenance work in the water distribution systems and gastrointestinal illness: a cohort study. *International Journal of Epidemiology, 36*(4), 873 - 880.

OECD (1999). *Household Water Pricing in OECD Countries*. Paris: OECD.

Og, A. J., and Schulz, C. E. (2006). Water Demand and the Urban Poor: A study of the factors influencing water consumption among households in Cape town, South Africa. University of Tromso.

Oshfeldt, R. L. (1983). Specification of Block Rate Price Variables in Demand Models. *Land Economics, August*, 365 - 369.

Park, H. M. (2005). Linear Regression Models for Panel Data using SAS, STATA, LIMDEP and SPSS. Indiana University.

Pattanayake, S. K., van-den Berg, C., Yang, J. C., and van-Houtven, G. (2006). *The Use of Willingness to Pay Experiments: Estimating Demand for Piped Water Connections in Sri Lanka*. Washington: World Bank.

Pindyck, R. S., and Rubinfeld, D. L. (1981). *Econometric Models and Economic Forecasts* (Second ed.). New York: McGraw-Hill.

Pindyck, R. S., and Rubinfeld, D. L. (1992). *Microeconomics* (4th ed.). New Jersey: Prentice Hall.

Pushpangadan, K., and Murugan, G. (1998). *Pricing with Changing Welfare Criterion: An Application of Ramsey-Wilson Model to Urban Water Supply*. Thiruvananthapuram: Centre for Development Studies.

Ramsey, F. P. (1927). A Contribution to the Theory of Taxation. *Economic Journal, 37*, 47 - 61.

Rees, J. (1969). *Industrial Demand for Water: A Study of South East England*. London: Weidenfield and Nicholson.

Renwick, M., and Archibald, S. (1998). Demand Side Management Policies for Residential Water Use: Who Bears the Conservation Burden. *Land Economics, 74*(3), 343 - 359.

Renwick, M., and Green, R. D. (2000). Do Residential Water Demand Side Management Policies Measure up? An Analysis of Eight California Water Agencies. *Journal of Environmental Economics and Management, 40*, 37 - 55.

Renwick, M., Green, R. D., and McCorkle, C. (1998). *Measuring the Price Responsiveness of Residential Water Demand in California's Urban Areas*: California Department of Water Resources.

Renzetti, S. (1988). An Econometric Study of Industrial Water Demands in British Columbia. *Water Resources Research, 24*(10), 1569 - 1573.

—. (1992a). Estimating the Structure of Industrial water demands: the case of Canadian Manufacturing. *Land Economics, 68*, 396 - 404.

—. (1992b). Evaluating the Welfare Effects of Reforming Municipal Water Prices. *Journal of Environmental Economics and Management, 22*, 147 - 163.

—. (1999). Municipal Water Supply and Sewage Treatment Costs, Prices and Distortions. *Canadian Journal of Economics, 32*(3), 688 - 704.

—. (2002). *The Economics of Water Demands*. USA: Kluwer Academic Publishers.

Reynaud, A. (2003). An Econometric Estimation of Industrial Water Demand In France. *Environmental and Resource Economics, 25*(2), 213 - 232.

Rietveld, P., Rouwendal, J., and Zwart, B. (2000). Block Rate Pricing of Water in Indonesia: An analysis of welfare effects. *Bulletin of Indonesian Economic Studies, 36*(3), 73 - 92.

Rogers, P., de Silva, R., and Bhatia, R. (2002). Water is and Economic good: How to use prices to promote equity, efficiency, and sustainability. *Water Policy, 4*, 1 - 17.

Ruijs, A. (2007). Welfare and Distribution Effects of Water Pricing Policies. Wageningen University.

Ryan, D. L., and Wales, T. J. (1998). A simple method of imposing local curvature in some flexible consumer demand systems. *Journal of Business and Economic Statistics, 16*(3), 331 - 338.

Ryan, D. L., and Wales, T. J. (2000). imposing local concavity in the translog and generalized leontief cost functions. *Economics Letters, 67*, 253 - 260.

Saleth, R. M., and Dinar, A. (1999). *Water Challenge and Institutional Response: A Cross-Country Perspective*. Washington: World Bank.

Saleth, R. M., and Dinar, A. (2000). Institutional Changes in Global Water Sector: Trends, Patterns and Implications. *Water Policy, 2*(3), 175 - 199.

Saleth, R. M., and Dinar, A. (2004). *The Institutional Economics of Water: A Cross Country Analysis of Institutions and Performance*: World Bank and Edward Elgar.

Saleth, R. M., and Dinar, A. (2005). Water Institutional Reforms: Theory and Practice. *Water Policy, 7*, 1 - 19.

Samad, M. (2005). Water Institutional Reforms in Sri Lanka. *Water Policy, 7*(1), 125 - 140.

Schefter, J., and David, E. (1985). Estimating Residential Water Demand Under Multi-tariff Using Aggregate Data. *Land Economics, 61*(3), 272 - 280.

Schneider, M. L., and Whitlach, E. E. (1991). User-specific water demand elasticities. *Journal of Water Resources Planning and Management, 117*(1), 52 - 73.

Seneviratne, L. W. (2000). Challenges to Urban Water Management in Sri Lanka. *Water Resources Development, 16*(1), 131 - 141.

Shah, T. (2005). *The New Institutional Economics in India's Water Policy.* Paper presented at the African Water Laws: Plural Legislative Frameworks for Rural Water Management in Africa.

Shin, J. (1985). Perception of Price when Price Information is Costly: Evidence from Residential Electricity Demand. *Review of Economics and Statistics, 67*(4), 591 - 598.

Sibly, H. (2006). Efficient Urban Water Pricing. *Australian Economic Review, 39*(2), 227 - 237.

Sri Lanka Water Vision Committee (1999). *Sri Lanka Water Vision 2025.* Paper presented at the South Asia Regional Water Vision Workshop, Colombo.

Stata Press (2003). *Cross-sectional Time-series Reference Manual.* Texas: Stata Press.

Stevens, T. H., Miller, J., and Willis, C. (1992). Effect of Price Structure on Residential Water Demand. *Water Resources Bulletin, 28*(4), 681 - 685.

Swallow, S., and Marin, C. (1988). Long-run Price Inflexibility and Efficiency Loss for Municipal Water Supply. *Journal of Environmental Economics and Management, 15*, 233 - 247.

Taylor, L. D. (1975). The Demand for Electricity: A Survey. *The Bell Journal of Economics, 6*(1), 74 - 110.

Terza, J. V. (1986). Determinants of Household Electricity Demand: A Two-Stage Probit Approach. *Southern Economic Journal, 52*(April), 1131 - 1139.

Tortajada, C. (2006). *Private verses Public in Water Provision: Encouraging Case of Sri Lanka.* Atizapan, Mexico: Third World Centre for Water Management.

Turnovsky, S. J. (1969). The Demand for Water: Some Empirical Evidence on Consumers' Response to a Commodity Uncertain in Supply. *Water Resources Research, 5*(2), 350 - 361.

Turvey, R. (1976). Analysing the Marginal Cost of Water Supply. *Land Economics, 52*(2), 158 - 168.

UNESCO Division of Water Sciences (2003). *Water for people water for life*. Paris: UNESCO.

United Nations Development Programme (2006). *Human Development Report 2006*. New York: United Nations Development Programme.

Uzawa, H. (1962). Production Functions with Constant Elasticities of Substitution. *Review of Economics and Statistics, 44*(4), 291 - 299.

Varian, H. R. (1984). *Microeconomic Analysis*: W.W. Norton and Company.

Vartia, Y. (1983). Efficient Methods of Measuring Welfare Change and Compensated income in terms of Ordinary Demand Functions. *Econometrica, 51*(1), 79 - 98.

Wang, P. (2003). *Financial Econometrics: Methods and Models*: Routledge, Taylor and Francis Group.

Warford, J. J. (2003). *Marginal Opportunity Cost Pricing for Municipal Water Supply*. Canada: International Development Research Institute

Wasny, G. (1986). Household Water Expenditures in Major Metropolitan Centres in Canada. *Canadian Water Resources Journal, 11*, 33 - 45.

Whittington, D. (2003). Municipal Water Pricing and Tariff Design: A Reform Agenda for South Asia. *Water Policy, 6*(5), 61 - 76.

Whittington, D., Pattanayake, S. K., Yang, J. C., and Balkumar, K. C. (2002). Household Demand for Improved Piped Water Service: Evidence from Kathmandu, Nepal. *Water Policy, 4*, 531 - 556.

Williams, M., and Suh, B. (1986). The Demand for Urban Water by Customer Class. *Applied Economics, 18*(12), 1275 - 1289.

Williamson, O. (2000). Economic Institutions and Development: A view from the Bottom. In S. Kahkonen & M. Olson (Eds.), *A new Institutional approach to Economic Development*: Oxford University Press.

Willig, R. (1976). Consumer's Surplus Without Apology. *American Economic Review, 66*, 589 - 597.

Wooldridge, J. (2001). *Econometric Analysis of Cross Section and Panel Data*: MIT Press.

World Bank (1992). *Asia Water Resources Study: Stage 1*. Washington Agricultural Division, Asia Technical Department.

World Health Organization (1997a). *Guidelines for Drinking-water Quality* (2 ed.): World Health Organization.

—. (1997b). *Health and Environment in Sustainable Development: five years after the earth summit*. Geneva: WHO.

—. (2002). Meeting the Millennium Development Goal drinking water and sanitation target: a mid term assessment progress Retrieved 09-02-2007, from http://www.who.int/water_sanitation_health/monitoring/jmp04.pdf

Worthington, A. C., Higgs, H., and Hofmann, M. (2006). Urban Water Demand with Fixed volumetric charging in a large municipality: the case of Brisbane, Australia. *Australian Journal of Agriculture and Resource Economics, 50*, 347 - 359.

Worthington, A. C., and Hoffmann, M. (2006). A State of the Art Review of Residential Water Demand Modelling. University of Woolongong.

WWC (2000). *A Water Secure World*. United Kingdom: Thanet Press: World Water Commission.

Ziegler, J. A., and Bell, S. E. (1984). Estimating demand for intake water by self-supplied firms. *Water Resources Research, 20*(1), 4 - 8.